Trade Negotiations in Latin America

Trade Negotiations in Latin America

Problems and Prospects

Edited by

Diana Tussie
Director, Research Program on International Economic Institutions
FLACSO
Argentina
Director, Latin American Trade Network (LATN)

First published 2003 by
PALGRAVE MACMILLAN
Houndmills, Basingstoke, Hampshire RG21 6XS and
175 Fifth Avenue, New York, N.Y. 10010
Companies and representatives throughout the world

PALGRAVE MACMILLAN is the global academic imprint of the Palgrave
Macmillan division of St. Martin's Press, LLC and of Palgrave Macmillan Ltd.
Macmillan® is a registered trademark in the United States, United Kingdom and
other countries. Palgrave is a registered trademark in the European Union and
other countries.

ISBN 0–333–98723–3

This book is printed on paper suitable for recycling and made from fully
managed and sustained forest sources.

A catalogue record for this book is available from the British Library.

Library of Congress Cataloging-in-Publication Data

Trade negotiations in Latin America : problems and prospects / edited by
    Diana Tussie.
        p. cm.
    Includes bibliographical references and index.
    ISBN 0–333–98723–3
        1. Latin America – Commercial policy. I. Tussie, Diana.

    HF3230.5.Z5 T73 2003
    382′.9′098–dc21   2002026954

10   9   8   7   6   5   4   3   2   1
12 11 10 09 08 07 06 05 04 03

Printed and bound in Great Britain by
Antony Rowe Ltd, Chippenham and Eastbourne

Contents

List of Tables and Figures

Tables

Figure

Acknowledgments

This volume represents only a portion of the considerably larger iceberg of the Latin American Trade Network (LATN), the now invisible supporting ideas and works that could not, for one reason or another, fit into the present framework. The initial questions posed by LATN were related to the implications of the novel and simultaneous trade negotiations taking place at multilateral, hemispheric and sub-regional levels in Latin America. What policy spaces were left for domestic policy-making in this context? Were there significant differences in the way issues were negotiated at each level? What was the comparative advantage of each level? Were certain levels preferable to others? Would it be possible to grade them? Our analysis had a practical intention: we were trying to draw out a road map for policy-making in a complex web of choices. We deemed ourselves to be doing something like the work of a test driver or a surveyor traversing unchartered land and mapping out the different plots.

We began with the support of a substantial grant from Canada's International Development Research Center (IDRC). The aim of the project was to unravel the strands of the trade agenda appearing in the period that began with the coming into being of the NAFTA and the entry into force of the Uruguay Round, strands that presented a distinctive character, different from those of any period that preceded it. Latin America together with other parts of the developing world appeared to be participating in full swing in trade negotiations and in multiple fora. The substantial opening of the economies seemed more akin to the events of the last third of the nineteenth century than post-1929 history.

LATN brought together people directly involved in public affairs as well as academics and experts from international organizations. It came together to make sense of different aspects of this recent piece of history and to monitor on-going developments. The initial stimulus came in 1998 from a paper by Rohinton Medhora, 'Emerging Issues in International Trade Relations: Some Research Directions', presented at the Facultad Latinoamericana de Ciencias Sociales (FLACSO) in Buenos Aires. The presentation engendered a discussion on the substance of the agenda, LATN's purposes and the process whereby those purposes could be attained. As productive and passionate arguments germinated, successive plenary meetings dissecting drafts of papers were held in UNCTAD and the WTO in Geneva in 1998, at the Consejo Argentino para las Relaciones Internacionales in Buenos Aires in 1999 and at the Inter-American Development Bank in Washington in 2000. Felipe de la Balze, Carlos Basco, Robert Devlin, Bernard Hoekman, Michael Finger, Sam Laird, Celso Lafer, Aaditya Mattoo, Patricio Meller, Theodore

Moran, Uziel Nogueira, Marcelo Olarreaga, Nicola Phillips, Vera Thorstensen, Hector Torres and Nicola Phillips provided generous ideas and comments at different stages.

As the embodiment of a vast research project carried out by LATN, this book would not have been possible without financial support from IDRC and the careful guidance of both Rohinton Medhora and Andres Ruis. As editor of the book and Director of LATN, I am especially indebted to the bountiful goodwill of LATN members throughout the world and additionally to the project's advisory committee composed of Robert Devlin, Enzo Grilli, Patrick Low, Patricio Meller and Rubens Ricupero. I was also fortunate to be able to lean on the talent of my colleagues at FLACSO Argentina: Valentina Delich, Miguel Lengyel, Cintia Quiliconi and Tracy Tuplin. Each has provided unflagging support to the project and to me personally. We all owe a special word of thanks to Brita Siepker for her time and energy dedicated to the content editing of the book in its entirety. Her diligence and unbending good humor with endless manuscripts polished our rough edges to perfection.

I cannot take full credit for what has come to fruition here but I will take full responsibility. All the usual disclaimers apply.

DIANA TUSSIE

List of Abbreviations

AB	Appellate Body of the WTO Dispute Settlement Understanding
AC	Andean Community
AD	Antidumping
APEC	Asian Pacific Economic Cooperation
ASCM	Agreement on Subsidies and Countervailing Measures
ASEAN	Association of South East Asian Nations
ATC	Agreement on Textiles and Clothing
BIT	Bilateral Investment Treaty
BPP	Basic Production Process
CACM	Central American Common Market
CANTV	Venezuelan National Telephone Company
Caricom	Caribbean Community
CER	Australia–New Zealand Closer Economic Relations Agreement
CET	Common External Tariff
CFS	Committee on Financial Services of the GATS
CNCE	Argentine National Foreign Trade Commission
CSC	Committee on Specific Commitments of the GATS
CUSFTA	Canada–US Free Trade Agreement
CVD	Countervailing Duty
DS	Dispute Settlement
DSB	Dispute Settlement Board of the WTO
DSU	Dispute Settlement Understanding of the WTO
EC	European Commission
EPZ	Export Processing Zone
EU	European Union
FAO	Food and Agriculture Organization of the UN
FCC	US Federal Communications Commission
FDI	Foreign Direct Investment
FTAA	Free Trade Area of the Americas
G-3	Group of Three – Colombia, Venezuela and Mexico
G-10	Group of Ten
G-20	Group of Twenty
GATS	General Agreement on Trade in Services
GATT	General Agreement on Tariffs and Trade
GDP	Gross Domestic Product
GNP–PPP	Gross National Product – Purchasing Power Parity
GSP	Generalized System of Preferences
GSTP	Global System of Trade Preferences
GVA	Gross Value Added at Factor Cost

ICPU	International Competition Policy Unit
ISO	International Standardization Organization
ISP	Internet Service Provider
IT	Information Technology
ITU	International Telecommunication Union
LAFTA	Latin American Free Trade Area
LAIA	Latin America Integration Association
MAI	Multilateral Agreement on Investments
Mercosur	Mercado Común del Sur
MFA	Multifibre Agreement of the WTO
MFN	Most Favored Nation
MNC	Multinational Corporation
NAFTA	North American Free Trade Agreement
NGO	Non-Governmental Organization
NT	National Treatment
NTB	Non-Tariff Barrier
OECD	Organization for Economic Cooperation and Development
PR	Performance Requirement
Proalcool	Brazilian National Alcohol Program
R&D	Research and Development
S&D	Special and Differential Treatment
SEACEN	South East Asian Central Banks
TMB	Textiles Monitoring Body of the WTO
TNC	Transnational Corporation
TRIMs	Agreement on Trade-Related Investment Measures of the WTO
TRIPs	Agreement on Trade-Related Intellectual Property Rights of the WTO
UN	United Nations
UNCOPUOS	United Nations Committee for the Peaceful Uses of Outer Space
UNCTAD	United Nations Conference on Trade and Development
UNESCO	United Nations Educational Scientific and Cultural Organization
UR	Uruguay Round
URAs	Uruguay Round Agreements
USDA	US Department of Agriculture
USDC	US Department of Commerce
USITA	International Trade Administration of the US Department of Commerce
USITC	US International Trade Commission
USTR	US Trade Representative
VER	Voluntary Export Restriction
WIPO	World Intellectual Property Organization

WLL   Wireless Local Loop
WPDR   Working Party on Domestic Regulations of GATS
WPGR   Working Party on GATS Rules
WTO   World Trade Organization

Notes on the Contributors

Marcelo de Paiva Abreu is a professor of economics at the Pontifical Catholic University of Rio de Janeiro. Marcelo received a PhD in economics from Cambridge University.

Luis Abugattas Majluf is a PhD candidate in political science and holds a Master's in political science and economics from the University of Pittsburgh. Luis is Executive Director of the Economic and Social Research Institute of the National Society of Industries.

Paulo Bastos Tigre received a Master's in production engineering and a PhD in science policy from the University of Sussex, England. Paulo is Professor of Industrial Organization at the Federal University of Rio de Janeiro.

Daniel Chudnovsky, who holds a DPhil in economics from Oxford University, is Director of the Centro de Investigaciones para la Transformación (CENIT) in Buenos Aires and is Professor of Development Economics at the University of Buenos Aires.

Valentina Delich received a law degree from the University of Buenos Aires and an MA in international relations from American University, Washington, DC. Valentina is a researcher in the International Economic Institutions Program at FLACSO Argentina.

Marisa Diaz-Henderson received a PhD in international political economy from the University of Warwick and a Master's in international relations from FLACSO Argentina. Marisa is currently Researcher and Analyst at the Argentine Mission to the UN Office in Geneva.

Andrés López is a researcher at the Centro de Investigaciones para la Transformación (CENIT). Andrés holds a doctorate in economic sciences from the University of Buenos Aires, where he is Associate Professor of Economic Development.

Pedro da Motta Veiga holds a PhD in economics from the Ecole des Hautes Etudes en Sciences Sociales and an MSc in production engineering from the Federal University of Rio de Janeiro. Pedro is President of the Brazilian Society for Transnational Business Studies and Economic Globalization and the Director of EcoStrat Consultants.

Amrita Narlikar is a post-doctoral research fellow at St John's College, Oxford University. Amrita's DPhil thesis was entitled, 'Bargaining Together in Trade: Developing Countries in Coalitions, 1982–98', which she completed at Balliol College, Oxford.

Sherry M. Stephenson is Deputy Director of the Trade Unit of the Organization of American States. Sherry received a PhD in international economics from the University of Geneva, Switzerland and an MA in economics from New York University.

José Tavares de Araujo Jr received a PhD in economics from the University of London, and is currently a professor at the Federal University of Rio de Janeiro and a consultant to the OAS Trade Unit.

Manuela Tortora is currently Coordinator of the Commercial Diplomacy Program at UNCTAD. Manuela received a PhD in political science from the University of Geneva, Switzerland.

Diana Tussie is Director of the Latin American Trade Network (LATN) and Director of the Research Program on International Economic Institutions of FLACSO Argentina. Diana received a PhD in international relations and economics from the London School of Economics and a BA in sociology from the University of Buenos Aires.

Ann Weston is Vice-President and Research Coordinator of The North–South Institute, a policy research organization based in Ottawa, Canada that focuses on international development issues. Ann was educated at the University of Sussex and the University of London.

Ngaire Woods is Fellow in politics and international relations at University College, Oxford and a Senior Research Associate of Oxford's International Development Centre, Queen Elizabeth House.

Introduction: On Shifting Ground – the Crossroads of Regional and Sectoral Associations

*Diana Tussie**

> 'So you think you're changed, do you?'
> 'I'm afraid I am, sir,' said Alice; 'I can't remember things as I used –
> and I don't keep the same size for ten minutes together! ...'
> 'What size do you want to be?' [the Caterpillar] asked.
> 'Oh, I'm not particular as to size,' Alice hastily replied: 'only one
> doesn't like changing so often, you know.'
> Advice from the Caterpillar, *Alice's Adventures in Wonderland*
> by Lewis Carroll

Trade generates mutual gains. The distribution of these gains both among and within countries remain matters of serious contention. The Stolper–Samuelson theorem argues that trade liberalization can make some members of a country even worse off; in other words, not only are the gains from trade unequally spread within a country, but losses can also ensue for some groups. Welfare economics also shows that unless those benefiting from a certain policy actually compensate those made worse off by it, that policy cannot be claimed as desirable. Even modern academic orthodoxy has opened the way to systematic exploration of links between trade and income distribution, turning away from the somewhat dogmatic view that dismisses the possibility that anybody may be hurt by liberalization. Simple assertions such as 'trade benefits everybody' or 'trade hurts everybody' reflect neither our knowledge nor reality. It all depends on the conditions of competition in which trade takes place. The sensitivity to the painful adjustment process is contained in what is known as the compromise of 'embedded liberalism' (Ruggie, 1982): the pursuit of an international division of labor compatible with the requirements of domestic stability. International rules encourage free trade but not at all costs; instead there is *pari passu* a commitment to minimize socially disruptive domestic adjustment costs as well as other economic and political vulnerabilities.

1

This conjunction of objectives is at the center of today's concerns. In Latin America it is taking the guise of a nuanced form of market rationality, one that comes in the hand of vigorous and vibrant regional negotiations. In this conjunction lies the question of the political limits that should be imposed on markets, a question of vast economic ramifications. The international trading system juggles with the two competing forces characterized by Karl Polanyi as a 'double movement' with two organizing principles interacting one with the other. Each principle sets specific institutional aims, has the support of discernible social forces and uses its own distinctive methods.

> The one was the principle of economic liberalism, aiming at the establishment of a self-regulating market, relying on the support of the trading classes, and using largely laissez faire and free trade as its method; the other was the principle of social protection aiming at the conservation of man and nature as well as productive organization, relying on the varying support of those most immediately affected by the deleterious action of the market.... (Polanyi, 1944: 132)

The common tendency to view trade negotiations as straight liberalization with cheating taking place on all sides fails to capture the complexity of this double movement. Policies have followed ebbs and flows to simultaneously accommodate these needs. Generally, global economic downturns have led to regulation and contraction, generating a situation where the hegemonic leader has to recast the rules for the new 'post-crisis' order. Since 1914 but especially from the 1930s onwards, the US felt responsible for leading a crusade towards free trade. This mission was conducted under a variety of political imperatives depending on the particular circumstances. As such, trade liberalization has become mixed with other causes, including the conflation of markets and political freedoms under US leadership. Often a menace or an enemy was necessary to garner consensus on further liberalization. When the First World War was over, a sense of moral revulsion led to the vision of a new international order on the basis of Woodrow Wilson's ideas of international cooperation hand-in-hand with trade liberalization. Wilson's 'Fourteen Points' contemplated 'the removal, so far as possible, of all economic barriers and the establishment of an equality of trade conditions among all the nations consenting to the peace and associating themselves for its maintenance' (Wilson, 1918). After the 1930 crisis, when countries adopted 'beggarthy-neighbor' measures, America's new role blossomed with Secretary of State Cordell Hull who claimed that the US had to take the initiative to halt the wave of protectionism and thereby reduce political tensions. As he fervently put it in an often quoted passage: .

> unhampered trade dovetailed with peace; high tariffs, trade barriers, and unfair economic competition, with war... if we could get a freer flow of

trade ... so that one country would not be deadly jealous of another and the living standards of all countries might rise, thereby eliminating the economic dissatisfaction that breeds war, we might have a reasonable chance of lasting peace. (Gardner, 1969: 9)

In essence, this was a universal projection of the American dream – a vision of economic plenty in the context of political freedom as expressed some decades later in the notion of a 'free world'. To retrace a step now, Cordell Hull actively lobbied Congress and managed to pass the Reciprocal Trade Agreements Act of 1934 which empowered the Executive to initiate trade agreements on the basis of reciprocal reductions in duties. In the period up to the outbreak of the Second World War, the US concluded reciprocal agreements with 29 countries on the basis of most favored nation treatment (MFN). While the impact on tariffs was small, the procedure stamped a mark of origin on post-war trading rules. The system of 'embedded liberalism' thus coupled trade liberalization with domestic policies to cope with market dislocations and provide social protection. These non-trade imperatives were considered at the outset of the General Agreement on Tariffs and Trade (GATT) and embodied in several articles: Art. XIX, the general safeguard; Art. XX, a safeguard for protection of human, animal and plant life; Art. XXI, a safeguard for security purposes; Art. XVIII a safeguard for the protection of the balance of payments and infant industries; and Art. XI allows the imposition of quantitative controls on exports and imports of agricultural products and fisheries. GATT thus codified a system not of absolute free trade; foreign suppliers could compete for a part of the domestic market in which domestic interests were afforded protection. While the US accepted the domestic compromise of embedded liberalism to safeguard its own stability, the domestic stability of others was harder to accept. Abroad, the quest for trade was hailed as a harbinger of redemption, subject to ideological utilization 'from the halls of Montezuma to the shores of Tripoli'.

Throughout the Cold War, successive rounds of trade negotiations within the GATT framework were animated by the containment of communism. With the fall of centrally planned economies, for a short interval, the GATT was stripped of its security role. The September 11 2001 terrorist attacks, however, pierced the US economy at its symbolic heart. In the aftermath, trade once again became wrapped up with value-laden imperatives and proselytizing. A round of negotiations in the World Trade Organization (WTO) was predicated on its contribution to the war against terrorism, much in the same fashion as trade was seen to stand against communism in the 1960s and 1970s. Thus, the notion of trade liberalization has become implicitly one of moral approval and political purpose. These claims clearly overstate the case for liberalization. Ultimately they lead to unrealistic expectations about the benefits of trade and the payoffs of negotiations, thus laying the ground for subsequent disappointment, frustration and resentment. Trade relations now constitute a gigantic Rorschach card into which different sets of people project their discontents and their solutions.

Candide's voyage through Latin America: the leap from exclusion to engagement

For a good 40 years after the Second World War, Latin America together with developing countries did not perceive the GATT as a friendly, fruitful institution in which to promote their interests, for a mix of both ideological and pragmatic reasons. Inward-oriented industrialization and nationalist ideologies of development prevailed, turning trade relations into the crux of the North–South debate. Few Latin American countries were members of the GATT, and those that were remained either detached altogether or sleeping partners in the GATT, with a nominal exception to this general trend marked by contributions to the working of the dispute settlement mechanism (see Weston and Delich, Chapter 10). But by and large, the insignificance of developing countries' markets had so far been perceived as not worth the effort of pressing for their opening. The result was negligible obligations for developing countries together with disproportionately small trade liberalization in those sectors of immediate interest to them (Tussie, 1987; Oyejide, 2000; Ricupero, 2000). The concoction of Art. XVIII:B and the Enabling Clause compressed the need to internalize the final results of each round into domestic policy. In other words, trade negotiations had at best a marginal impact on the domestic policy process. By the mid-1980s this picture had changed significantly. To begin with, several Latin American countries became major exporters of manufactured goods, including in sectors in which it was previously assumed they lacked comparative advantages. Further, as competition among the major trading players intensified, the continued opening and greater contestability of Latin American markets became a more valued asset. Finally, the US was firmly determined to extend GATT into services and other new areas and no longer willing to leave developing countries out-of-the-loop on such issues as intellectual property. Either out of conviction or triggered by fears of closing markets and the implications of conditional MFN treatment, Latin American countries abandoned their former defensiveness and made a U-turn in the 1990s when a Panglossian approach to trade and financial liberalization took root. Hand in hand with unilateral reforms, Latin American countries participated in the UR to signal the path to medium-term economic objectives and provide an anchor for reforms.

The challenges soon proved highly demanding. Countries learned in the early stages that participation did not automatically translate into leverage. Similarly, with the expansion of the agenda through the inclusion of very complex and slippery issues (services, intellectual property, technical, sanitary and phytosanitary standards) many countries found their capacity for analysis and for turning such analysis into sound negotiating positions completely overstretched. As some authors have stated, '...a pro-active, constructive approach was frequently out of reach for many countries because of resource and research capacity constraints' (Chadha *et al.*, 2000: 432–3). The impact of these difficulties on the final commitments made during the UR should not be underestimated. First, countries had to accept a new approach to special and differential (S&D) treatment that undermined their former rights. Second, because of the rules packed under the single undertaking, they had to make significant concessions. The gains from these commitments have been leaner than envisaged. The effect on growth has yet to materialize, as have the alleged benefits of market access. If market access problems could once have been attributed to detachment, activism has not provided the solution.

To be sure, developing countries did not leave negotiations empty-handed: the inclusion of agriculture, the commitment to phase out the restrictions on textiles and the creation, with the birth of the WTO, of a much stronger dispute settlement mechanism were significant gains. Yet, these were more than compensated by concessions, the most significant of which included a more restrictive S&D approach, commitments made in the intellectual property and services agreements, the binding of all tariffs on goods, and new disciplines on subsidies and customs valuation. Furthermore, the very creation of the WTO added new challenges for effective participation. The overextended trade agenda was rapidly consolidated, calling for additional institutional capacity in member governments. In a similar vein, the WTO in contrast to the GATT accommodated on-going negotiations, demanding perpetual involvement. Finally, while the new dispute settlement mechanism is without doubt an asset, it has imposed the need to finance and develop expertise on international trade law in order to take full advantage of it. Given the level of technical expertise required, questions have been raised about developing countries' capacity to efficiently bring cases as complainants, and/or to protect their interests as defendants. Even though some technical assistance is available from the WTO Secretariat, it is not intended to assist countries on specific cases. External legal counsel usually comes from an international law firm or consultant at considerable cost (see Weston and Delich, Chapter 10).

Yet the resolve to continue negotiating has not abided, but rather led to the pondering of the dilemmas of involvement anew and searching for ways to turn participation into more meaningful or effective leverage. Disappointment with the returns of the WTO process has spurred a keen interest in regional initiatives as a complement, rather than an alternative, to the global regime. Latin America has been quick to accept the promise of the Free Trade Area of the Americas (FTAA) setting in motion a low-profile machinery which has minced through complex technical issues while at the same time a network of sub-regional agreements have channeled increasing volumes of trade. After a decade of blossoming regional and sub-regional trade agreements, three results have become clear. First, the benefits reaped by Latin American countries from multilateral trade agreements fall short of expectations. Second, regional arrangements risk becoming small areas of hegemony where predominant countries can increase their power. Third, the regional, sub-regional and multilateral arenas are in constant and revolving interaction. Multiple games take place simultaneously; each level has an intrinsic value but it also serves to play off the other two (Motta Veiga, Chapter 3).

Thus the expansion of international trade negotiations today covers far more than traditional North–North or North–South relations, painting a scenario in which intra-South relations are as important as more traditionally conceived relationships. Much of this activity takes place on shifting ground in the shape of issue- or sector-specific coalitions, which do not fit with a traditional view of across-the-board intergovernmental trade negotiations (see Narlikar and Woods, Chapter 2). Thus mini-trade regimes abound not only in the proliferation of regional trade accords; but also in sector-specific agreements: in the General Agreement on Trade in Services (GATS) (see Abugattas Majluf and Stephenson, Chapter 5); in textiles which rest on the quotas of the Agreement on Textile and Clothing; in the car sector for which the quantitative restrictions of the Trade Related Investment Measures (TRIMs) agreement are crucial (see Chudnovsky and López, Chapter 7); and in the steel sector which drafted the antidumping agreement in its own image and likeness (see Tortora and Tussie, Chapter 9). Behind much of the ostensible bargaining of governments lie internationally organized networks of business, which coalesce across borders keeping with market conditions and opportunities. What previously was experienced as fate, North–South conflict and South–South solidarity, is now an arena of choices in all directions. Interlocking relations of conflict and association require an *à la carte* approach, not a recipe to increase confusion but a compulsion to be alert and nimble on many fronts in order to prize open foreign markets. In spreading in all directions relations have acquired variety and novelty. The bargaining agenda can be fully and deeply understood by focusing less on overtly visible conflict in the North–South directions and by focusing more on neglected areas of agreement in North–South relations and disagreement in intra-South relations. This procedure will allow a clearer display of the multiple games present in each bargaining context.

On shifting ground

This book shows to what extent the cumulative effect of multiple trade reforms has dramatically altered the context in which each individual reform now operates. The removal of trade repression and the liberalization of financial markets have increased cross-border investment and regional interdependence. At the same time, thinly disguised forms of administered protection have flourished, not as a deviation from the norm but as an integral part of the liberalization effort. Almost all countries are resorting to ad hoc protection, intensively using safeguards, countervailing duties and especially antidumping measures to protect domestic producers (see Tortora and Tussie, Chapter 9). In other words, as negotiations reduce conventional barriers, trade relief policies are being used and abused to protect domestic interests. This practice now goes far beyond the North–South agenda, branching out into intra-Latin American relations. Indeed, in tandem with regional trade agreements, a covert war of mutually paralyzing trade relief measures has mushroomed. Many Latin American countries have actively applied trade relief measures on 'sensitive' sectors precisely against neighbors that, simply because of geographical proximity, had been able to benefit most from trade liberalization. The intra-Latin American dimension has also emerged over investment policies, against the backdrop of a potential race to the bottom over incentives. As countries compete to attract investments, transnational corporations shop around for the most 'market-friendly' jurisdictions and thus engage in what has come to be called regulatory arbitrage. New multilateral trade negotiations could still offer an opportunity to strike a balance between the need to avoid the irrationality of a costly race and the convenience of retaining room for incentives to encourage specific investments. Countries would benefit greatly from efforts to increase transparency and limit competition over rules of origin or even antidumping regulation as a means of attracting investment (Tavares de Araujo, Chapter 8, and Chudnovsky and López, Chapter 7). The Uruguay Round Agreements (URAs) left large degrees of freedom in these areas, freedom which regional agreements did not choose to circumscribe. Neither regional nor multilateral agreements offer appropriate dams of contention for the proliferation of these measures, now the cutting-edge of reciprocal protection and the foci of trade disputes.

Trade relations, traditionally a re-enactment of cycles, have now become an open-ended series of moments of choice which demand agile responses, less adept to the strategic planning world in which most policy-makers have been trained. Market access requires engagement and engagement requires agility to play on shifting terrain. On the eve of the FTAA and a new round in the WTO, there are new challenges and priorities. In the first place, there is broad consensus that the market access promises of the UR were deceptive. Agriculture products continue to have high protective tariffs as do the classic footwear, clothing, textile and steel sectors, even after allowing for the Generalized System of Preferences. In agriculture, tariff peaks as high as 350 per cent remain in important export products, some of them particularly sensitive for Latin American countries (see Diaz-Henderson, Chapter 4). Second, neither did the UR reverse the bias in developed countries' trade policies that obstructs export diversification and reduces incentives for processing commodities, with serious implications for export growth of more value-added products. In a related domain, commitments on subsidies limited the maneuvering room to implement support policies for growth and exports (Lengyel and Tussie, 2000). These issues of the classical North–South agenda do not, however, exhaust the complex menu on the table. The intricate issue of trade in services has become a locomotive for many negotiations (see Abugattas Majluf and Stephenson, Chapter 5). Complexity is related to several factors: negotiations are simultaneously proceeding at multilateral, regional and sub-regional levels; a choice must be made between regional or sectoral associations; a similar choice is to be made between sectors with distinct importance in the domestic economy and, therefore, different producer interests (see Bastos Tigre, Chapter 6); and, lastly, results spill over into other areas such as intellectual property rights, foreign direct investment and competition policy (see Chudnovsky and López, Chapter 7, and Tavares de Araujo, Chapter 8). The weaving of negotiating positions has thus become a staggering task, both technically as well as politically. As countries diversify their export products and markets, it becomes more difficult to concentrate their bargaining resources in a few selected areas. With the agenda expansion, opportunities for friction expand as well, making it almost impossible to remain a single-issue country nowadays. Argentina was among the early learners of this lesson, which, in spite of its efforts to concentrate on agriculture, was drawn into disputes over intellectual property with painful trade-offs between these sectors (see Casaburi *et al.*, Vol. II).

These shifting trends make it hard for Latin American countries to find common grounds and build joint negotiating positions, even when there is agreement that such cooperation could increase their leverage at the bargaining table. As Narlikar and Woods (Chapter 2) forcefully argue on the basis of UR experiences, many factors – including the political context, the availability of rewards and incentives, leadership, income levels – heavily condition the constitution of trade coalitions, alliances or any other similar collective endeavor. The growing heterogeneity of trade interests within and among Latin American countries stemming from these trends only contributes to weaken the likelihood of such initiatives (see Paiva Abreu, Chapter 1). The case of the Antidumping Agreement (see Tortora and Tussie, Chapter 9) exemplifies how the WTO scene is now serving to play out South–South issues and even to tie and untie loops in regional agreements. Brazil and Chile, usually 'victims' of antidumping measures, were keen to reopen the discussion of the Agreement with the aim of reaching stricter disciplines. Other countries in the region, frequently applicants of antidumping procedures, maintained exactly the opposite stance.

These are but a few examples of the multiplicity of dimensions that need to be addressed by Latin America in trade negotiations. The complexity of the new issues has also led to changes in the locus of responsibility for trade bargaining. Traditionally, most countries have assigned this function to foreign affairs ministries, which represented the 'national interest' single-handedly. As the interests of 'the nation', and even those of particular sectors within it, become less clear, and as the issues become more technical, input from other ministries is indispensable. Decentralization may improve the quality of decision-making, but it can also lead to bureaucratic wrangles and reduced effectiveness by opening a wider range of targets for lobbying by other countries. As governments turn away from their traditional role of regulatory control to one of facilitating investment and trade, the capacity to draw the contours of the 'national interest' with a minimally adequate degree of consensus has been undermined. The situation has posed governments with new challenges to provide a suitable response to trade policy-making in terms of their management capacity. Not only is there a vast need to generate greater technical capacity in government agencies; there is also a consensus about the need to establish mechanisms to ensure greater internal coordination between agencies, and to develop formulas for including civil society and business in the decision-making process.

Leverage or participation?

Disappointment with results of trade negotiations has come to be closely connected with the notion of participation or rather lack of participation. As Susan Strange puts it, we are faced with 'the old questions of all political analysis: Who gets what out of it? Who benefits, who loses? Who carries the risk and who is spared from risk? Who gets the opportunity and who is denied an opportunity?' (Strange, 1994: 18). At the governmental level, participation in international trade policy-making involves a first dimension related to building up capacities. For one, countries must improve their skills and institutional capacity to analyze, take stock of and manage existing agreements in order to frame positions in follow-up negotiations. The importance of this analysis can hardly be dismissed with reciprocity of concessions at the heart of negotiations; market access payoffs must not be overestimated and costs of domestic implementation must not be underestimated. Moreover, the reform of domestic regulation and its impact on development must be more carefully analyzed on its own merits, rather than on its value as a bargaining chip. In order to avoid the capture of issues by vested interests, the conditions of competition and the need for regulation in each sector must be carefully evaluated to achieve both efficiency and equity. Gone are the times when multilateral bargaining could be broadly articulated by a grand coalition of developing countries; thus the need for each country to do its own homework with extensive background research cannot be dismissed. The acquisition of knowledge, technical skills and an adequate institutional capacity should be priorities, particularly taking into account that all other trade institutions (except the Andean Community), and above all the WTO, are member-driven organizations with very small secretariats.

The analysis of issues and framing of positions is largely left to members, necessitating extraordinary attention for the South–South, intra-Latin American, and intra-bloc implications of trade rules.

Enhanced capacity to participate also requires tackling the lack of coordination and turf wars at the national level, a problem that has worsened with the multiplication of issues now addressed in trade negotiations, and thus require the inclusion of more government agencies. Coordination problems stem from various sources, including competition regarding the location of real compared to nominal authority with respect to trade negotiations as well as differences in terms of which agency is responsible for trade policy and which has the power to negotiate and sign international agreements. The need for coordination is pressing not only among government agencies but also with business. Trade policy is inherently a redistributive instrument whereby interests among sectors and between winners and losers within a sector will be at odds. The trade-offs must be clarified and negotiated so that compromises are allowed to emerge during rather than after the process when compliance is socially and politically costly and lack of compliance leads to international disputes which bear financial as well as credibility costs (Chudnovsky and López, Chapter 7, and Tortora and Tussie, Chapter 9, tellingly reflect the magnitude of the institutional adjustment required at the domestic level).

Proposals to address these capacity-building and implementation problems have stressed the need for increasing technical assistance within international bodies. These are welcome initiatives yet stop short of actual needs. Beyond these 'top-down' initiatives, Latin American countries must continue the search for additional, self-generated and homegrown ways to build their technical and institutional capacity. Only those with expertise typically have the knowledge necessary to codify and interpret arcane trade information. No doubt, the task is daunting and seems out of reach for many countries if approached on an individual basis. Feasibility could be augmented, however, if scarce financial resources were pooled, for instance, in the context of regional groupings of countries which share many trade interests, allowing actions to be jointly designed, organized and managed. Such an endeavor could result in a more demand-driven and customized process. The fact that trade negotiations have expanded their sway over so many aspects compounds the seriousness of this problem.

Another dimension of participation is related to sharing in the decision-making process. To escape the neglect of their interests in the WTO, and in an effort to gain some leverage over the agenda, Latin American countries strove to take advantage of bilateral negotiations and preferential treatment. They have tried to increase their room to maneuver exploring the potential of regional agreements and have shown a keen interest in the proposal launched by the US for a FTAA. In contrast to the WTO decision-making process which is seen as costly, distant and arcane, in the FTAA the bulk of the process lies in a dense network of regular and systematic exchanges among negotiators, which has so far advanced issues according to schedule. The FTAA has managed to engage a considerable group of middle-ranking civil servants whose job is to move the process along. Bureaucratic inter-penetration has evolved so that now all governments have a stake in not let-ting the agenda come unglued. Karl Mannheim (1952) once noted that the fundamental tendency of all bureaucratic thought is to turn problems of politics into problems of administration. The extraordinary growth of this administrative and bureaucratic involvement now encompasses a large vari-ety of bodies, ministerial departments, central banks, and regulatory com-missions. Insofar as bureaucracies become part of a process of mutual penetration and socialization, a new pro-trade, pro-negotiating ethos with values, symbols, and goals of its own gains ground, a feature which lends the process a measure of self-preservation. Because negotiators continue to reside in their own countries and only travel to meetings periodically, they are able to remain more in touch with their constituencies than in the WTO's Geneva-based process. Still the FTAA agenda mirrors that of the WTO. Not surprisingly, issues that are problematic in the global arena are particularly difficult in regional fora. Agriculture and trade relief measures appear to be the most polemic and exhausting issues in the FTAA as well as in any free trade agreement (see Diaz-Henderson, Chapter 4, and Tortora and Tussie, Chapter 9). The leverage of Latin American governments in the FTAA process so far has been clearly more effective through a negative veto power than through positive control of the agenda-setting process. This veto power has allowed Latin American countries to reject the linkage of trade with labor and environment issues. However, Latin American countries have had less success, for instance, in agriculture. Still, possibilities for triangular, mul-tipolar and inter-regional diplomacy are limited only by the imagination. For example, one of the latest proposals put forward by Mercosur suggests a '4+1' negotiating process between the members of Mercosur on one side and the US on the other, designed to bring about an 'early harvest' of some of the expected benefits of the FTAA.

Above and beyond the involvement of domestic bureaucracies, the concept of participation now also carries an 'anti-elitist', 'anti-technocratic' tone, seek-ing to debunk the pretensions of technocratic elites. In the FTAA process civil society has managed to include a Social Agenda after the Santiago Summit of 1998, to create a committee to channel their demands, and, more impor-tantly, to publicize the complete draft of the FTAA agreement for the first time ever. Moreover, Latin American governments have opened formal channels for business participation, marking a clear departure from the past. Business participation has also been given a foothold in the Americas Business Forum, which monitors negotiations very closely. The new pledges engaging civil society in foreign policy-making reflect a gradual transformation in the rela-tionship between government and civil society. The process of participation is fragmented, ambivalent and largely dominated by business, but it has opened opportunities nonetheless. However, the tendency to arrogate superior understanding of trade problems is just as strong among elites presently in power as among those only aspiring to it. It is not clear that the loose alliance of strident non-governmental organizations (NGOs) that leapt to global prominence at the 1999 WTO meetings in Seattle is well suited to advance the case for change. The instincts that usually accompany both military conflicts and global economic slowdown may serve their anti-trade protectionist purposes; nonetheless, changes in government policy require a more systematic engagement with the state.

The twin questions of who ought to participate in the design of public policy, and when, raise two important issues. First, new demands pose a major challenge to the traditional mechanisms embedded in representative democracies. Once the secure terrain of electoral representation is abandoned, one is confronted with a slippery slope where the rights and responsibilities of various social groups have to be redefined. Traditional democratic practices give priority to the majority, while they formulate a range of approaches to address the interests of minorities. The dilemma poses a challenge to politicians insofar as it exposes a democratic deficit. Second, is the question of when those entitled can participate. So far, participation has been restricted to side issues, as in NAFTA, with precious few examples of participation and accountability at higher levels of the decision-making process. The risk posed by having embryonic participatory mechanisms without adequate institutionalization is that such mechanisms may only serve to increase the legitimacy of bureaucrats without contributing much to solving the discontent over the questions of who benefits, who grows, and whose market is at stake.

The WTO procedures since Seattle have also become more transparent and inclusive with important matters passing through the General Council on which all WTO members sit. Still much more is required to allow an expanding set of players to increase their voice in the affairs of the organization. The WTO process could be decentralized, delegating the task of finding common grounds 'downstream' to, for instance, regionally based committees which bring together developing country constituencies with the mission of assembling joint positions on major issues to be later brought to the negotiation table. Hence, participation and interest representation could be broadened, thus strengthening the legitimacy of the whole decision-making process without undermining the quest for efficiency.

The removal of trade repression together with the call for participation pose new challenges of inclusion, in contrast to fifteen years ago when countries faced the challenges of exclusion. Strategic dilemmas had traditionally revolved around whether or not, and in what way, to get engaged in trade negotiations. Today, the central concern is at what level (multilateral, regional, sub-regional) and to what extent commitments should be made and how to face and assess the expansion of the trade agenda. Beyond contriving a strategy they need to break down the rules governing trade, to deal with the consequences of past commitments, and, foremost, to handle the intricacies of each negotiation in order to put together the right mix of incentives for business. It is not surprising, therefore, that at this juncture countries are pondering bargaining relations anew. If in the early 1990s the major concerns were to anchor domestic reform with international commitments and to become good systemic players, today, other development considerations – mainly related with the new mix of incentives required for the attraction of investments – have (re)gained relevance. These questions, it should be stressed, do not in themselves invalidate the main thrust of mainstream trade theory. To understand the conditions of trade liberalization is not tantamount to overall rejection of trade as such.

The internationalization of competition has redrawn both geographic and political borders. In essence, internationally organized networks under the aegis of interlocking trade agreements, be they regional, sub-regional or multilateral, have provoked and endorsed new bargaining relations in which trade liberalization can provide economic gains without relatively large adverse impact on individual firms or countries. Is this the birth of 'embedded liberalism' in a new guise in Latin America? If so, this vintage of 'embedded liberalism' comes without safety nets to cushion the plight of losers. A safety net of sorts resides in the web of regional agreements, which allow trade liberalization to advance gradually bit by bit, literally bartering the pains of liberalization with the gains of market access and export growth. Thus negotiations have become a centerpiece of embedded liberalism. It is in essence not free trade at all costs, but a risk-minimizing strategy resting on concrete trade-offs between liberalization in some sectors and increased market access for others: textiles for agriculture, telecommunications for financial services. If trade liberalization is effectively carried out in quid pro quo terms, the costs of adjustment can hopefully be mitigated. However, the entrenched emphasis on reciprocity in trade negotiations has added a previously absent domestic dimension. With the need to offer reciprocal concessions, every international negotiation necessarily gives rise to a parallel domestic negotiation, whereby the gains of one sector abroad require another sector to adjust to heightened import competition. Hence the sensitivity of domestic actors to the distributional impact of trade concessions has tended to generate conflicts and resentment, adding a source of further fragility.

In these intensely micro-managed regional negotiations, the pace of sectors is accommodated in double movements, leading to the coexistence of camps of swift liberalization and camps of protracted progress. Sectors move at different paces following the interplay of three variables – internationalization, labor-intensity and concentration. The more internationalized and the less labor-intensive and concentrated a sector's production is, the more likely it is to accept the removal of trade regulation. Once we move away from perfect competition and consider vertical integration across borders, firms find benefits in the reduction of tariffs on products they both import and export. The coalition supporting and spurring free trade is not a 'loose lobby', but a powerful locomotive (see Narlikar and Woods, Chapter 2) as exemplified by the telecommunications sector (see Bastos Tigre, Chapter 6). Agriculture, in contrast, remains mostly a price-competitive market where market niches cannot be as easily carved into differentiated products. These special features make it a particularly unruly sector (see Diaz-Henderson, Chapter 4), whose reluctance to liberalize might be mitigated at times but is replicated in all fora. Because sectors move differently, a dual policy is hammered out feeding upon and fuelling movement in different directions for different sectors with different outlooks.

If differences between sectors are wiped away, international trade might be seen as an incrementalist process in which failure to sustain the momentum towards liberalization precipitates retreat into mutually destructive protectionism – the 'Alcoholic Anonymous' view of international trade: one swig from the bottle will bring the fall; the 'capitulation' to protectionist pressures in one industrial sector compels capitulation in others. In practice, because sectors move differently, there is no logically necessary correlation between protectionism in one sector and protectionism in another.

The idiosyncrasies of sectors have given rise to specific trade regimes in which distinctive coalitions now operate. Sectoral and sub-sectoral coalitions will no doubt continue to move on shifting ground, and thus change focus, shape and membership as negotiating goals transmogrify. But they are an increasing part of the new scenario, a function of rapid technological change and the broadness of the agenda *vis-à-vis* crisscrossing interests. They will coexist and compete with the mushrooming of regional coalitions, thus demanding that countries deal with multiple memberships and split loyalties. In fact, the coexistence of sectoral and regional forms of association allows countries to not put all their eggs in one basket. If regional arrangements risk becoming small areas of hegemony where predominant countries can increase their power, the dovetailing with sectoral and sub-sectoral coalitions, even on shifting ground, could possibly allow smaller countries room to pursue interests which risk being subdued or even smothered by regional coalitions. If one sees these two forms of association in sharp relief, a host of empirical questions become bracketed. If it is not only possible but necessary to veer back and forth from regional to sectoral coalitions, the value of defection is heightened and sooner or later it will have to be faced. Defection is not only morally but also politically indicated, making concepts such as victims and victimizers entirely off the mark.

Structure of the book

A first thread spun by the book is a dissection of the extent to which the new trade agenda is genuinely as threatening to Latin American countries as is assumed *a priori*. Much has been said about how the setting up of a very comprehensive trade agenda leads to the loss of policy autonomy and reduces development options. The passage from so-called shallow to deep integration is seen as a threat by Latin American countries because, compared to the past, large degrees of freedom have been curtailed. Massive support policies for industry may be out of bounds. But this book strives to go beyond this broad assertion and look more closely at the opportunities and the probably still ample scope for policy maneuver. In essence, the objective is to examine where the trade agenda is not only broad but also thin, in order to put into perspective the widespread sense of increasingly open-ended and encroaching negotiations. Emphasis is placed on the interlocking games of cooperation and conflict in intra-regional relations, and how these are played out in the WTO arena. The focus on these neglected games allows us to move away from one-dimensional views of multilateralism, with the overcast of North–South tensions. The purpose here is to capture the novel ways in which the WTO is used by Latin American countries. Most of the literature posits the links between regionalism and multilateralism as a dilemma and looks at the impact *of* regionalism *on* multilateralism; but it fails to capture the contribution of multilateralism to healthy regional relations. Regionalism thrives in the policy spaces left by multilateral commitments, but when interstices are too many or too wide, they quickly become a source of regional friction.

The second thread woven throughout the book is the level of analysis of trade issues, paying special attention to how issues are broken down along regional, hemispheric and global lines, and to national and sub-regional responses to shifts in the agenda. The view across levels not only provides insights into the strengths and limitations of each level but also shows how the levels interact with each other. As several chapters suggest, it is not clear that the multilateral forum is more convenient or amenable than the others to negotiate on particular issues, even if commitments made at that level serve to both propel and anchor regional initiatives. As will be seen, issues in slow motion at the global level (agriculture, antidumping) are also conflict-ridden at the regional level. Issues on fast track globally (services) also glide rapidly regionally. But the book tries to go beyond this merely additive character of the whole process. Each issue provides scenes for regional agreement and disagreement, both of which are projected onto the screen of negotiations. On a single occasion the impulse to collaborate invisibly vies with the impulse towards conflict. Members of a regional unit will seek out an opportunity to mutually tie each other's hands, and, at the same time, an opportunity to build a common front against outsiders. Once again, this is the increasingly intensive South–South dimension that the book tries to capture.

The book is structured in three parts. Part I combines three chapters with an overarching perspective on interests, coalitions and emerging scenarios. The chapters consider convergent interests that are creating or have created opportunities for coalitions at various levels, drawing out possible scenarios in the different fora. Part II addresses the management of sectoral market access, with three chapters focusing on agriculture and services, the major areas emerging after the Uruguay Round. Here the interests of the region and individual countries in specific sectors is magnified at a more disaggregate level. Part III deals with the management of competition and conflict, with chapters delving into policy competition for foreign direct investment, competition and its policy implications, general trade-defense policy issues, and trade disputes.

These sectoral and institutional issues will continue to grind along in the ongoing multilateral, hemispheric and regional processes. The circumstances surrounding and shaping the interaction between the FTAA and the WTO will be a crucial determinant of the turbulent scenario in the region. Progress towards the FTAA continues to chug along steadily and quietly, with negotiation teams meeting week after week in Panama City. Similarly, the post-Doha work project will dirty its hands in issues of services, antidumping, and so on. With the region destabilized by crisis in Argentina and a new round of multilateral negotiations opening that promises to be more concerned with anti-terrorist alliances than development issues, regional and sub-regional negotiations could offer safety nets to reign in the most painful displacement effects of global competition. When adjustments are very high the politically optimal and even economic way of removing trade barriers may be in phases rather than all at once. Here regional, sub-regional and sectoral coalitions intersect and spread out leading to a variety of compromises and mutual adjustments, with the outcome varying greatly from case to case.

Note

* Many of the ideas contained herein were drawn from meetings and discussions with LATN colleagues. I must mention in particular Valentina Delich, Marisa Diaz-Henderson, Manuela Tortora, Daniel Chudnovsky, Rohinton Medhora and Nicola Phillips who generously read and provided comments on previous drafts. Gabriela Rodriguez López and Cintia Quiliconi also deserve special mention. I owe a vast debt to Brita Siepker for her time and energy in putting together this introduction. Some sections draw on a previous essay with Miguel Lengyel. Needless to say, the responsibility for the interpretations that finally emerged from these discussions, insofar as they are reflected in the text, is mine alone.

Part I
Interest, Coalitions and Scenarios

1
Latin American and Caribbean Interests in the WTO

Marcelo de Paiva Abreu

1.1 Introduction

Despite the successful launching of a new round of multilateral trade negotiations in Doha, a wide gap between the priorities of developed and developing countries in the World Trade Organization (WTO) persists. The
position of Latin American members tended to converge with that of other
developing economies. Latin America made considerable concessions in the
Uruguay Round (UR), with many economies binding their tariffs at relatively low levels. Even in the middle of macroeconomic turmoil in the late
1990s, with the successive financial crises in Asia, Russia and Brazil, commitment to liberal trade policies has been on the whole preserved. The liberalization process has, of course, raised severe problems related to the
accommodation of conflicting interests. Problems arising out of the political
economy of trade are not the monopoly of developed economies. After the
very significant reduction of high tariffs entailed by the UR, tariff concessions
by developing countries by further lowering their bound tariff levels will
severely affect established interests which are favored by protectionist policies. Most of the region's economies may face problems in adjusting in the
mid-term to substantial additional tariff reduction undertakings. To create
the political conditions required for further liberalization, Latin American
governments need to be able to show to domestic interests that the developed countries are willing to make significant concessions by opening their
markets in all sectors.

Attempts to launch a new Millennium Round in Seattle at the end of 1999
were principally thwarted by the stances adopted by the European Union
(EU), Japan and the United States (US). The EU and Japan persistently
resisted considering further reductions in protection affecting agricultural
products. The US, on the other hand, made it clear, in a surprising move,
that it would consider as a *sine qua non* the inclusion of labor standards in
the new round. These stances were partially ceded at Doha, as a new recognition of the interests of developing countries arose among a desperate

search for consensus. On one hand, a new round was only possible with an acceptance of the growing importance of developing countries in the WTO. On the other, poor countries newly signified important allies to the US in the war on terrorism, especially as they sought to further their role in multilateralization and globalization. In this context of acquiescing to the interests of developing countries, the launching of a new round was possible.

Liberalization originating in multilateral trade negotiations should in principle affect both industrial and agricultural products in a balanced way. There is, for instance, no economic reason to limit offers of total tariff elimination to industrial products. In the same way that developing economies in the UR were expected to, and did, fall in line with more liberal trade regimes affecting industrial products, the new round should remove the obstacles that still affect agricultural trade at a much faster pace than further liberalization affecting industrial products. Convergence in the direction of less distorted world agricultural markets may, however, require the international mobilization of resources to cope with the consequences of price increases on vulnerable food importers.

The inclination of developed economies to include a number of new issues, such as environment and labor rights, which had not been traditionally dealt with by the WTO and the General Agreement on Tariffs and Trade (GATT) in the past, introduce a new range of difficulties. The situation is not dissimilar to that before the launching of the UR in the early 1980s concerning trade-related intellectual property rights (TRIPs), trade-related investment measures (TRIMs) and services. However, economic arguments for the inclusion of such themes were sounder than those used today in the policy harmonization debate. In spite of initial suggestions by developing countries in the UR negotiations, there is no essential difference between arguments in favor of the liberalization of goods or services as long as the differences concerning modes of supply are considered thus raising problems related to the treatment of foreign investment. Similarly, there is little doubt about the importance of protection of intellectual property to foster invention. The arguments in favor of linking labor and environmental standards to trade measures are much more controversial as there are significant doubts on what would be the end impact on exactly those targets which are thought to be worthwhile to pursue. Compulsory minimum standards enforced through trade retaliation measures may end up further hurting abused workers and the environment, a result which is directly in contradiction with the alleged aims of such trade measures (Bhagwati and Srinivasan, 1996, and Brown, Deardorff and Stern, 1996).

Section 1.2 of this chapter will focus on the analysis of concrete interests of groups of economies in terms of market access. Account will be taken of the potential differences between Latin American countries in terms of their interest in multilateral negotiations and regional integration. Section 1.3 will consider other negotiating issues of interest for Latin America, especially issues not traditionally dealt with in the WTO/GATT such as environment, labor rights and competition policies. Section 1.4 will include an assessment of how to cope with the issue of special and differential treatment taking into account the different levels of development of Latin American economies. This will also consider how such provisions worked under the arrangements negotiated in the UR. Section 1.5 will deal with the difficulties of implementation of prior agreements, taking into consideration the impact those experiences may have in the new round. The final section concludes with the establishment of taxonomies according to converging interests of Latin American and Caribbean countries in the post-Doha agenda.

1.2   Market access: potential interest in multilateral negotiations and trade geographical concentration

To gauge what is at stake in multilateral trade negotiations in the WTO from a Latin American perspective, it is important to have a clear idea of the present trade flows and size of domestic markets of Latin American economies. Table 1.1 summarizes such information, presenting statistics on gross national product at purchasing power parity rates (GNP-PPP) and total (imports plus exports) trade for most Latin American and Caribbean economies. While the impact of further trade liberalization is likely to be greater in economies with greater trade flows, the impact of other issues under discussion in the WTO, such as intellectual property or services, is likely to be proportional to the size of the domestic markets of member economies.

What emerges from such trade data is that Mexico is by far the most important trading economy in Latin America: its total trade in 1999 accounted for nearly 45 per cent of total Latin American trade, representing almost three times total trade from the second most important Latin American trading nation – Brazil – and 80 per cent more than total Mercosur trade. Mercosur's total trade was about 45 per cent of total trade in all other Latin American and Caribbean economies, Mexico excluded. Mercosur's 1999 GNP-PPP represented 48.7 per cent of total GNP-PPP of the region (of which Brazil accounts for 33.9 per cent), Mexico 24 per cent, the Andean Community (AC) as a whole about 16.7 per cent and Chile 4 per cent. All other economies together thus account for around 6 per cent of the aggregate. These data, as represented in Table 1.1, may speak to the countries' comparative leverage in negotiations, given the small size of all Latin American and Caribbean economies compared to major developed economies. However, little indication is made of multilateral negotiations' importance for each particular economy.

The coincidence of the culmination of negotiations in both the WTO and the Free Trade Area of the Americas (FTAA) for the year 2005 will divide the attention and efforts of developing countries. It seems reasonable to believe that the more concentrated trade in Western Hemisphere markets is,

Table 1.1   Latin American and Caribbean Gross National Product and total trade

	GNP (in US$ billion)	Total trade (in US$ billion)
AC	523.0	79.4
Bolivia	17.8	3.3
Colombia	237.2	22.2
Ecuador	32.3	8.6
Peru	110.7	12.7
Venezuela	124.9	32.6
Caricom	30.6	17.8
Bahamas	3.0	3.8
Barbados	3.3	1.4
Belize	1.1	0.5
Dominica	0.4	0.2
Grenada	0.6	0.2
Guyana	2.8	1.2
Jamaica	8.5	4.4
St Kitts	0.3	0.1
St Lucia	0.7	0.1
St Vincent and Grenadines	0.5	0.6
Trinidad and Tobago	9.4	5.3
CACM	109.7	39.6
Costa Rica	20.7	13.6
El Salvador	25.1	6.5
Guatemala	39.0	9.3
Honduras	14.3	8.1
Nicaragua	10.6	2.2
Mercosur	1525.7	154.1
Argentina	414.1	46.6
Brazil	1061.7	98.1
Paraguay	22.5	3.6
Uruguay	27.4	5.8
NAFTA		
Mexico	752.0	278.4
Other		
Chile	125.7	29.9
Dominican Republic	39.1	14.5
Haiti	11.0	1.4
Panama	14.1	5.0
Suriname	1.7	1.0

Source: GNP-PPP data for 1999 (for Bahamas, Barbados, Belize and Suriname, data for 1998) from World Bank (2000). Trade data from International Monetary Fund (1998).

the more intense the interest will be in a regional hemispheric integration initiative as opposed to multilateral negotiations. Indeed in the case of Mexico, already a member of a preferential trade area that includes the US, this adjustment in evaluating the issues at stake is essential.

Table 1.2 presents data on the relative importance for each economy or set of economies in Latin America and the Caribbean of both intra-free trade agreement (FTA) trade and of trade within the Western Hemisphere. Interpretation of the data changes quite dramatically when trade orientation is taken into account. The concentration of Mexican and, to a lesser extent, Central American and AC trade with Western Hemisphere partners, and especially the US, significantly reduces their potential stake in new multilateral negotiations. What marks a difference between the two cases is that while Central American economies would wish to be included in the FTAA, Mexico already has access to the US market through its membership in the North American Free Trade Agreement (NAFTA). On the other hand, Mercosur and Chile, with a large share of their exports to economies outside the hemisphere, would in principle have more at stake in the new multilateral round in spite of Mercosur being less open than many other Latin American economies. This is indeed the reciprocal of the argument that justifies the less than enthusiastic stance of a country such as Brazil concerning the FTAA. The bottom line is that there is not enough trade with the hemisphere to justify becoming a partner of FTAA at least in the time span initially preferred by the US and in competition with multilaterally agreed liberalization. The AC, especially Colombia, and the Caribbean Community (Caricom) economies, are in the intermediate group in terms of share of trade with the hemisphere.

Table 1.2 Share of intra-FTA exports in total exports and of exports outside the hemisphere

	Share of intra-FTA exports in total exports	*Share of exports outside the Western Hemisphere*
AC	0.0789	0.259 (0.281)
Colombia	0.141 (AC)	0.237 (0.276)
Venezuela	0.038 (AC)	0.154 (0.161)
Caricom	0.154	0.319 (0.376)
CACM	0.116	0.234 (0.264)
Mercosur	0.205	0.460 (0.579)
Argentina	0.302 (Mercosur)	0.433 (0.621)
Brazil	0.140 (Mercosur)	0.528 (0.614)
Mexico	0.902 (NAFTA)	0.062 (0.618)
Chile	—	0.583

Note: Share of exports outside the hemisphere excludes intra-FTA trade.

Source: Data for 1997 from IMF (2000).

But much of Caricom trade outside the hemisphere rests on special arrangements under the EU preferential regime for AC countries.

For Latin American economies most likely to consider multilateral negotiations as vital because a significant share of their current trade is with countries outside the hemisphere, the main distortion to be removed in relation to market access is the asymmetrical treatment between agricultural and industrial products. This is certainly the case for Mercosur members and also to a lesser extent for Colombia. At the other extreme of the spectrum, Chile, Peru and some of the Central American and Caribbean economies may be rather less enthusiastic about collective commitments to reduce agricultural protection rapidly (see Diaz-Henderson, Chapter 4, for a discussion on agricultural protection in the Americas).

The major trading economies have reflected their intention to preserve such distortions. On one hand, the US has stated its interest in a selective approach based on sectoral liberalization showing, implicitly, its resistance to the application of tariff reduction formulae that would affect tariff peaks protecting sensitive products. On the other hand, the EU voiced its preference for the application of formulae to reduce tariffs in order to assure automatic trade liberalization across the board. But this explicitly excluded agricultural products. The inclusion of industrial products will confront resistance from developing economies unless a credible quid pro quo can be presented. The effects of recent financial crises in most Latin American economies have given a new lease of life to protectionist lobbies under pressure, but is counterbalanced by the export interests committed to a reduction of industrial tariff peaks which significantly affect the exports of most economies in Latin America, especially those with a higher share of manufactured exports in total exports: Mexico, Brazil, Colombia and Argentina.

New empirical work by Hertel and Martin (1999) has shown that a standard tariff cut of 40 per cent in the next round of multilateral trade negotiations would relatively benefit developing more than developed economies. Possible welfare gains would amount to a maximum in the region of 1.5 to 2.0 per cent of total income for some Asian economies contrasted to 0.1 to 0.2 per cent for most developed economies. Brazil's income would increase by 0.5 per cent and the rest of Latin America's by 0.2 to 0.3 per cent. This difference between developing and developed countries reflects the fact that tariffs on industrial products in developed economies are much lower than those in developing economies.

A complication involving market access is that tariffs applied by most Latin American and Caribbean economies are below tariff levels bound in the UR. There have been suggestions that developed countries would be unwilling to accept that additional liberalization commitments by developing economies would take bound tariff levels as reference, on the grounds that applied rates offer a more appropriate benchmark. This demand, besides interpreting 'bound tariff rate' in an innovative way, would introduce an undesirable additional source of unequal treatment between developing and developed economies, since most developed country applied and bound tariff rates coincide. Many countries in the region bound their rates at 35 per cent in the UR but applied rates are typically below 15 per cent for bigger economies.

The application of either of the tariff reduction methodologies proposed by the US and the EU would assure that tariff peaks remain as unwarranted exceptions in the long-term trend towards across-the-board trade liberalization, which should be the thrust of the multilateral negotiation effort. Ideally, tariffs should be reduced by the application of formulae but in such a way as to assure that tariff (or tariff equivalent) levels above a relatively high threshold, either 30 or 40 per cent for agricultural products, would rapidly converge to such a threshold. An additional formula, perhaps of the Swiss type, would then be applied to reduce tariff levels under the threshold. In a second stage of trade liberalization a formula could be universally applied without the exclusion of any product.

The big effort to gain market access for agricultural trade will have to be accompanied by the elimination of export subsidies and the curtailment of domestic support, which is a very heated issue. Latin American and Caribbean economies that are food importers, especially in Central America and the Caribbean, will have a strong interest in contingent measures of financial support to cope with possible price increases. New estimates of the impact of agricultural liberalization on the price of agricultural commodities, however, have tended to qualify the results obtained earlier which suggested a significant rise in world prices. Anderson, Erwidodo and Ingco (1999) have once again stressed the benefits of agricultural liberalization and the fact that one-third of the gains entailed in a total liberalization scenario would result from removing market distortions for agricultural products in OECD economies though their agricultural producers contribute only 4 per cent of global GDP.

The emphasis placed by Mattoo (1999) on competition in the provision of services rather than the simple increase of foreign ownership is welcomed. Assuring competition together with widening the scope for foreign ownership depends crucially on effective regulation. There is significant opportunity for technical assistance in this area. Indeed, some developed economies have been reticent to commit to a multilateral competition policy agreement because it would lead to the removal of the inter-country heterogeneity of the legal frameworks; exactly the same arguments should be applied to developing economies (see Tavares de Araujo, Chapter 8). The services agenda includes both negotiation of rules such as those on safeguards and subsidies and commitments covering new sectors. There are important discrepancies between developed and developing countries on the desired timing of such negotiations as the latter would of course prefer to further the negotiation of rules that would enhance their capacity to compete both domestically and abroad. Of special interest to developing economies, and especially to the larger Latin American economies with a particular interest in the market for construction services, is the improvement of rules on the temporary presence of natural persons (see Abugattas and Stephenson, Chapter 5).

1.3   Non-traditional issues

Many developing countries argue that there is already too much to be done in relation to the built-in agenda and pending implementation, but there are a number of issues not traditionally dealt with by the GATT or the WTO that could draw attention. Hence, broadening the agenda would not be a major priority. The WTO ministerial meeting at Singapore in 1996 agreed to have work programs in four issues which were included in the negotiating agenda of the Doha work program: competition policies, trade facilitation, transparency in government procurement, and investment. There was no particularly strong objection from developing countries to the inclusion of competition policies and trade facilitation. In the case of competition policies difficulties are more likely to occur among developed economies because of the extreme disparity in the maturity of institutions and policy preferences. Developing economies have traditionally resisted signing multilateral agreements on government procurement and it is unlikely that such a stance will change radically. It is reasonable to suppose that the relatively larger Latin American economies would tend to resist undertakings on government procurement since present domestic suppliers would quite likely be displaced by foreign suppliers. On the investment issue, Latin American countries are unlikely to resist the very cautious stance of most WTO members limiting their efforts to stressing the desirability of 'educational and analytical work' on foreign direct investment (see Chudnovsky and López, Chapter 7).

In other important non-traditional issues such as labor rights and environment, not only was it difficult to see a *demandeur* role for Latin America, but they seem to provide a strong case for the adoption of obstructionist stances, especially in the case of labor rights. It is difficult to single out a developing country not suspicious of a possible misuse of a so-called harmonized approach to labor standards. Thus the US insistence on the creation of a working group on labor standards in Seattle in fact blocked the launching of a new round in Seattle, and was left by the wayside in the Doha agenda. The obstructionist stance of Latin America and the Caribbean in relation to trade-related environmental matters is likely to be less homogeneous. In contrast with the history of US–Mexico difficulties on environmental matters in the NAFTA negotiations (see Ortíz Mena, Vol. II), cross-border issues tend to be unimportant for other Latin American countries. The potential difficulties converge on the policy harmonization context concerning global externalities generated by the emission of gases and deforestation. The bigger economies are more likely to be targeted as generators of undesirable externalities and more so, countries such as Brazil where environmental issues related to the preservation of the rainforest are superimposed on the more general problem of fuel emissions.

The fact that relatively more damage to the environment per unit of output results from economic activity in developing economies than in developed economies does not justify the adoption of policies that are not the result of multilateral agreements. An effective system of incentives to curb pollution multilaterally does not include the possibility of creating WTO enforcement mechanisms. It probably includes side payments, mainly funded by developed economies, to foster the preservation of resources now facing depletion at an undesirable rate.

It is ironic that environment and labor standards, issues that pose a threat to the multilateral consensus, are those around which there also is the most pressure to include non-governmental groups purporting to democratically represent the interests at stake. Given the political economy of protectionism and the asymmetrical perceptions of economic actors on the impact of protection on their income, it is not unreasonable to have sympathy with those who are skeptical about the positive role (from an efficiency point of view) of such lobbies. Inefficient steel makers, for example in the US, are able to obtain protection from the US government in the form of antidumping duties in spite of the cost entailed by higher steel prices in the domestic market because steel consumers have more diffuse interests and are unable to resist their lobbying power (see Tortora and Tussie, Chapter 9, for a discussion on the US steel industry's use of antidumping). There are no guarantees to avoid the capture of non-governmental organizations (NGOs) involved in the 'harmonization' of environment and labor standards by such protection lobbies that are keenly seeking a modern argument to cover up their lack of competitiveness.

The linkage of democracy and the WTO with the role of the NGOs is highly artificial. It is only reasonable that many governments vented their dissatisfaction in Seattle with supposed manipulation by aggressive NGOs with the electoral platform of the host country. Some observers did not fail to mention that if the theme of democracy in the WTO was to be considered seriously, analysis should start with the different weight attached to the participation of member countries as attested to by 'green room' negotiations and other traditionally WTO opaque practices (Tussie and Lengyel, 2001).

1.4 Special and differential treatment

Special and differential treatment (S&D) remains one of the most difficult issues in multilateral trade negotiations. In the UR, special concessions were mostly confined to the adoption of extended periods to cope with new rules compared to the periods allowed in the case of developed economies as well as to possible provision of technical assistance. Typically, extended periods for full implementation have been generally assured to developing countries and exemption from implementation has been granted to least-developed countries. In many cases the treatment of least-developed and other developing countries has been different.

Different deadlines for adjustment were applied to agricultural liberalization commitments concerning domestic support and export subsidies, application of sanitary and phytosanitary measures, customs valuation, withdrawal of existing TRIMs, imposition of safeguards, use of export subsidies and commitment to TRIPs disciplines. In the case of trade-related exceptions, it is likely that industrial interests would welcome a revision of the constraints imposed by the present commitments, especially in the case of the automotive industry which relies on main offices to extend special arrangements. The economic rationality of such arrangements, which generally involve subsidies tied to export performance, is scant from the point of view of the country that attracts foreign investment. The inclusion of such an instrument in the negotiating agenda in spite of its inefficiency is a reflection of the clout of such sectors in the political economy of protection rather than of any genuine 'national interest'.

TRIPs are of more general interest for Latin American and Caribbean economies than TRIMs. There is a much better case for the inclusion of TRIPs in a revision agenda from a social point of view as the increased cost of the relevant protected products is likely to affect the poor and the very poor in developing economies, especially in the case of pharmaceutical products. However, in contrast with TRIMs there is no hope that the bargaining power of multinationals could be used to further a revision of the agreed implementation periods. Rather the reverse is the case, as pharmaceutical multinationals are very keen on the importance of the agreed implementation period to assure increased revenues if intellectual property rules are better enforced in developing economies. Nevertheless, initiatives led by Brazil, India and South Africa, with support from the ally-seeking US, won the inclusion of TRIPs and pharmaceutical issues in the Doha agenda, and more importantly the recognition of members' rights to protect public health and promote access to medicine in cases of AIDS, tuberculosis, malaria and other epidemics.

In other cases the references to differential treatment for developing countries is extremely vague such as those related to technical barriers, import licensing, the imposition of antidumping (AD) and countervailing duties (CVDs) and rules and procedures related to dispute settlement. In the case of AD, the exhortation to take into account levels of development when duties are imposed seems to have been completely disregarded (see Tortora and Tussie, Chapter 9).

There is a very strong feeling among developing countries that this approach has been an unsatisfactory way to cope with sharp contrasts in development levels. The simple extension of implementation periods implies that given time and/or sufficient technical assistance it will be possible to remove inherent disadvantages which affect the competitiveness of develop-ing economies. Criticisms imply that such difficulties will only be solved by the convergence of levels of development. The essential problem here is that to reopen the issue of how the S&D issue has been addressed in the UR agreements and renegotiate such terms is likely to have a cost in terms of addi-tional concessions by the developing country members. The main proponents of such a move seem to turn a blind eye to such likely costs.

Another pending issue related to S&D refers to preferential treatment accorded to imports of developing countries in the markets of developed economies under Generalized System of Preferences (GSP) schemes.[1] There is also a near consensus in developing countries that rules concerning such preferences should be more automatic and stable over time so that the con-cession of preferences is not unilateral and does not turn into a negotiation to extract specific concessions from beneficiaries. There may be room for a more formal set of rules to be adopted for preferences under the umbrella of the GSP and the Global System of Trade Preferences (GSTP). It could include a universal system of variable preferences decreasing with the level of income of the recipient economy until graduation and withdrawal of pref-erences. Low-income countries would receive 100 per cent preferences from all other groups. Countries in an intermediate group would receive perhaps 50 per cent preferences from the high-income group. The system would be of automatic application as thresholds would be defined by GNP-PPP levels.

1.5   Difficulties of implementation: an agenda in itself

The clash between liberalization timetables from the URAs and from the onset of a new round has been significantly reduced by the postponing of a new round. Two major themes emerge in relation to the implementation timetable of the UR results: agriculture, and textile and clothing. The timetable of the aborted Millennium Round was to be effective beginning in 2003, but the round begun in Doha has until 2005. Problems concerning overlapping of liberalization commitments are perhaps less likely to surface in the case of agriculture as full implementation of reduction commitments for economies other than developing and least-developed countries was to be completed by the end of 2001. Nevertheless, implementation has not gone smoothly, especially on expedient notification of allowed subsidies and transparency in relation to quota allocation. There have been complaints by agricultural exporters on importers' lack of expediency in providing full information on issues like quotas as required by the URA on agriculture with the consequence that agricultural imports are reduced (see Diaz-Henderson, Chapter 4). In the case of the WTO Agreement on Textiles and Clothing (ATC) a Textiles Monitoring Body supervises the pace of the liberalization according to the three-phase schedule, the enlargement of existing quotas and the use of transitional safeguards. The implementation period runs until the end of 2004. It is well known that importers have padded their list of products included in the transitional list so as to artificially extend the regime of high protection typical of the Multifibre Arrangement (MFA). The issue of the balance of concessions between developed and developing country members was bound to arise due to a possible overlapping and the related danger of procrastination to dismantle the remnants of the MFA.

The revision of implementation and related issues foreseen in the Doha ministerial declaration is essential for the success of the round. International disciplines concerning the application of antidumping duties need to be improved, since their determination process is often crowned by the imposition of disguised voluntary export restraints. The constraints imposed by present rules on panel findings, which limit their scope to the verification of proper and objective establishment of the facts and their objective evaluation, pose a severe curtailment to their capacity to adequately solve antidumping grievances at the multilateral level. Given the present rules it is extremely unlikely that multilateral dispute settlement will be able to dilute the asymmetries of bilateral bargaining power involved in the imposition of antidumping and countervailing duties (see Weston and Delich, Chapter 10).

Another important issue involves strengthening the WTO's multilateral capacity to restrain countries' ability to unilaterally adopt measures without recourse to the full possibilities of the multilateral dispute settlement system. There is a grey area related to the WTO-legality of unilateral actions used in the past by the US under Section 301 of the Trade Act of 1974 and of similar EU regulations which may be created. A WTO panel found that parts of sections 304, 305 and 306 of the US Trade Act of 1974 were not GATT or WTO-inconsistent but with the proviso that its findings were based in full or in part on US undertakings articulated in the Statement of Administrative Action approved by the US Congress at the time it implemented the URAs and confirmed in the statements by the US to the panel. The panel stated that should those undertakings be repudiated or in any other way removed, its findings of conformity would no longer be warranted. The question of whether the use of such instruments is compatible with WTO's multilateral disciplines and if these latter contribute to dampen the disparities between the bargaining clout of different WTO member countries remains dormant.[2]

1.6   Converging interests in the post-Doha agenda

In the face of continuing multilateral trade negotiations, Latin American and Caribbean countries converge on various issues. Their participation in the new round could be stepped up by the formation of coalitions among converging interests. Taxonomies can be formulated based on the concrete interests of different Latin American and Caribbean economies given the material presented in the previous sections. Three different sets of economies can be distinguished: Mercosur, and perhaps also Colombia; Mexico, with Peru and Venezuela; and all small economies of the Caribbean and Central America. The only group with specific emphasis on the issue of access of goods would be Mercosur and Colombia. The more advanced economies, and more prominently Brazil, Mexico, Argentina and Chile, would have common interests in a whole set of access-related issues which would cover services, AD, CVDs, and unilateral measures like Section 301. Finally, almost all economies in Latin America and the Caribbean converge on both a heart-felt reluctance to harmonize environment and labor standards and a keenness to reopen the transition period of the TRIPs so as to reduce the impact of remittances on balances of payment. Participation in the new round will surely center around fending off developed country environmental demands and pushing for special treatment in TRIPs and pharmaceuticals.

Latin American and Caribbean economies should not limit their role to a defensive agenda. In response to the defensive strategy pursued in the UR, it has been deemed a mistake to abandon the role of *demandeur* based on points of principle (Tussie and Glover, 1993). It should be recognized, however, that the defensive stance of developing economies concerning harmonization of policies related to labor and the environment seems to provide a much firmer coalition ground than opposition to the inclusion of services in the UR negotiations (see Narlikar and Woods, Chapter 2). From a *demandeur* point of view there are opportunities for the Latin American members of the Cairns Group to press for a more significant effort to liberalize agricultural trade (Diaz-Henderson, Chapter 4). Although the Doha Ministerial Declaration committed members to a reduction in export subsidies towards a complete phasing out of their use, it also provided for the negotiations to be carried out without prejudice to their outcome, which dilutes the solvency of commitments made. There is also scope for a more widespread, informal coalition of the bigger economies in Latin America related to services (see Narlikar and Woods, Chapter 2), limitations of dispute settlement machinery in the case of AD, CVDs, and the imposition of unilateral 301-esque measures by the US and the EU.

Notes

1. It is of course true that the spread of regional agreements tend to blunt the effectiveness of arrangements following GSP lines. But the same is true for all previous preferential schemes such as Lomé. Resistance to effective graduation may also be weakened by growing regionalism.
2. See Jackson (1998), sections 4.5 and 4.6. See also the WTO documentation on *United States – Sections 301–310 of the Trade Act of 1974*, complaint by the European Communities (WT/DS152/1). The panel report was adopted on 27 January 2000 and the dispute was dated 25 November 1998.

2
Sectoral Coalitions: the Case of Services

Amrita Narlikar and Ngaire Woods

2.1 Trade and new coalitions in a globalizing world economy

In the arena of international trade, coalitions have traditionally formed within countries, and occasionally, among countries, in order to protect the domestic production of particular goods, services, or sectors of the economy (Rogowski, 1989). However, oil and interest rate shocks in the world economy during the 1980s, coupled with debt crises and the rise of a more market-oriented economic philosophy, brought about a dismantling of organized protectionism in many countries, eroding the coalitions which had so tightly resisted trade liberalization (Goldstein, 1998). Furthermore, the completion of the Uruguay Round (UR) led to the creation of the World Trade Organization (WTO), and the flourishing of regional trading blocs that can lead to small areas of hegemony in which predominant states enjoy yet more unfettered power. Far from obviating the need for developing countries to form coalitions on the basis of interests both within regions and across them, regionalism can underline the ongoing need for other coalitions. Within these regional and international fora, many countries have come sharply to recognize that the impact of trade liberalization is highly uneven. New interests have arisen which they must fight for – either alone or with other countries in a coalition.

Alongside regionalism, the world trading order in the last decade has been marked by increased institutionalization. This has opened up a new, wider set of issues and interests around which future coalitions of countries may well form. Prior to the UR, and during the pre-negotiations of that round, developing countries had formed a coalition of 'the South'. The Group of Ten (G-10), led by a 'Big Five' comprising Argentina, Brazil, Egypt, India and Yugoslavia, formed as soon as the US began its push to launch a new round of trade negotiations. The coalition of developing countries successfully blocked some aspects of the US initiative. However, the G-10 soon found itself split in trying to formulate negotiating positions on the various aspects of trade to be discussed in the Round (Narlikar, 2000 and Kumar, 1995). The coalition was overtaken by other smaller groupings of states sharing more specific trading interests. The UR included new issues such as services, trade-related investment measures (TRIMs) and trade-related intellectual property rights (TRIPs), as well as bringing agriculture into GATT negotiations. This range of issues gave almost all countries some stake in the outcome. It also altered various alignments of interests among states, opening up new possibilities for coalitions in trade negotiations. The inclusion of agriculture, for example, produced serious rifts within the so-called Quad (the US, the European Union (EU), Canada and Japan), as well as defections from the G-10, and led to the formation of the Cairns Group coalition. The inclusion of services, on which there was only a very limited epistemic consensus, underlined the potency of coalition bargaining. The inclusion of a range of issues such as tropical products, linkages through the Single Undertaking and cross-retaliation further increased the potential for side-deals and interest-based coalitions. All states continue to have an interest in coalescing as groups both try to alter the structure of bargaining in which the Quad enjoy so much power, as well as to gain more leverage on specific issues or in specific sectors which most affect them.

This chapter investigates the potential role for trade coalitions beyond Latin America and across regions. Section 2.2 investigates the nature of trade coalitions, focusing in particular on the issue-based diplomacy of recent years and its contrast with former coalition practices. Section 2.3 explores interests in services, and finds cross-regional issue-based coalitions in the area a possible and viable option. Section 2.4 explains why this expected outcome has not materialized, and finds that interest alignments can be traced to various sources at the sub-sectoral level. It is these interest alignments that have determined the pattern of coalition formation, as the experience from 1986–94 reveals. Section 2.5 explains the implications of these limitations, and elaborates on the types of countries for which issue-based coalitions have much bargaining value. Conclusions are highlighted in section 2.6.

2.2 Characterizing the new diplomacy

The origins of the issue-based diplomacy can be traced to the so-called Jaramillo process that arose in the context of the issue of services. The 1982 GATT decision had urged countries to undertake studies and exchange information on the new issue of services. Both developed and developing countries recognized that services played a crucial role in national development, and hence any 'concessions' in this issue area necessitated great vigilance and voice in the next negotiation. Conceptual uncertainties increased the possibility of developing countries getting cornered into agreeing to definitions and an agenda that excluded their interests. But the same epistemic uncertainties also provided developing countries with an opportunity to find a niche in the negotiations through alternative conceptualizations. Under the pressure of these new dangers and opportunities, some developed and developing countries came together informally to explore the issue. Colombia's ambassador to the GATT, Felipe Jaramillo, was selected to chair the meetings. A recalcitrant refusal of the G-10[1] even to discuss the services issue catalyzed the transformation of the Jaramillo process into the Group of Twenty (G-20) coalition.[2] The emergence of the G-20 revealed that the traditional bloc diplomacy of developing countries was riven with some serious differences. It demonstrated that the common front was now a thing of the past: Colombia, Chile, Jamaica, Mexico and Uruguay became enthusiastic members of the G-20, while Argentina, Brazil, Cuba, Nicaragua and Peru pledged allegiance to the G-10. Quite explicitly a negotiating rather than a blocking coalition, the G-20 realized that if stalemate was to be avoided, negotiation with the developed countries was necessary. The Café au Lait coalition resulted, led by Jaramillo and Pierre Louis Girard from Switzerland, which was key to the launching of the UR.

The successes and prominence of Café au Lait proved crucial in two ways. First, they discredited the methods of bloc-type coalition diplomacy that developing countries had traditionally used in the GATT and elsewhere. Second, they showed developing countries an alternative model that they could adopt with considerable success. This alternative model was characterized by an issue-based focus, intensive research initiative, a largely positive rather than blocking agenda, and simplicity of coalition structure that was based on issue-specific interests rather than elaborate log-rolling. A succession of coalitions with an issue-based focus followed, and continues to date.

Examples of issue-based coalitions are not limited to the services area. In fact, one of the most prominent examples of an issue-based coalition is the Cairns Group in agriculture, which further reinforced the faith of diplomats and academics alike in issue-based coalitions. The Food Importers maintained a similar issue-based focus. The International Textiles and Clothing Bureau has been established by developing countries with keen interest in the area. Some attempt has been made by developing countries to build coalitions that focus on the issues of labor and environment. In the services sector, too, Café au Lait persists in a new incarnation – the Friends of Services Group. Coalitions with narrower sub-sector foci such as telecommunications, financial services, and liberalization particularly of mode 4 have also emerged.

The remainder of this chapter examines the record of issue-based coalitions in the area in which they first evolved – that is, services.[3] On the basis of such an analysis, it highlights the extent to which the high expectations from the new diplomacy have been borne out, and where the search for alternatives is necessary. It also identifies the direction along which the alternative diplomacy might usefully progress.

2.3   Issue-based bloc on services

The first coalition attempt that followed the successes of the Café au Lait based itself on a restricted membership of developing countries with a shared interest in services. In many ways, such a coalition was an expected and natural one. This section highlights the interests that underlay the attempt, and traces what became of it. The former hardliners, having learnt their lesson from the Café au Lait experience and the beating that they had received in its follow-up, began a rigorous research initiative. Such an initiative, at least at the broad aggregate level, indicated that it was possible to speak of Latin America together with all developing countries as sharing a common set of interests. As a group, they ran a deficit in trade in services (with the exception of tourism and services delivered through the movement of labor, though the latter are often categorized as labor remittances rather than 'other services'). In traded services, nine of the top ten exporters and importers in 1982 were found to be developed countries. This dominance had been increasing over the previous decade, and developed countries had succeeded in converting their US$1.3 billion deficit in 1970 to a US$9.8 billion surplus in 1980. In contrast, developing countries had gone from a moderate deficit of US$3.8 billion in 1970 to a substantial deficit of US$57.3 billion (Gibbs, 1985). This position worsened with the inclusion of factor services, particularly foreign direct investment (FDI). Trends in Latin American countries, in general, corresponded to the trends in the rest of the developing world. The over US$9 billion surplus of developed countries in 1980 was matched by a corresponding deficit of about US$9 billion in Latin America.

At the disaggregated level too, some similarities among developing countries suggested that they had the potential to form a natural coalition on services. For instance, most developing countries revealed a deficit in 'other services'. Trade deficits in a particular sector may not be a problem per se, but they certainly become one when generated in critical sectors such as producer services. Producer services, a key component in the category of 'other services', have been found to have the highest growth potential and are also a source of developing country deficits. In the case of the Andean Community (AC), for instance, the largest import item in the services category in the period 1980–85 was travel. The second service import comprised 'other services' and grew more rapidly than imports of goods in all the AC economies, even during periods of declining demand. Imports of 'other services' constituted between 20 and 30 per cent of services imports. Like most developing countries, the AC economies were characterized by increasing surpluses in merchandise trade, but also continuous growth in the deficit of all services (UNCTAD, 1988). Some qualitative similarities in the services component of the domestic economies of developing countries were also noticeable. First, in many developing countries, services are critically influenced by colonial links – railways or banks for instance. Second, contrary to predictions of the product-cycle model or the historical experience of the North, an important segment of labor has moved directly from the primary sector into services (without the intermediate manufacturing stage) in developing countries. This employment in the services sector, however, has usually not been in jobs demanding a skilled output, largely due to the absence of supportive infrastructure or education. For instance, in the AC, the services sector was characterized by a large informal sector with a concentration in low productivity activities like personal services. The high services content in the import figures of the region derives from 'the insufficient and/or inadequate Andean supply of services related to merchandise trade, of producer services, and of services of exportable activity. The situation is reflected, on the one hand, in the high concentration of employment in low productivity or low value-added activities, most of them operating in the informal economy, and, on the other hand, by the low share and limited growth rate of potential dynamic services' (UNCTAD, 1988: 203). Third, even in the 1980s, producer services constituted close to 20 per cent of the GDP of developed countries. This figure was limited to 5 per cent in low-income developing countries, 7.5 per cent in the middle-income developing countries and 10.5 per cent in the upper-income developing countries. The high tradability of these services, linkages that they generated and their contribution to value-added, all implied that the weakness of the sector in most developing countries deterred their international competitiveness in other sectors as well. In services trade, most developing countries showed deficits, with the tourism section providing the notable exception.

The reduction of potential export earnings of developing country producers due to the loss of value-added revenues can only be estimated by comparing f.o.b. prices with those obtained in the domestic markets of importing countries. There is also an opportunity cost involved as export of goods may be hindered due to the absence of appropriate services such as transport networks. A close inspection hence indicated that there existed common interests among developing countries that could be tapped into to build a new coalition base.

The attempt to capitalize on these well-researched similarities among developing countries was led by the former hardliners in association with the UN Conference on Trade and Development (UNCTAD), but the attempt never went far enough to create a solid coalition. It found its initial expression in an attempt to revive the Informal Group of developing countries, soon after the Punta del Este declaration.[4] It persisted in UNCTAD documents, which continued to stress the differences in the position of developed and developing countries. It was also possible to speak of a joint developing approach with a common agenda. As a part of this agenda, developing countries emphasized that the discussions should first focus on statistical issues, definitions and identification of sectors covered by the multilateral framework. They laid stress on the mandate of the Ministerial Declaration and the stated objective therein of 'promoting economic growth of all trading partners and development of the developing countries' (Gibbs and Mashayekhi, 1989: 98–105). Brazil and India took the lead, though individual submissions were also made, for example by Mexico, Argentina, Brazil and Peru, emphasizing an approach broadly similar to the joint one. But once this point was reached, the attempt never went much beyond.

Having declared their support for these joint positions, developing countries parted ways. A plethora of coalitions along narrower interests was also attempted. Coalitions emerged, demanding that greater importance be accorded to movement of laborers; others emerged on still narrower issues like air transport. Except for the occasional UNCTAD official's suggestion of a renewed common position on services as a whole or similar suggestions from some of the former hardliners, little of the approach survives today. The reason why it proved difficult to maintain an issue-based focus on services and the associated tendency of coalitions to form along sub-sector lines, is examined below.

2.4 Disaggregating services: sub-sector coalitions

The tendency of an issue-based services coalition to disaggregate into sub-sectoral ones was partly a product of the stage that the negotiations had entered with the launch of the Uruguay Round. Once services were on the two-track agenda, grandiloquent statements that swept away sub-sector differences were no longer adequate. Concrete give-and-take necessarily devolved to the level of the sub-sector. The result was the emergence of several coalitions with overlapping and cross-cutting loyalties. Three sources of disaggregation of the services sector in a divergence of interests away from the coalition may be discerned. The first was resource-based. Developing countries in general found that, depending on the source of their competitive advantage, their interests in particular sub-sectors varied. The second source of division was the actual vs. potential advantage that the country saw for itself in the services sector. This in turn, depended on factors like the size and nature of the domestic market, fixed costs already invested in services, and the infrastructural context. Third, developing countries found that their interests in services differed according to the extent of specialization in one sub-sector vs. diversification of the economy that disallowed a concentration of diplomatic resources in one sub-sector category in the case of diversified economies. These sources of diversification persist today, and have considerably complicated the range of sub-sector coalitions that developing countries join. A summary of these differences and resulting coalition structures follows.

Different resource endowments

Developing countries have found that their competitive advantage lies in services that can be labor-intensive, technology-intensive, or based on geographic, strategic or cultural advantage. Different sources of their competitive advantage determine their coalition alignment.

Sanjaya Lall suggests how some developing countries, even when capital-poor, may enjoy a comparative advantage in technology-intensive services. Many services, like shipping, require specificity of knowledge, which can be drawn from diverse national sources on the basis of historical, institutional, social, cultural and strategic peculiarities, and is not simply dependent on capital investment in knowledge. 'Certain skills, for instance, are best learnt with low labor endowments, low levels of human capital, small R&D investments and relatively restricted markets' (Lall, 1986: 131). Three sources of a competitive edge for developing countries in technology-based services have been suggested. First, developing countries may be more competitive in producing technology adapted to local needs of other developing countries. Second, they may be able to provide technologies complementary to the developed countries as franchised sub-contractors or partners particularly when taking on simpler (though highly skilled) tasks of detailed engineering, construction and so forth. Third, non-overlapping with developed countries, there are some services that are specific to developing countries (such as gasohol in Brazil) and where developed countries are not competitors at all. Often these advantages are culture, education, language, or location-specific, giving some countries a competitive edge in sub-sectors that do not provide a common competitive advantage to the entire group.

Other examples of services that thrive on a location-specific comparative advantage include tourism. Strategic position is a similar advantage, often enjoyed by small island economies that are especially suitable for providing logistics services such as staging posts, refueling stations and siting of communications, meteorological and paramilitary functions, and even educational facilities, and the sale of shipping services. Singapore is hoping to exploit its time zone as a vital link for 24-hour financial transactions. Uruguay, Panama and the Dominican Republic similarly, use their geographical and political positioning to transship services and manufactures. In those services where there is a good deal of personal interaction with customers, cultures that place emphasis on maintaining good interpersonal relationships (rather than simple task efficiency) would be at an advantage. Air transport services may be a case in point. Not unrelated to the cultural ethos is the knowledge infrastructure of a country. A sustained institutional and cultural advantage in knowledge translates directly into professional services. Professional services that are usually associated with the temporary relocation of labor through increasingly disembodied services have been facilitated by telecommunication technology. A number of countries in Latin America are characterized by competitive standards of education. Despite Economic Needs Tests and other barriers to the movement of professionals (see Abugattas and Stephenson, Chapter 5), the potential in this sub-sector is significant. The recent hire of soldiers from Argentina to meet the shortfall in Spain provides one example of the use of such comparative advantage. Technological change has facilitated the development of off-shore software and data-processing services in Uruguay. Many leading firms such as Apple, IBM, Intel and Oracle have also set up joint R&D and production ventures throughout Latin America. Data processing firms in Jamaica similarly work for clients in Canada, the US and the UK, on the strength of a comparative advantage of an English-speaking workforce and competitive telecommunication prices. Several niche markets have also been found in the audio-visual industry in Brazil, Venezuela, Colombia, Mexico and Argentina. Language plays a critical role in these sub-sectors as well, with not only entertainment programs and films in English, but also a market for subtitling and smaller tasks in the industry that can be won on a franchise basis. Such knowledge-based advantage is characteristic of several countries, being often accompanied by advantages of language as a remnant of colonial ties. But it is also present in some developing countries that had consciously tried to develop institutions promoting science, engineering, electronics, health, consultancy and others. Latin America, particularly Cuba, Brazil and Argentina, had developed institutions in at least some of these areas.

Labor comprises the third resource from which several developing countries derive their comparative advantage. The most direct result of the low wages in developing countries is trade in services through the movement of natural persons. Many services activities are labor-intensive: labor in hotel operations accounts for about half of costs, and construction and engineering design services, maritime transport (the wage bill of the crew is a principal element in shipping costs), and the distribution side of banking and financial services all thrive on significant components of labor.

Already, the different sources of comparative advantage and differing levels of competitiveness have some serious implications for coalition formation. At the simplest level, we can expect countries with similar sources of advantage to coalesce together. Such coalitions are indeed evident; countries sharing a comparative advantage based in low-cost labor have been particularly active. A coalition of like-minded countries (Argentina, Colombia, Cuba, Egypt, India, Mexico, Pakistan and Peru) was responsible for the initiative and subsequent inclusion of the Annex on Movement of Natural Persons in the GATS.[5] Similarly, all the smaller tourism-oriented economies were privy to the deliberations of the Jaramillo track, and continue to work in the Hotel de la Paix Group and Friends of Services Group. The emergence of these coalitions, however, cuts across alternative alignments of which some developing countries were already a part, and resulted in a very complex pattern of overlapping coalitions working at cross-purposes.

Equally interesting, there were several other obvious groupings that could have emerged with a focus on sub-sectors based on the source of competitive advantage. One obvious coalition in which developing countries would have enjoyed considerable bargaining power as weighty exporters, and yet did not emerge, was the potential coalition on professional services. The competitive advantage in professional services enjoyed by countries of Latin America as well as some in Asia, was described earlier in this section. This competitive advantage was and continues to be threatened as a result of exclusionary regional arrangements within the North such as the EU, and the North American Free Trade Agreement (NAFTA). These arrangements have heightened restrictions on the supply of professional services through the movement of natural persons through quotas and non-tariff barriers (NTBs) like non-recognition of qualification requirements (see Abugattas and Stephenson, Chapter 5, for recognition in trade agreements). But no coalition to counter these measures has yet emerged.[6]

Another coalition with some potential among developing countries across regions is one that focuses on the construction and engineering design industry. It is true that there is considerable divergence in the nature and extent of competitiveness of construction and engineering design services in the developing world. However, Brazil and India continue to dominate in disembodied technical and consultancy exports (Lall, 1984). But no such coalition is in the offing. In part, the absence of such a coalition is a product of the diverging sources of the comparative advantage in construction and engineering design of different developing countries. The labor component of construction and engineering design gives India an incentive to continue with former coalitions such as the group of like-minded countries on the inclusion of labor movement under mode 4, while Brazil is an important absentee from this eight-member coalition. The different sources of competitive advantage hence, induce divergence even at the sub-sector level among countries with a competitive advantage.

The bargaining strength of at least some developing countries in sub-sectors of services lies not only in their role as suppliers of services but also markets for services imports. Irrespective of the differences in current figures of the growth of the construction and engineering design sector in developing countries, the largest potential market for these services exists in the developing countries. The dependence on construction and engineering design services could be transmogrified into a bargaining strength. In this case however, developing countries get caught up in their dual roles as exporters and importers of construction and engineering design services, rendering coalition formation on the basis of either interest difficult.

Common to all the cases where developing countries have shown a reluctance to seek obvious allies on the basis of sub-sector advantages and common resource endowments is a simple explanation. Divisions within the developing world and affinities among countries, even at the sub-sector level, had two other sources besides the origins of comparative advantage. These sources and their influence are elaborated below.

Realized vs. potential advantage

A common resource base provides only one basis to the convergence of interests at the sub-sector level. Fissures within the developing world and the search for other allies were and can still be located in the level of potential vs. realized advantage in the particular issue. This level of advantage has to be considered in the context of the development level of the economy. Three groups may be noted. Group I comprises a small number of developing countries that have acquired a well-founded material advantage in the particular sub-sector. Most of these countries have found it easiest to build alignments with each other, as also with the developed countries. Costa Rica, the Dominican Republic, Uruguay, Argentina and Chile feature most frequently in this category though memberships vary according to the sub-sector. Group II comprises countries that have a developing advantage in the sub-sector, with Brazil providing the obvious Latin American example. These economies have already invested a form of 'fixed costs' in the particular sub-sector and expect returns from them to materialize within the short to medium run. For these countries, the opportunity cost of yielding domestic markets to foreign competition is the highest. Group III includes some of the smallest and poorest of countries that have opened their services markets. The high proportion of their services imports also allows these countries to buy arguments of efficiency gains from liberalization; their resource base and level of development offer them little opportunity of building their competitive advantage in the area. Trade-offs and linkages within the North offer cheaper access to services imports, as well as possible trade-offs on other issues. Countries of Group I and III are more likely to form bandwagons with the developed countries; the possibility of forming a blocking or agenda-setting coalition was and continues to be much higher with Group II countries.

The telecommunications negotiations provide an instance of all these groups in action. Most developing countries generally maintained a stance of blocking, as market power wielded by the developing countries provided the basis for such a position. Smaller coalitions also emerged among developing countries. The attempt in the Telecom annex to strike a balance between the needs of users for fair terms of access and needs of the regulators and public telecommunications operators to maintain a system that fulfils trade needs but also public policy objectives (see Bastos Tigre, Chapter 6) resulted from two submissions made by India, Egypt, Cameroon and Nigeria. The bloc of developing countries, however, remained ineffectual because it combined all three groups of countries and hence was a divided attempt. The thrust of the attempt came from the stalwarts of the former G-10, India and Brazil, which had already invested considerable resources into building their indigenous telecom industry (see Bastos Tigre, Chapter 6). In relation to these investments, their telecom industry still bore a promise of success, but was not competitive enough to withstand world competition. The telecom sectors of many of the smaller countries had already been at least partially penetrated by the industrialized countries and the possibility of their building an indigenous industry was small. The opportunity cost of yielding the remainder of their market to foreign competition was smaller for these countries than India and Brazil. Minimal influence of the attempt is not surprising, given that members of the coalition experiment were at cross-purposes.

Similar stages of comparative advantage also yielded strange bedfellows. India and the US, traditionally at loggerheads for ideological as well as economic reasons based on structural differences of resource endowment, found common interests in liberalization of their audio-visual services. In the context of the Annex on Air Transport Services, Malaysia and Singapore combined with Australia, New Zealand and the Nordic countries. Together, the group urged caution, stressing the use of reviews that were to be held every five years. The Association of South East Asian Nations (ASEAN) countries and Australia embarked on a joint research project. On the basis of similar levels of development in the sub-sector, there were alliances between state and domestic actors. The push for services by the US had derived considerably from internal business interests. The Financial Services Annex was significantly influenced by a proposal submitted by Malaysia, on behalf of the South East Asian Central Banks (SEACEN) comprising Indonesia, Korea, Malaysia, Myanmar, Nepal, Philippines, Singapore, Sri Lanka and Thailand. As a result of this proposal, the annex did not impose liberalization obligations. Its provisions on domestic regulation were based on the overriding importance of prudential considerations, monetary policies and the integrity and stability of the financial system. Argentina, Colombia, Cuba, Mexico and Peru jointly sponsored the proposal on movement of personnel as a mode of supply, along with Egypt, India and Pakistan.[7] India's frequent ally and a leader of developing countries in the pre-negotiation and negotiation phases of the Uruguay Round, Brazil, was notably absent from the group.

Depending on how 'real' or developed the competitive advantage in the sub-sector was, several examples of counter-intuitive behavior become more explicable. Irrespective of some resource endowments, such as skilled labor or professional services, that they might share with other parts of the developing world, the East Asian countries had already realized their competitive advantage in other services sub-sectors. Their high level of development implies a productive bandwagoning with the developed countries that shared similar interests. In contrast, countries like India and Brazil have still not realized their comparative advantage in some of the key producer services. However, having already expended considerable effort in the development of some of their producer services under former ISI models, they see potential yields from them in the medium to short-term. Hence for instance, these economies resisted any concessions on telecom or financial services at least in the earlier stages of the negotiations.

The third category is occupied by smaller economies. Even if they enjoy certain endowments such as educated labor or prime location (especially in the case of island economies) and reveal a high services export content in terms of tourism, they rely upon services imports due to inadequate economies of scale. In the absence of some revolutionary technological breakthroughs, these economies see little potential of developing an advantage in the key services. Greater liberalization as per the agenda of some developed countries at least allows them certainty of supply of the critical producer services. The level of translated advantage thus dilutes similarities based purely on similar resource endowments.

The specialization principle

The formation and survival of a coalition at the level of the sub-sector depends on a third factor, besides the resource base and consideration of the immediate vs. potential advantage: the extent of diversification of the economy, and the importance of the particular sector therein. Specialization of the economy allows a greater concentration of diplomatic effort and commitment in selective coalitions, dissuading conflicting loyalties and cross-cutting linkages. Such a specialization is characteristic of several LDCs, reflecting a tendency to obtain the greater part of their services export receipts from a single sub-sector in services (Hoekman, 1988). This means that the inclusion of the particular sub-sector on the agenda would make trade-offs worthwhile on other sub-sectors.

The implications of this specialization principle are simple. Dilemmas about loyalty to particular coalitions are easily resolved, especially for small developing island economies. These countries have higher than average export intensities in all three services sectors, but are clearly most specialized in tourism (Hoekman, 1996). The categorical export advantage in the tourism sub-sector is complemented by an absence of national economies of scale in the production of several essential services such as telecommunications. These countries must devote larger shares of their resource base for the provision of basic infrastructural services than bigger countries (UNCTAD, 1985). For small countries very close to the continent or to each other, the costs of this provision may be reduced through scale economies of trade. This involvement in international trade could be unilaterally conducted to the benefit of the country concerned. But the case of services and their inclusion in the agenda provided these small economies with a bargaining chip. They could extract concessions, better terms and inclusion on the agenda of areas such as tourism, and also gain from any inclusion of other services within the multilateral agenda as was desired by the developed countries. Most countries of the Caribbean fell into this pattern of behavior, and Jamaica's leading role in the G-20 may be traced to the same imperatives. Many of the small countries of the Caribbean found that multilateral measures that promote travel services far outweigh any gains they make by extending their activity to other sub-sectoral coalitions or compensatory arrangements.

Few countries, however, have such unambiguously defined interests. Especially in the bigger and more advanced of the developing economies interests in a range of sub-sectors prevent concentrated loyalty and attention to one coalition. Brazil and India provide classic examples of countries faced with such a conflict of loyalties. Brazil was an active player in the Latin American group, most of which shared the demand for the preferential treatment of developing countries.[8] Yet Brazil, along with India, had also expressed dissatisfaction with S&D treatment.[9] The Indo-Brazil partnership in presenting a common front in multilateral trade negotiations was endangered by the multi-directional pulls exercised by alternative coalition memberships. India and Argentina joined forces over the inclusion of labor as a mode of supply, in which Brazil had little interest. But India's former alliance with Brazil continued over telecom. Unprecedented de facto commonalty of interest emerged with the US over audio-visual services.

That effective leadership in coalition formation has been largely unforthcoming in the case of the larger developing countries, is hence, on closer inspection, unsurprising. The diversified interests of these economies produce a conflict of loyalties and memberships. Resulting linkages and concessions adversely affect the efficacy of most sub-sector coalitions involving these countries. Note that the impact of diversification is different in developed economies, where irrespective of diversified production and trade in different sub-sectors, the primacy of the services sector as a whole renders broad sector coalitions and sub-sector linkages possible.

2.5   Constraints and conditions for success – sub-sector coalitions

At least in the case of services, it has been difficult to maintain a broad issue-based coalition, due to the proneness of the sector to disaggregate into narrower interests.[10] Moreover, the resulting coalitions that operate at the sub-sector level have a mixed record. Only a few have actually emerged among the many potential ones, and even fewer among them have had any lasting duration or achievements. However, the few successful cases suggest that the sub-sector coalition would work well, but within a set of constraints and only for a sub-set of developing countries. This section highlights the problems and limitations that affect this coalition type, and further assesses which countries are likely to be able to utilize them to their advantage.

The first problem of cross-cutting sub-sector interests is distracted and ambiguous commitment to particular coalitions. It is possible for some of the more specialized economies to overcome this problem, and concentrate diplomatic initiative in the relevant sub-sector. Occasionally, additional gains might be derived through linkages. The small island economies, such as the

Caribbean countries, with similar geographic and strategic endowments, concentrated interests in tourism exports and imports of producer services, present one example of countries that can build such coalition successfully.

The identification of a coincidence of narrower interests by the more specialized economies, however, generates the second problem affecting sub-sector coalitions. Most of the more specialized economies are also small in economic size. This has meant that even their combined market influence would still be limited. Bandwagons provide a solution to the problem. But bandwagons with the bigger developing countries yielded few successes and were even detrimental to the maintenance of the coalition. The bigger developing economies were also the more diversified ones, so that including them increased the combined economic size of the coalition, but it also adulterated the sub-sector agenda and expanded it to cross-cutting issues. Bandwagons with the developed countries, however, provide a promising alternative because, in spite of diversification, the developed countries offer two advantages as coalition partners over the bigger developing countries. First, the sub-sector shares of the developed countries are likely to be substantive enough to allow sufficient bargaining weight to the coalition. Second, the interests of the developed economies in the services sector are enormous, irrespective of differing sub-sector priorities. These interests present a contrast with the larger developing economies, where interests in particular sub-sectors are often at cross-purposes with each other. The initiative of the smaller developing countries with higher stakes in the sub-sector concerned would provide diplomatic momentum to the coalition, while the presence of developed economies would lend greater market shares.

Developed–developing country coalitions with a sub-sector focus also resolve the third problem that afflicts this coalition type. The problem may be identified as a leadership problem, and was also responsible for the limited tangible successes of sub-sector coalitions. The former leaders of the developing countries continued to take the leadership initiative in most coalitions. Due to their diversified economies and varied levels of competitive advantage that had been translated across sub-sectors, their leadership and commitment to each sub-sector coalition was divided and confused. Smaller, more specialized economies are able to overcome this problem, while an alliance with the developed countries allows them economic weight. The leadership niche that smaller countries may have found for themselves in the sub-sector coalitions marks, in some ways, the culmination of the initiative taken by the 'less important' developing countries in the Jaramillo track and later the middle powers of the Cairns Group.

Coalitions focusing on the relevant sub-sector provide a viable policy option for smaller developing countries, particularly when formed with the developed countries. The importance of bandwagoning with the developed countries, however, also circumscribes the negotiating leeway that such coalitions might enjoy, particularly when differences within the developed world are minimal. The previous sections indicated that for Groups I and III in the level of advantage scale, plus for the more specialized countries, there is a similarity of interests with the developed countries. However, if faced with a conflict of interests (perhaps in a non-service sector), the formula will have to be revised.

There remains a large group of countries for which coalitions with a sub-sectoral focus do not provide the answer. The question of coalition strategies for the countries classified as Group II, particularly when overlapping with the diversified economies, is not an easy one. The problem here is not a lack of awareness of interests, or the stupidity or ideological reluctance of politicians to acknowledge them. Rather, this group of countries includes the former leaders of the G-10, and represents interests that are too diversified to fit within any sub-sector coalition. Their large markets and potential in services are also too great to be unilaterally surrendered or bartered away for concessions in any one sub-sector with lesser growth potential or one in which lesser fixed costs have been invested. For such countries, a bloc-type approach which allows them a broad sweep of log-rolled, diversified interests holds greater promise. Regionalism might provide a possible springboard for such coalitions, exemplified by ASEAN in the WTO and the Caribbean countries and Mercosur in the FTAA.

2.6   Conclusion

This chapter has covered the phenomenon of issue-based coalitions that characterize the new trade diplomacy. It found that at least in the services sector, issue-based coalitions have proved difficult to sustain due to the tendency of interests to disaggregate into sub-sectors. Coalitions at the level of the sub-sector, however, display longevity and efficacy in only some cases. The tripartite disaggregation into sub-sectors, and further the conditions in which the sub-sector specific coalitions work, are recapitulated here.

Three sources of division were discovered, which influence the pattern of coalition formation at the level of the sub-sector. The first source of division was found to be resource-based, resulting in the dominance of labor-intensive services in some countries, technology-intensive in others and so forth. Factor proportions, however, are not the sole determinant of the competitive advantage and resulting coalition loyalties. The second factor determining the interest and diplomatic effort that a developing country is willing to invest in a particular sub-sector is the actual or medium to long-term potential advantage that it enjoys in the sector. Advantage considered in these terms is only partially dependent on resource endowments and might even ignore them. Rather it is a product of other factors such as the size and nature of the domestic market, fixed costs already invested in services production, and the infrastructural context. The third determinant of coalition membership and loyalty at the sub-sector level is the extent of specialization in the sub-sector disallowing a concentration of diplomatic resources in one sub-sector category for the more diversified economies.

Based on the simultaneous operation of all three constraints, some economies would find the opportunity costs of yielding to pressures to open their markets particularly high. Diversified economies with a medium-term potential competitive advantage across sub-sectors, exemplified by Brazil and India, fall into this category. Not surprisingly, even after having surrendered their bloc-based strategies, they have frequently participated in coalitions that attempt to slow down the liberalization process. However, the widespread and diverse levels of the sub-sector interests of these diversified economies have also led to their multiple memberships and conflict of loyalties regarding coalitions with a narrower focus. For smaller countries with a greater dependence on services imports, or the dominance of a particular sub-sector in exports, the choice has been simpler. Once interests in the particular sub-sector are met, their loyalties to other coalitions become superfluous. Bandwagoning possibilities and their limitations were examined in the previous section.

The evidence demonstrates that the bloc-type sectoral coalition is rendered difficult due to the lack of shared interests. The coalition type with a sub-sector focus has been a mixed blessing. For the smaller developing economies, it has offered a viable coalition strategy, admittedly amidst a set of constraints. The participation of bigger developing countries in the same coalition type, however, has actually reduced the efficacy of this sub-sector coalition. The precarious world of 'shifting coalitions' (Medhora, 1998) is dotted with coalitions of the sub-sector type. Their makeshift character is, in good measure, a product of the participation of the larger developing countries with their conflicting priorities (across sub-sectors) and divided aims. It is only by avoiding dominance by the more diversified developing economies with a medium-term interest in the particular sub-sector, and by bringing in the developed economies with more consistent interests across sub-sectors, that the sub-sector coalition can hope to provide a stable alternative.

Sectoral and sub-sectoral coalitions in services will no doubt continue to move on shifting ground, and thus change focus, shape and membership as negotiating goals transmogrify. But they are an increasing part of the new scenario, a function of rapid technological change and the broadness of the agenda *vis-à-vis* crisscrossing interests. They will coalesce and compete with the mushrooming of regional coalitions, thus demanding countries to deal with multiple memberships and split loyalties. In fact, the coexistence of sectoral and regional forms of association allows countries to not put all of their eggs in one basket. If regional arrangements risk becoming small areas of hegemony where predominant countries can increase their power, the dovetailing with sectoral and sub-sectoral coalitions, even on shifting ground, could possibly allow smaller countries room to pursue interests subdued or even smothered by regional coalitions.

Notes

1. The G-10 epitomized the traditional bloc-type diplomacy of developing countries in the GATT, akin to the G-77 in the UNCTAD. In its hardline version, the group comprised the Big Five (Argentina, Brazil, Egypt, India, Yugoslavia, along with Cuba, Nicaragua, Nigeria, Peru and Tanzania). The negotiating position of the G-10 was simple: members would resist the opening of a new round until issues of standstill and rollback were attended to. Most important, they would resist the inclusion of services within GATT purview.

2. The G-20 included Bangladesh, Chile, Colombia, Hong Kong, Indonesia, Ivory Coast, Jamaica, Malaysia, Mexico, Pakistan, Philippines, Rumania, Singapore, Sri Lanka, South Korea, Thailand, Turkey, Uruguay, Zambia and Zaire.

3. Given that the first issue-based coalition had its origins in the services sector, it seems appropriate to expect that coalitions continuing with the same strategies are likely to have the greatest promise within the same issue-area. Further, as issue-based coalitions have usually portrayed themselves as explicitly negotiating coalitions rather than purely agenda-setting ones, they would have considerable relevance for the built-in agenda and services negotiations, which have moved beyond the agenda-setting stage (see Abugattas and Stephenson, Chapter 2).

4. Both the former hardliners (the G-10 and the G-20) pledged allegiance to this grouping in a personal communiqué from Ambassador Shukla, January 2000.

5. The joint document submitted by the coalition was entitled, 'Temporary movement of services personnel' (MTN.GNS/W/106). The proposal offered ways of concretizing the principles relating to the movement of personnel as a mode of supply, as agreed in paragraphs 4 and 7, Mid-Term Review, Brussels.

6. Like many sub-sectoral coalitions, this one would divide the developing countries into importers and exporters of professional services (with large parts of Africa and West Asia importing services).

7. MTN.GNS/W/106, 18 June 1990, Communication from Argentina, Colombia, Cuba, Egypt, India, Mexico, Pakistan and Peru, Annex on Temporary Movement of Services Personnel.

8. One example of the proposal for preferential treatment is found in the joint statement of 11 Latin American countries, 26 February 1990, Proposal to the Group of Negotiations on Services (GNS), MTN.GNS/W/95.

9. 'We believe that we should not base our approach on the assumptions borrowed from [the] familiar area of trade in goods supplemented by carving out exceptions in terms of special and differential treatment for developing countries.' (Statement of India at the GNS meeting on 23 February 1987 cited in Mark and Helleiner, 1988: 26).

10. It is also worth noting that most prescriptions for issue-based coalition diplomacy do not tell us whether the coalition would best operate at the level of the sector as a whole or much narrower sub-sectors.

3
Unfolding Scenarios

Pedro da Motta Veiga[1]

3.1 Introduction

Scenarios are simplified representations of reality. This simplification becomes evident when scenarios are applied to complex systems characterized by a high degree of instability and sensitivity to exogenous variables. The simultaneous ongoing trade negotiations involving Latin American and Caribbean countries at the multilateral, hemispheric and sub-regional level interact in a complex web of uncertainty. Complementary and competitive relationships subject each individual process and the collective outcome to vast indefiniteness. The scenarios developed in this chapter map out paths for the negotiations, leading to a synthesis of the possible paths regionalism could take in the hemisphere. The design of unfolding scenarios for the region as a whole does not mean to suggest Latin American and Caribbean countries have convergent interests. In fact, as Abreu points out in Chapter 1, the Latin American and Caribbean common trade agenda is quite restricted.

After painting a contextual backdrop, this chapter proposes possible scenarios for the negotiation processes. Section 2 summarizes the recent evolution of negotiation processes in the World Trade Organization (WTO), the Free Trade Area of the Americas (FTAA) and sub-regional and bilateral trade agreements and their context. Section 3 comments on the architecture of trade negotiations emerging in Latin America and the Caribbean in the 1990s. Section 4 presents alternative hypotheses for the evolution of trade negotiations.

3.2 Contextual variables

The scenario exercise is based on hypotheses about the interaction between four groups of variables. First, an 'external' block of variables reflects the global context in which each of the processes develops, capturing the tensions and pressures of global economic organization, regulatory order and the prevailing bargaining power framework. Next, three blocks of 'internal' variables represent trade negotiation processes at the multilateral, hemi-spheric and sub-regional levels.

The global context

The outlook for the growth of trade flows within and between blocs turned favorable with the satisfactory conclusion of the Uruguay Round (UR), US budget deficit reductions, and rejuvenation of US exports. Pessimistic scenar-ios that had augured a 'war between blocs' and a worsening of protectionist trends lost relevance. Trade growth and liberalization was bolstered by the reintegration of major Latin American and Caribbean economies to interna-tional circuits, the emergence of a third generation of Asian 'tigers' (Indonesia, Thailand, Malaysia and the Philippines) and the increasing integration of Russia and China into the world market. Not even the December 1994 Mexican Crisis was sufficient to debunk this scenario in which liberalization of goods and services continued with greater mobility in capital and trade flows.

A wind of change swept through the global arena in 1997 with the Asian financial crisis and the Japanese economic downturn. Recession and devalu-ation in Japan brought back worries about trade imbalances between the major international trade players and especially about the growing US trade deficit. Moreover, difficulties faced by former Soviet countries (Russia, mainly) and Latin American economies (Brazil, mainly) in market-oriented transi-tions coincided with a global recognition of the increasing importance of developing economies. These economic omens were accompanied by a shift in public opinion swayed by sociopolitical forces arguing that 'globalization has gone too far' (Rodrik, 1997). Proactive opposition to further multilateral and regional liberalization initiatives fought against trade promotion author-ity in the US and impeded the conclusion of the Multilateral Agreement on Investments (MAI) negotiations (see Chudnovsky and Lopez, Chapter 7). Furthermore, the anti-liberalization forces called for participation of environ-mental non-governmental organizations (NGOs) and labor representatives in the trade negotiation fora, arguing that international economic integration is managed by a small group of governments and big corporations which exclude labor, the environment and consumer interests. This modality of protectionism must not be equated to the 'crude protectionism' of the 1970s and 1980s, but is a more nuanced reaction to globalization that accepts the phenomenon's inevitability yet seeks to manage it in potentially destructive ways or calls for a halt in further liberalization. At least in its motivations and social base this phenomenon is new (Bergsten, 1998).

Not surprisingly, the consolidation of these tensions occurred ten years after the end of the Cold War, as positions and interests of major players were rede-fined. The political rationale for US leadership and the consensus around trade liberalization is no longer derived from the goal of reinforcing the Western Bloc against the Socialist Bloc (Gilpin, 2000). As Tussie argues, 'the end of these collective organizing principles has allowed the de-ideologization of trading arrangements' and led to a weakening of the political foundations of the post-War liberalizing order (1998: 41). In this new environment, the US reconsidered its position and leadership style, abandoning its previously unflagging support of multilateralism and evolving towards a multifaceted foreign economic policy that prioritized regionalism, and later towards a strategic trade policy of unilaterism. The European Union (EU) first turned its attention inward and then confronted US proposals on sensitive issues such as agriculture, environment, and consumer health and safety. Asia, in turn, also increasingly focused on regional issues, turning from exclusive multilateralism to bilateral trade agreement proposals. Moreover, the Asian crises set in motion a new type of groupings (such as the Asian Pacific Economic Cooperation (APEC)) somewhat in tension with the prevailing tone of multilateralism given worries about de-nationalization of Asian firms and economies (Tan, 1998) and strong nationalistic tendencies.

In this adverse context globalization faced a legitimacy crisis plagued by a lack of even minimal consensus between the major players on WTO issues, the international financial architecture issues and the regulation of financial flows. The debate is gradually shifting to governance of globalization, a subject that will draw the attention of both integration defendants and opponents. From a tunnel vision of trade and investment liberalization and harmonization, to a bifocal lens split between liberalization and cohesion concerns, the global vision has changed focus.

Negotiations in the WTO

The failure of the WTO Ministerial Conference in Seattle was not without precedent: the launch of a new round in Geneva in 1982 also failed, and the Brussels meeting in 1990 led to a temporary suspension of the UR. Nevertheless, the Seattle fiasco is seen as the first major failure of the organization and has been accorded higher political and symbolic value than the previous failures. The decisively weak link in the chain of events leading up to Seattle was an unfavorable political and economic context. Specifically, four anti-liberalization forces doomed the launch of a new round: defensive agricultural policies in the EU, increasing antidumping measures and voluntary export restraints in the US, inclusion of environment and labor on the agenda, and demands for a 'development dimension' by poor countries. Thus the 'hard core' traditional protectionism of rich countries coincided with a new protectionism of 'trade regulation'. Compounded with pro-liberalization business groups favoring sector-specific negotiations and developing countries seeking to limit the scope of the agenda and force discussions on Special and Differential Treatment (S&D) and Uruguay Round Agreements (URAs) implementation (see Abreu, Chapter 1), the launching of a new round was predestined to be stillborn.

Seattle has left an indelible mark on the international trade system. The most obvious impact has been on the content and pace of negotiations: negotiations on the UR built-in agenda, whose main topics include agriculture and services, began in January 2000 without a deadline or precise objectives while the launching of a new round was delayed until November 2001 in Doha. Another permanent mark has been the mushrooming of regional integration initiatives, evidenced by the gradual embrace of the FTAA and the negotiation of preferential trade agreements in Asian-Pacific countries previously indifferent to such initiatives.

The context is now marked by the tension between, on one hand, the trend towards market liberalization and policy harmonization that marked the first half of the 1990s, and on the other, the regulation efforts that submit these processes to national development goals, labor issues and international financial stability conditions. The launching of a new round in Doha confirms that the liberalization agenda will be counterbalanced by the regulation agenda, especially regulations aimed to confer political legitimacy on multilateral negotiations. The translation of decisions made at Doha into concrete results may prove insurmountable given global economic downturns and flagging pro-liberal, pro-multilateral consensus in developed countries.

The Free Trade Area of the Americas

The FTAA bears the influence of the free market ideas that shaped the first half of the 1990s, by now considerably eased by the evolution of trade and industrial policy reforms in Latin American and Caribbean countries. The Buenos Aires Ministerial Meeting in April 2001 marked the conclusion of another phase in the FTAA negotiating process, with a decision to set the agreement into motion in 2005. Concern for S&D for less developed economies was explicitly emphasized in the Ministerial Declaration and labor and environmental issues were given prominence although also clarifying that these issues can not lead to trade restrictions or sanctions. Initial US reluctance to agricultural discussions at the hemispheric level has been attenuated, though antidumping remains a heated, untouched issue. Obstacles may be posed by the conditions attached to granting trade promotion authority to the US Executive or the possible turn to the left in Brazil's 2002 elections, but a reversion in hemispheric momentum is out of the question. Since the coming to office of President Bush, efforts to accelerate the negotiations have been stepped up and some Latin American countries have jumped onto the bandwagon. The US and Chile began negotiating a free trade agreement in November 2000, and the US Trade Representative stated that, in the face of eventual difficulties, the US might appeal to bilateral agreements with Latin American countries to reinforce its position in the hemisphere.

Sub-regional and bilateral agreements

Latin American and Caribbean countries have a long history of bilateral and sub-regional preferential liberalization and economic integration agreements.

Dating from the 1960s and early 1970s, the Latin American Free Trade Area (LAFTA), the Andean Community (AC), the Caribbean Common Market (Caricom) and the Central American Common Market (CACM) rarely met their goals, because of the inherent clash between integration and import substitution industrialization. However, a new wave of preferential agreements rocked the region in the 1990s, now linked to a re-hauling of trade and development strategies. Traditional arrangements, such as the Latin American Integration Association (LAIA) – LAFTA's successor – and the AC, gained strength and Mercosur broke off as an important sub-regional initiative in South America. Various bilateral agreements (many of them under the Montevideo Treaty that created LAIA in 1981) were struck, generally with the goal of establishing free trade areas. Moreover, Mexico negotiated NAFTA with the US and Canada during the 1990s.

This wave of agreements went one step further than the liberalization of trade in goods with the establishment of disciplines on such issues as services and investment, replicating the thematic scope of the WTO. Hence the arrangements signed and the treatment given to issues could be defined as WTO-plus. These agreements often managed to form sub-regional free trade areas; many even explicitly seek to become common markets. For example, Mercosur was created with the intention of gradually evolving towards a common market and the AC has reaffirmed its goal of forming a common market in 2005. Neither has the Caricom abandoned its strategic goal of building a common market, evidenced by member statements in the Protocol of Guatemala in 1993.

With ambitious integration goals and modest results, taken together the initiatives present similar trends and prospects. Most remain in a free trade area stage incapable of turning into full-fledged customs unions. Divergent foreign policies, domestic political and economic restraints, and border conflicts plague nearly all. Conflicts flare up from disparities in size, economic structure and patterns of trade, in addition to often contradictory cost-benefit evaluations of undertaking a common external tariff. Moreover, sub-regional agreements risk being drowned out by the deepening of unilateral preferential trade schemes in the US and the EU that benefit the small economies of Central America and the Caribbean.

Lastly, the FTAA project introduces radical changes in the depth and scope of economic integration. On one hand, it brings together all the countries in the hemisphere (except for Cuba) and will thus potentially umbrella the vast web of trade preferences woven during the last decades among countries. The FTAA will redefine the preferences established by these agreements and extend them to all countries in the hemisphere. On the other hand, the project will 'compete' with prevailing agreements, both in terms of trade preferences and trade and non-trade norms and disciplines. Given the scope of FTAA negotiations, the competition with those sub-regional and bilateral agreements will be intense.

3.3 The architecture of negotiations: interactions between processes

The multiplicity of negotiations (multilateral, regional, bilateral and sub-regional) conflicts and coalesces because of simultaneity and thematic convergence. The 'architecture' of the negotiations is grounded on the following pillars.

- *Thematic Convergence around the WTO.* The URAs are the basic point of reference for all regional projects, which, by definition, aim to be WTO-plus by either widening commitments and deepening disciplines, or by dealing with issues not fully integrated into the multilateral agenda. Convergence creates competition between negotiation processes.
- *Institutional Hierarchy.* Commitments undertaken at the regional level must be compatible with WTO rules. Compatibility does not preclude those agreements from going beyond the WTO agreements.
- *Substantive Hierarchy.* Commitments assumed in a given negotiation sphere tend to become a reference point and eventually a ground zero for subsequent negotiations, especially if large economic players are involved. For instance, the negotiation of an agreement within the FTAA or the EU is bound to become a reference point for a subsequent multilateral negotiation, whereas a Mercosur agreement can hardly promise to move the agenda. The substantial liberalization of agriculture carried out by Mercosur with negligible impact so far on other policy arenas is a case in point (see Diaz-Henderson, Chapter 4).
- *Logistical Differences.* Despite thematic convergence, negotiations can proceed along distinct paths due to logistical differences including distinct negotiation dynamics, goals, methodologies, number of parties, economic power, or private sector participation. Coordination of a country's negotiation strategy is complicated by the overlapping timings of negotiations. These hurdles are heightened by asymmetrical distributions of power.

Two patterns of interaction among trade negotiation fora have been distinguished by Granados (1999): cross-fertilization and blocking interaction. In FTAA–WTO relations, Granados identifies positive cross-fertilizations in subjects such as antidumping, subsidies, investment, services, technical barriers, and sanitary and phytosanitary barriers. In these same issues, however, blocking interactions between the two negotiation processes are entirely possible, as will be shown below.

A clear hierarchy among the world trade system, the WTO, the FTAA and sub-regional negotiations dictates the restrictions and conditions that each process imposes on the rest. First, the evolution of the world trade system defines the prevailing mood of trade negotiations. The world trade system and multilateralism reciprocally affect each other, so that the world trade system's progress impacts the prospects of multilateralism while simultaneously being victim to the dynamics of WTO negotiations. Second, the evolution of multilateral negotiations sets the frame for FTAA negotiations, and less directly for sub-regional negotiations. Conversely, developments in the FTAA can influence the evolution of WTO negotiations and to a lesser extent the world trade system. In addition, the FTAA may either induce accelerated sub-regional integration or dilute the sub-regional entities within a dominant hemispheric agreement. Finally, the internal evolution of sub-regional negotiations, despite marginal impact upon the world trade system and multilateral negotiations, can influence the FTAA's viability, rhythm and policy convergence. Moreover, the internal evolution of sub-regional negotiations influences members' participation in negotiations as a whole and each individual process. These interactions suggest the existence of a clear hierarchical relationship between the four groups in terms of their capacity to mutually affect each other. Nevertheless, assuming that each process enjoys a reasonable degree of autonomy, the effects of one process on another need not be deterministic.

3.4   Evolving scenarios

Interdependence is particularly intense between the world trade system and multilateral negotiations, and between the FTAA and sub-regional negotiations. Hence, the following exercise is organized around those two fields – one global, another regional. The world trade system and multilateral negotiations will run up against each other in the liberalization and harmonization of 'non-border' policy issues. These tensions may be resolved in two distinct fashions: a liberalization cycle fueled by a renewed consensus among OECD countries, or the perpetuation of an uncooperative, unstable equilibrium between major players. These possibilities would impact multilateralism and the relationships between the major world trade players in distinct ways, as developed in the scenarios of Table 3.1.

The first field combines four global variables: (i) the macroeconomic international environment and its impact on the trade flows and policies of major players; (ii) the extent of market integration; (iii) the global hegemonic power structure; and (iv) the international cooperation or governance mechanism. Three scenarios emerge from the combinations of these variables: anti-multilateral globalization, new multilateral consensus and uncooperative equilibrium (see Table 3.1).

The regional field is built from the interaction between the FTAA and sub-regional agreements rekindled in the 1990s, as liberalization and policy convergence between neighboring countries became powerful escape mechanisms from the constraints of small markets. The FTAA, however, competes directly with each of these sub-regional agreements, which will likely lose functionality for their members, especially given their inability to move beyond free trade areas to become full-fledged common markets. The competition posed

Table 3.1   The world trade system and multilateral field

	Variables			
	Macro environment and trade impact	*Market integration*	*Hegemony*	*Governance*
Scenarios				
Anti-multilateral globalization	Stable with few negative impacts	High	Unilateral (US)	Low
New multilateral consensus	Stable with few negative impacts	High to medium	Shared	High
Uncooperative equilibrium	Unstable with negative impacts	Low to medium	Challenged and fragmented	Low

Table 3.2   Regionalism in the Americas field

	Variables		
	Market integration and policy harmonization	*Hegemony*	*Sub-regional agreements*
Scenarios			
FTAA predominance	High	Unilateral (US)	Stagnation/ impasse
Trade 'balkanization'	Unequal: bilateralism of US + Southern Agreements	Unilateral (US) with sub-regional hegemonies	Defensive deepening
Plural regionalism	Unequal: FTAA + Deep Southern Agreements	Shared, with divergences	Deepening
Regionalism in crisis	Medium	Challenged internally and externally	Stagnation/ impasse

by the FTAA is the main erosion factor in the sub-regional initiatives. As developed in Table 3.2, the regional field is built with reference to three variables: (i) the extent of hemispheric market integration; (ii) the hemispheric power structure; and (iii) the dynamics of sub-regional agreements, especially in Mercosur and the AC. Four scenarios for the development of regionalism in the Americas are drawn out in this field: the predominance of the FTAA, trade 'balkanization', the FTAA coexisting with intense integration in South America, and a crisis of regionalism.

The synthesis of the fields contained in Tables 3.1 and 3.2 leads to 12 alternative scenarios, as each field could follow convergent or divergent paths. In a convergent path both fields evolve in an analogue way, creating

Table 3.3   A synthesis of unfolding scenarios

	Fields	
	World trade system and multilateralism	Regionalism in the Americas
Scenarios		
Unipolar hegemony	Anti-multilateral globalization	FTAA predominance
Building blocks	New multilateral consensus	Plural regionalism
Regional hegemony	Uncooperative equilibrium (new multilateral consensus)	FTAA predominance
Fragmentation and bilateralism	Uncooperative equilibrium	Trade balkanization
Impasse in negotiations	Uncooperative equilibrium	Regionalism in crisis

'anti-multilateral globalization and FTAA hegemony', 'new multilateral consensus and plural regionalism in the Americas' and 'uncooperative equilibrium and regionalism in crisis'. The first scenario would be characterized by unipolar globalization (with the US as the sole pole), the second scenario by multilateral/regional and regional/sub-regional equilibrium, and the third scenario by crisis. Divergent scenarios point to the possibility that the two fields counter-evolve, speaking to a reasonable degree of autonomy for regionalism in the Americas. This hypothesis of divergence gives way to combinations like 'uncooperative equilibrium and FTAA hegemony' or 'uncooperative equilibrium and trade balkanization in the Americas'. In both cases, US hemispheric trade initiatives evolve in the vacuum of multilateralism and in a crisis-ridden world trade system, giving impulse to regional initiatives.

Five scenarios surface as possible paths for the global and regional fields in Latin American and Caribbean negotiations: unipolar hegemony, building blocks, regional hegemony, fragmentation and bilateralism, and impasse in negotiations (see Table 3.3). The features of each scenario follow.

- *Unipolar Hegemony Scenario.* The combination of FTAA hemispheric predominance in the regional field with anti-multilateral globalization in the global field would result in a scenario of unipolar hegemony. The US, presiding as the world's economic engine, would face increasing pressure given the growing disparity between US economic performance and that of other OECD economies. Institutional and regulatory competition would lead Europe and Japan to continue liberalizing domestic policies, despite domestic social resistance. The US would use multilateralism to get plurilateral agreements in subjects and sectors of their sole interest, such as international diffusion of the so-called new economy. The paradigms of these arrangements would include the Information Technology Agreement and the URA on government procurement. Leaders would exert minimal pressure to launch a new multilateral negotiation round and there would be little to no room for governance or development issues in the international economic agenda. Developing countries would divide between those seeking preferential trade schemes with the US and those opting for South–South alternatives. FTAA predominance would prevail in the Americas, combining FTAA advances propelled by domestic pro-hemispheric integration coalitions with persistent economic and political difficulties that slow down integration in sub-regional schemes. The FTAA would arise as the preferred option, leading to a swift suffocation of sub-regional projects. The combination of anti-multilateral globalization with the FTAA as the dominant trade integration pole in the Americas would present Latin American and Caribbean countries with asymmetrical regionalism characterized by pressures towards intense trade liberalization and policy harmonization with the US.

- *Building Blocks Scenario.* This scenario of building blocks would result from a new multilateral consensus in the world trade system and plural regionalism in the hemisphere. The global arena would enjoy a relatively stable macroeconomic and financial situation, a balanced distribution of power between the US, the EU and Asia, and a mutually fertilizing relationship between multilateralism and regionalism. With this backdrop, the domestic and international pro-globalization consensus could be rebuilt around new foundations including labor and environment issues. The underpinnings for a new international and domestic social pact capable of sustaining a new liberalization cycle would be gradually laid through labor training programs like the US Workforce Investment Act of 1998 and international agreements like the June 2000 Guidelines for Multinational Corporations. A global extrapolation of these initiatives could give way to a fresh *modus vivendi* for ideas of embedded liberalism (see Tussie, Introduction). On the other hand, the multilateral agenda would take into account the increasing weight of emerging markets in the world economy, particularly in terms of the international division of industrial labor. The new round of multilateral negotiations would include substantial reform of subsidies and sector-specific protection systems. China's entry into the WTO and Asia's economic recovery would significantly step up investment flows to that region. While Asian countries advance towards regional free trade areas, the leverage of the 'South' would increase in international arenas. US unilateralism would be limited by Asian and European economic and political consolidation. In the Americas, Mercosur, the AC and the FTAA would successfully evolve. The FTAA would come into effect in 2005 with transition times and temporary safeguards for sensitive sectors and smaller economies as well as environmental and labor clauses as required by the US Congress. Mercosur and the AC would merge in 2003 through a free trade agreement and consolidate as individual customs unions, opening a space for the negotiation of those issues logjammed in the FTAA. The sub-regional blocs, which maintain their identity within the FTAA, would contemplate constitution of fully integrated common markets in a ten-year period. Hence a united hemisphere characterized by the coexistence of several preferential trade arrangements with different degrees of depth would be created. In this scenario the consolidation of a global consensus would be complemented by a pluralist hemisphere. These building blocks would present Latin America and the Caribbean, and especially South American countries, with a less asymmetrical scenario than the unipolar hegemony scenario. Governance and development issues would become legitimate agenda items in the distinct trade negotiation fora, offsetting the trends towards market liberalization and policy harmonization around orthodox paradigms.

- *Regional Hegemony Scenario.* A scenario of regional hegemony would emerge should the US face difficulties in pushing its agenda and interests in an uncooperative global scenario, combined with the FTAA's consolidation of trade liberalization and policy harmonization. The essential feature of this scenario would be the US's resort to regional fora to advance its interests, especially policy harmonization, in the context of either a cooperative or uncooperative multipolar global scenario. At the global level, the outlook most compatible with this scenario would be an uncooperative equilibrium where liberalization is blocked by both developed and developing countries in an unstable economic environment with impacts on trade flows. Protectionism and unilateralism would return recharged to the scene, and the 'stumbling blocs' version of regionalism would gain impetus. Regional leaders would use these initiatives to reinforce their economic power against rivals in other geo-economic blocs. The tripolar polarization between the US, the EU and Asia would surge with worsening trade conflicts around the three blocs and emerging anti-Western regionalism in Asia. The WTO legitimacy crisis would not be overcome despite the launching of a new round. Even negotiations within the built-in agenda would fail, and multilateralism would enter a deep funk. Major players would allot priority to domestic agendas and regional initiatives would gain strength propelled by players unsatisfied with the multilateral inertia (like Asia and the US). The FTAA would embody the hemispheric expression of these new regionalist trends. Negotiations would conclude in 2005 with a far-reaching integration project WTO-plus in areas such as services, investments and intellectual property rights. Sub-regional integration initiatives in Latin America and the Caribbean would go through a period of impasse but would not disintegrate. US pressure on hemispheric trade partners for an immediate and unconditional alignment on economic struggles with the EU and Asia would meet with considerable resistance from South American countries. The implementation of the FTAA would confront the foot-dragging of South America's large countries that use the economic competition between the blocs to their advantage.

- *Fragmentation and Bilateralism Scenario.* Convergence of an uncooperative equilibrium in the global field and the inability of the FTAA to consolidate in the regional field would generate a scenario of fragmentation and bilateralism. US trade strategy would focus on the negotiation of bilateral agreements with Latin American and Caribbean countries as regionalism would replace the shortcomings of multilateralism in US strategy. However, unlike the previous scenario of regional hegemony, the FTAA would not gather enough support in the US and other large countries. In the face of a balanced international environment and domestic and external difficulties the US would resort to bilateral agreements to promote the FTAA, attracting not only Central American and Caribbean countries but also members of South American sub-regional agreements, and would thereby stoke internal divergences within each bloc. This divide-and-conquer method would provoke defensive political reactions and stimulate nationalism and anti-US sentiments. These backlashes would have an economic component with the intensification of industrial policy activism and trade protectionism in these countries. Integration scheme leaders, like Brazil, could promote the deepening of the sub-regional bloc as a defense against US bilateral initiatives and the subsequent dilution of regional projects. Hence the Americas would live among intense, fragmented negotiations and trade conflict with political consequences, dividing the region into two distinct blocs: one attracted by US initiatives, and a Southern bloc anchored in defensive sub-regionalism and extra-hemispheric trade and economic alliances.
- *Trade Negotiation Impasse Scenario.* A scenario of complete impasse would combine the uncooperative global equilibrium with regionalism in crisis. Latin American and Caribbean sub-regional agreements would enter endemic crisis and negotiating paralysis. The FTAA would also be affected by the lack of domestic consensus around new US liberalization initiatives and by countries' resistance, especially Brazil's, to the project. The political deterioration in the AC could also factor in. The dynamism and motivation that sustained regional initiatives in the Americas in the 1990s would be exhausted. The prevalence of an uncooperative global equilibrium and fragmentation would practically prohibit Latin American and Caribbean countries or sub-regional agreements from seeking refuge in extra-hemispheric diversification strategies. Trade and political tensions would mushroom, even between sub-regional partners, who would face a complex and intricate process.

These five scenarios make it clear that Latin America and the Caribbean could face quite heterogeneous contexts, though the hemispheric arena would hold special weight in three out of five scenarios. Should multilateralism retain a relevant weight and sub-regional agreements not dissipate, Latin America, and especially South America, would tend to be less restricted.

These scenarios, like the building block scenario, favor development-oriented issues and offer an equilibrium between additional liberalization efforts and governance issues. To end on an optimistic note such scenarios may provide space for a new embedded liberalism in which regional and sub-regional negotiations offer the quid pro quo bargaining necessary to form a new safety net in the face of multilateral globalization (see Tussie, Introduction).

Note

1. Translated by Ignacio Labaqui and Brita Siepker.

Part II
The Management of Sectoral Market Access

4
The Negotiation on Agriculture: the Regional-Multilateral Relationship

Marisa Diaz-Henderson

4.1 Introduction

The relationship between the proliferation of regional economic agreements on the one hand, and the process of global economic integration on the other, is largely complementary with influences travelling on a two-way street. Most of the time one is inclined to think of the impact of regionalism on multilateralism; but attention should also be paid to the contributions made by multilateral rules to a sound ground for regional trade flows. This complex dual relationship can be exemplified by the case of sugar, revealing the linkages between the political economy of regional and international policy-making. Mercosur brought about a convergence of policies among its members, which reverberates on the countries' participation in the World Trade Organization (WTO). On many issues Mercosur speaks with a single voice, potentially yielding more market power for its members. However, many of the conflicts inherent to a regional integration initiative are played out by Mercosur members using WTO norms and rules including its dispute settlement system.

The argument of this chapter is developed in the following steps. Section 4.2 traces integration in the agricultural sector and looks at the patterns of agricultural trade and production in Mercosur. Section 4.3 details domestic agricultural trade regimes, which will help place the agricultural situation in the wider context of multilateral negotiations. Section 4.4 illustrates the political economy of the residual protection in the case of sugar, showing how domestic political and socio-economic objectives have prevailed over regional and multilateral trade liberalization. Finally, section 4.5 examines the developments taking place in WTO negotiations on agriculture, shedding light on the unstable relationship between domestic and regional compromises and the contributions that the WTO agenda can make to cement the regional bloc.

4.2   Mercosur: the building blocks

Coordination of agricultural policies in Mercosur has been the subject of technical discussions on harmonizing domestic policies and modeling the emerging regime on the Uruguay Round Agreement (URA) on Agriculture. While there are to be some limitations on national autonomy on measures subject to reduction commitments at the WTO, governments retain full autonomy regarding the use of domestic support measures that have minimal or no effect on trade (subsidies which are decoupled from production). Most tariffs applicable to intra-Mercosur trade were dismantled in January 1995 and some 85 per cent of intra-trade became duty free. Practically all agricultural tariffs applicable to intra-Mercosur trade have been reduced to zero, though sugar is a notable exception. In 1995, a common external tariff (CET) was created for trading partners subject to most favored nation (MFN) rates. Each country has been allowed a list of exceptions to the CET until 2006. Overall, Mercosur is the regional initiative that has attained the deepest and most complete liberalization worldwide and in fact much more than was affordable multilaterally.

By dismantling agricultural tariffs within Mercosur and undertaking commitments at the WTO, agricultural sectors have been opened to competition from within and beyond the region. Governments have, to varying degrees and through various measures, assisted the transition to more efficient and profitable farming, but with mixed results. Dismantling certain support measures has proven difficult and led to controversies, with the lack of a common sugar regime as a case in point. The pace and scope of change has also been hampered by the overriding problem of farm debt and access to the markets of developed countries, many of which remain highly protected. Nevertheless, more market-oriented adjustments in patterns of production and improvements in productivity have been made resulting in a new mix of farming capabilities.

Trade and production patterns

The agricultural sector is of enduring importance for Mercosur countries in terms of contribution to GDP, employment and trade. Agricultural products, such as Argentine beef and wheat and Brazilian coffee and sugar, are competitively priced and of internationally renowned quality. The agriculture, hunting, forestry and fishing sector contributes 12 per cent of Mercosur's GDP, making it the fourth largest sector. Agriculture employs about 15 million people, representing over 20 per cent of the economically active population. Mercosur is one of the world's main food producers and the agricultural sector experienced strong growth in production from 1991 to 1999 in sectors such as rice (41 per cent), soy (91.8 per cent), wheat (34.4 per cent) and corn (45.8 per cent) (CEI, 2000). Growth has been facilitated by greater mechanization of the means of production, improved transportation infrastructure and the regional integration process. Mercosur is ranked fourth among global exporters of agricultural products, claiming a 7 per cent share of the world's total agricultural exports in 2000, up from 5 per cent in 1990. Over the same period, the value of extra-Mercosur agricultural exports increased from US$1.7 billion to US$2.97 billion, or by 72 per cent. In 1998, Brazil and Argentina were fifth and seventh respectively among the top food exporters and Mercosur countries were responsible for a relatively large proportion of the world's exports in some key agricultural commodities (soybean oil 44 per cent, honey 20 per cent, coffee and sugar 17 per cent, corn 15 per cent and poultry 9 per cent).[1] Mercosur countries hold significant comparative advantage in agriculture and would gain considerable market share in a multilaterally freer market.

Agricultural exports are of varying importance for Mercosur countries. In 1999, they contributed as much as 71 per cent of Paraguay's total exports, 48 per cent of Argentina's (1998), and 48 per cent of Uruguay's (1999) but only 30 per cent of Brazil's (1999).[2] The Brazilian figure represents a high percentage in world terms, but it is a figure that has been in decline and given the extent of Paraguay's dependence on agriculture, Mercosur countries' long-term agricultural trade priorities may continue to diverge. The large variances in size and industrial activity among the countries will inevitably be reflected in their trade interests.

While Mercosur countries export agricultural products to distinct destinations, the similarities suggest that they should have a common outlook on trade talks (Table 4.1). The European Union (EU) has always been the most important market and the rate of growth has exceeded that of intra-trade. Mercosur's lack of market penetration in the US is a concern given the relevance of its market. Negotiations in the WTO and also in the Free Trade Area of the Americas (FTAA) could lead to the adoption of beneficial policies in this area.

Evidence suggests that the integration process has given impulse to specialization. David and Nonnemberg (1997) have shown that patterns of specialization in production, based on indices of revealed comparative

Table 4.1 Share of agricultural exports by main markets of destination

	Mercosur (%)	US (%)	EU (%)	Rest of world (%)
Paraguay	34.6	6.2	47.0	12.2
Argentina	22.4	4.8	25.0	47.8
Brazil	6.9	8.2	44.0	40.9
Uruguay	41.0	5.3	21.0	32.7

Source: Based on FAO database. Paraguay and Uruguay calculated using 1999 data. Argentina and Brazil calculated using 1998 data.

advantage, have increased in Brazil, Uruguay and Argentina. Wheat and soybeans are just two of the many sectors in which specialization has followed comparative advantage. As a key exporter of wheat, Argentina's trade with third parties is growing at an even faster rate than trade within the bloc. Brazil is the main consumer and importer of Argentine wheat but it also imports from other countries to meet growing demand. Argentine wheat exports more than doubled in 1996–97 and were sold to more than fifty countries in Africa, Asia, Europe and the Americas. Since the wheat sector in partner countries seems to be in decline as Argentine exports increase, wheat is clearly a sector in which intra-regional specialization is evolving. Argentina, together with Brazil, has also long specialized in soybean products, and the bloc is now one of the major production centers in the world. The region is also one of the major world suppliers of soybean by-products as larger volumes of oilseeds are being processed domestically, and consequently there is a smaller exportable surplus of oilseeds. Mercosur accounts for 25 per cent of world production of soybean oil and 50 per cent of global trade. Brazil is the largest soybean oil producer but since the 1980s Argentina has replaced Brazil as the region's main exporter. Argentina has managed to gain this dominant position in soybean oil exports through substantial investment in oil crushing plants and technology.

Sector investment patterns in processed products prior to the formation of Mercosur still affect intra-regional trade patterns. Brazil has found a growing market for poultry and pork products in Argentina. In contrast, Argentina and Uruguay are exploiting their competitive advantage in other products such as temperate climate fruits (apples and pears), beef, leather and leather products, milk, and dairy products. However, for a few products, such as corn, no clear pattern of specialization has yet emerged. The rate and extent of reform has not been even across all agricultural sectors and residual protectionism remains the skeleton in the closet for the countries of Mercosur.

4.3   Domestic politics: the contrasts

The building blocks of Mercosur depend upon the foundations laid in each member country. Throughout the region, liberalization has tended to benefit large export-oriented farmers at the expense of small, less efficient producers. The problems that farming communities face tend to be similar but the ways in which governments have dealt with them have varied. The restraints on domestic governments as well as their choices have laid the cornerstones from which the integration process has grown. A country-by-country review shows not only the building blocks of Mercosur's regional agricultural policies but also how each country has been able to operate individually within the boundaries of the WTO framework. The resulting differences become the source of intra-regional frictions.

Paraguay

The contribution of agriculture to Paraguay's economy exceeds that of the industrial and construction sectors. It accounts for about 30 per cent of GDP, is responsible for the greatest share of total export earnings and provides a source of gainful employment for 45 per cent of the country's 4.95 million people, particularly the subsistence cotton farming families, who make up about 20 per cent. Productivity and efficiency are unevenly distributed and a small percentage of farmers enjoy the greatest share of the income. High interest rates have tended to discourage investment in agriculture and rural poverty has become a major concern, especially as the subsistence cotton sector has faced low production and prices. Farm indebtedness is a serious problem, in particular for subsistence farmers.

In the 1990s, the mix of Paraguay's agricultural production and exports changed. As cotton and wheat exports became less profitable, production and exports shifted towards other crops, such as soybeans. Modern, larger farmers were able to shift production and take advantage of the fertile, uncultivated land available. To help the indebted and cotton-dependent subsistence farmers, the government provided loans and technical assistance for farmers willing to switch from traditional crops. As a result, agricultural output diversified as farmers increased the production of speciality and high-value products, such as fruits and vegetables. However, the government's diversification program has not been without its share of disillusionment; producers' relatively limited technical knowledge and the shortage of appropriate storage and handling facilities have restricted progress. By the end of the decade, production of fruit and vegetables had declined and a number of farmers either returned to cotton or left the land altogether. The government's support to the agricultural sector has been very limited in the last years. Paraguay's total expenditure on domestic support measures was US$27.9 million in 1999,[3] including subsidies that are exempt from WTO commitments as they are considered to have no or minimal trade-distorting effects.

Uruguay

In the mid- to late-1990s, Uruguay greatly expanded its production so that agriculture accounts for about 10 per cent of GDP. Preferred access under Mercosur to the Brazilian market increased demand for many products including rice, wheat, dairy, beef and fruits. Processors find it difficult to compete with large, internationally competitive industries in Argentina and Brazil because of their small size and less modern technology. With relatively high processing costs, a number of local processing facilities have had to close. Without further assistance, the crushing sector faces continued decline and many of the seeds and grains Uruguay produces will be sent to Argentina or Brazil for processing.

In addition to rural unemployment, debt also remains an issue. After a recovery in the early 1990s, not only did indebtedness of the agricultural sector continue to grow, but it did so at an increasing rate. In 1996, total bank debt of the agricultural sector was about 45 per cent of the agricultural gross production, compared with 41 per cent the previous year (USDA, 1997). There was simultaneously a rise in the number of farms in a worsening financial condition. By the end of the 1990s, debt as a proportion of agricultural GDP was no better than it had been before Uruguay entered Mercosur. One sector that performed better than expected was wheat, despite increased competition from Argentina. While Uruguayan soils are generally less fertile, yields have improved as farmers have adopted new technology and increased fertilizer use. Also, farm operations have increased in size, allowing them to use larger, more modern machinery and thereby benefit from economies of scale.

Government subsidies to the sector have mainly been in the form of pest and disease control and inspection services, marketing and promotion services and investment subsidies. Under WTO rules, these so-called 'green box' subsidies are considered to have minimal impact on trade and production and are exempted from reduction commitments. Total expenditure on these kinds of measures by Uruguay represented US$33.1 million in 1999. In addition, Uruguay has provided product-specific direct payments within the context of the 'Farm Conversion and Development Program'[4] and non-product specific subsidies in the form of an exemption from payment of CET on imports of agricultural inputs from non-Mercosur countries.[5] These last two support measures are considered to have distorting effects on trade and production within WTO rules. While the former affects mainly producers' returns, the latter raises output by lowering input costs. However, Uruguay has not been obliged to reduce subsidy levels as they have not reached 'de minimis' levels.[6]

Argentina

The agricultural sector in Argentina adapted reasonably well to the changing circumstances of the 1990s. While agriculture's contribution to GDP dropped from 8.3 per cent in 1991 to 6 per cent in 2000, nearly half of Argentina's exports still come from the agricultural sector. Farmers are rapidly adopting new technology and their more extensive use of fertilizers and agricultural chemicals has allowed them to increase yields and productivity. An upgraded transportation infrastructure handles the expanding supply of products more efficiently and at lower costs. Hence, farmers are now able to produce, process, and transport greater quantities of agricultural products than ever before.

Whereas overall trade has shown a slight tendency to be directed towards Mercosur, agricultural trade has diversified considerably. Agricultural trade with Mercosur countries accounted for only 20 per cent of total agricultural trade. Since the devaluation of the Brazilian real in January 1999, Argentine exporters have had to search even further afield as their produce became overpriced for the Brazilian market, a trend that may be quickly offset by the crumbling of the peso in early 2002.

In addition to the problem of access to highly protected international markets, Argentine farmers face serious farm debt. In response to high world grain prices in the 1996–97 season, farmers sharply increased their investment in planted area, expensive inputs such as genetically modified seeds and fertilizers, and farm machinery and other capital goods. However, since 1998, commodity prices have fallen considerably, making it increasingly difficult for farmers to repay their loans. A third of farmers have gone bankrupt over the past decade. Therefore, with some commodity prices at their lowest level in years and rising interest rates, and despite rising productivity and output, farmers were faced with declining incomes and rising debts in the year 2000. The government has allowed the market to operate freely and thus the pattern of landownership has become increasingly concentrated. To date, the government's financial support to farmers consists of making credit available to smaller agricultural producers. However, few producers are able to obtain credit and those that do have to pay very high interest rates. In the absence of affordable credits, groups of small and medium farmers have formed so-called 'investment pools' as a means of spreading financial risks. Government subsidies to agriculture have been mainly used for green box measures including investment aids and research. Government expenditure on such measures in 1997 was US$237.4 million.[7] The government has also maintained a price-support program for leaf tobacco which in 1997 stood at US$84.1 million.

Brazil

Brazil is the largest country and economy in Mercosur with an estimated GDP of US$1.13 trillion and 80 per cent of the bloc's population. Agriculture accounts for about 9 per cent of GDP and 23 per cent of total employment. Brazil is the world's largest producer of coffee and sugar (from sugarcane) and is amongst the largest producers of soybean products, orange juice, cocoa, beef, tobacco and cotton. Agricultural products account for around 30 per cent of Brazil's total export revenue, making the country one of the world's leading exporters of cocoa, coffee, orange juice, soybean products and sugar. Its market share has allowed it a degree of influence over price formation in international markets.

Characterized by a large number of smallholdings, almost half of the rural establishments are under 10 hectare and account for less than 10 per cent of the total area. A relatively small number of large farms make up around 40 per cent of total area. These tend to be run inefficiently, with as little as 30 per cent of the area in production. In addition, farming incomes are uneven and characterized by significant regional differences. The Landless Rural Workers Movement has been instrumental in organizing large-scale occupations of land in order to draw attention to these phenomena and to encourage the government to speed up land reform.

The agricultural sector has recently suffered from a number of setbacks that have hindered the adoption of a more liberal trade regime, including increasingly high levels of farm debt and the impact of stringent monetary policy on profitability. Though the 1994 Real Plan increased consumer purchasing power and real incomes, it had negative financial repercussions in the agricultural sector. First, several farmers were caught off guard by the cuts in inflation, as they had relied on the previously high inflation to erode their debt. Second, the government's reduction in funding for subsidized credit programs placed loans out of reach for many farmers, as loan criteria became more selective.

Various government subsidies have aided the sector. The government has financed a wide range of general services related to the agricultural sector including infrastructural services, marketing and promotion services, and activities related to agrarian policy, agrarian reform and settlement projects. Budgetary expenditures on these kinds of green box subsidies were US$2420 million in 1998.[8] The government has also provided product-specific subsidies in the form of price support, direct payments and production and marketing credits for products such as wheat, soybean, rice, maize, sugar cane and barley.[9] Finally, the government has helped farmers with production and investment credits. These are government and private funds allocated to production at preferential interest rates or directed to improve rural infrastructure. In 1998, for instance, expenditure on this category of subsidies was US$373 million. As part of the special and differential (S&D) treatment given to developing countries in the Uruguay Round (UR), these production and investment credits are exempt from reduction commitments.

At the beginning of 1999, the devaluation of the real gave an extra push to exporters' and farmers' incomes. Brazil became more competitive and increased its export surplus. This surge in exports contributed to the lowering of the international commodity prices of products such as soybeans and soy products, sugar, rice and poultry. Mercosur partners were particularly affected by the devaluation of the real, facing stiffer competition in competing products and a decline in producer prices. Whereas Mercosur countries had dismantled intra-regional tariffs, third countries with protective tariffs, such as the US in sugar, could prevent the passing through of lowered prices from international markets to consumers. Even though Mercosur countries called upon antidumping measures, these defense mechanisms are not as easily applied as tariffs and created further regional tensions.

All told, Mercosur countries built a WTO-plus agreement in terms of liberalizing border tariffs on agriculture. However, they neglected to coordinate domestic support policies beyond the border, paralleling the laxity of the WTO framework in this area. Minimal regional coordination was based on the minimalist commitments at the multilateral level. A double standard has thus been created, juxtaposing liberalization with inherently contradictory domestic support policies. On one hand, this proved problematic in the regional fora as Mercosur had attained meaningful liberalization of agriculture, causing friction between the members. On the other hand, the persistence of high tariff protection at the multilateral level posed no such contradiction to continued domestic support. When the multilateral framework fails to address an aspect of protection, Mercosur is unable, on its own, to unravel domestic protectionist policies against the lingering multilateral current of protection. Thus regional trade liberalization in agriculture is inherently unstable. Sugar is the clearest case of a sector that fell through the cracks of liberalization.

4.4 Residual protection: the case of sugar

Sugar is the only sector in which intra-trade in Mercosur has not been liberalized,[10] interconnecting the sectoral issue at the regional and multilateral levels. When Mercosur partners met at Ouro Preto in 1994, they agreed to exclude sugar from liberalization, due to Argentina's concern over the trade-distorting effects of Brazil's National Alcohol Program (Proalcool). All sugar imports to Argentina (including those from Mercosur countries) pay a 35 per cent tariff plus a variable levy based on the difference between the average world sugar price over the last four years and the closing price of the previous month's importation. Without this tariff, Argentine sugar, which is more expensive than Brazilian sugar, would find it hard to compete. Argentine producers justify the tariff as rectification for the imbalance created by the unfair advantage created by Proalcool.

The most obvious characteristic of sugar is its versatility and popularity. Not only an essential household commodity, sugar is also used throughout industry, such as in food processing. Sugar enjoys a relatively high inelasticity of demand since it has had, until recently, no near substitutes. Historically, high demand for sugar has meant that taxes on it have been a useful source of revenue for governments. However, unlike most agricultural commodities, sugarcane is an unstable product and must be processed immediately upon harvest or suffer from rapid sucrose decomposition. Any delay in getting the sugarcane to the crusher would result in loss of revenue for the producer and require imports to make up for the shortfall. Since these imports may be more expensive, governments have also resorted to taxing exports of sugar at times of shortage. Sugar producers therefore require the proximity of local millers, who in turn, seek a regular and dependable supply of sugar in order to produce at near capacity and get a reasonable return on their investment in capital. To ensure the viability of production therefore, farmers and producers have tended to concentrate in certain geographical areas. Geographical concentration that enables strong lobbying pressure on governments allows higher levels of protection. Protection is also connected to the volatility of production levels and therefore the world price for sugar. Yields of sugar from sugarcane have tended to vary considerably – for example, in Brazil, where the year on year fall in sugar production from June 1999 to June 2000 was 29.7 per cent. While the area under cultivation is estimated to have shrunk by 5 per cent due to low prices

(USDA, 2000), the main cause was a long drought followed by severe frosts. Another factor that characterizes the production of sugar is the amount of industrial processing required. Traditionally, raw sugar was, and in some parts of the world still is, produced by cutting and crushing sugarcane to extract its juices, which are then boiled down in open containers until a sludgy mass of crystals is formed, separated and left to dry. Large quantities of water and containers resistant to high temperatures are required. Modern-day milling, distillation and refining processes are long, highly complex and capital intensive, requiring sophisticated equipment and technical expertise.

Using data provided by Yeats (1998), a comparison, between prepared sugar and other commodities can be drawn. A value of 100 is given for products whose labor intensity is average relative to all manufacturing activity with increasing values above 100 indicating increasing capital intensity. Sugar production has a value of 140, which is almost as capital intensive as Iron and Steel Castings (145) and is more so than road motor vehicles (122), underlining the assertion that sugar incurs a relatively industrialized process and is therefore different from other agricultural products. Hence sugar can be distinguished by a number of characteristics: it is a highly versatile and popular commodity; it is vulnerable to supply shocks; and it is as much an industrial as an agricultural product. Protection of sugar may be partly explained, therefore, by a combination of factors: versatility; irregular supply and inelastic demand; and a particular symbiosis of agricultural-industrial production with a geographical concentration.

The Argentine sugar sector is far smaller than that of Brazil but usually produces enough sugar to meet domestic demand. The main sugar-producing provinces in Argentina are Jujuy, Salta and Tucuman, the latter contributing as much as 70 per cent of the country's total acreage. In recent years, relatively high stocks, a weak international market, limited credit and mills' financial strains have led to a crisis in the local sugar sector. Only the most efficient producers have managed to cover costs, forcing many farmers to abandon production. Nevertheless, the remaining farmers have benefited from good weather and invested more than in the past, which has resulted in a more efficient use of resources and increasing levels of production. Most producers are improving crop management and are incorporating new technology. Due to expanded production, Argentina has become more than self-sufficient in sugar, generally fulfilling its portion of the US sugar tariff rate quota, and exporting refined sugar to Chile and raw sugar to Uruguay. Exporters have requested a subsidy of US$150 per metric ton to allow further exports, but the government is unlikely to ever accede to this demand because it would mean abandoning its historic opposition to export subsidies for agricultural products. The tariff on intra-regional imports, however, is seen to be justified on charges that the Brazilian Proalcool program effectively subsidizes sugar exports.

Proalcool was set up in 1975 with goals of reducing dependency on external supplies of energy, encouraging scientific and technological development and internally supplying bio-mass fuel of renewable origin, and securing environmental advantages from the use of 'clean' fuel. The program began with the expansion of traditional sugar areas and distillation of anhydrous alcohol for blending with gasoline in plants annexed to existing mills. A few years later, this was followed by production of hydrous alcohol from sugarcane for use in alcohol-only engines in autonomous distilleries located near new sugarcane regions. Alcohol production expanded from practically nil in 1975 to about 14.5 million cubic meters in 1997. Practically all the demand for fuel alcohol was met by massive expansion of sugarcane production (WTO, 2000a). Government quotas and guaranteed prices ensured that sugarcane producers would be able to sell their crop at attractive prices.

Yet, soon after Proalcool was introduced relatively large oil deposits were discovered in Brazil and international oil prices fell steadily. These developments markedly reduced the value of ethanol as a gasoline substitute and by the mid-1980s, the WTO found that Brazil no longer had comparative advantage as a producer of a substitute fuel for gasoline (WTO, 1997). The cost differential between gasoline and ethanol increased throughout most of the 1980s and 1990s, requiring extensive government intervention. The industry incurred large debts with Banco do Brasil, estimated at some R$4.6 billion in early 1996. The program therefore required heavy subsidization from the Brazilian government and depended on tax incentives to stimulate consumer purchases of alcohol-burning vehicles. While its supporters have been lobbying the government to adopt special measures to keep the program afloat, the program's detractors have been calling for it to be dismantled. However, since 1998, the price of oil has tripled and demand for fuel alcohol has risen sharply, thereby strengthening the argument of Proalcool supporters. To support the fuel alcohol program, the mandatory content of anhydrous alcohol in gasoline was increased to 24 per cent in June 2000. Also the Green Fleet Law of 1998 provides for the replacement of gasoline-fuelled vehicles owned by the public sector by hydrous fuel vehicles. The law also requires that vehicles bought under the benefit of a fiscal incentive, such as taxis, run on renewable fuels. The government estimated that this measure would result in the purchase of 120,000 alcohol-powered vehicles per year, up from 600 when the measure was adopted.

A major criticism leveled at the Brazilian government is that producers are cushioned from the effects of the world market price for sugar. When sugar prices are low, unsubsidized producers are discouraged from increasing sugarcane production and may even take some land out of cultivation. When world sugar prices rise again, it takes time to put land back into production to take advantage of higher prices. Farmers may even delay doing so until they see whether the price rise will be permanent. The sheer size of the sugarcane growing base needed to support both the sugar and fuel alcohol industries means that Brazil has the potential to expand sugar exports more rapidly than any of the major world exporters by diverting more cane into sugar production when sugar prices are high. When world sugar prices fall,

Brazilian producers simply produce more fuel alcohol and less sugar. What is more, when gasoline prices are high, Brazilian farmers will actually cultivate more sugarcane even if the price of sugar falls dramatically, because the price of fuel alcohol will also rise in relation to gasoline. Brazil will therefore be in a position to capture an even greater share of the world sugar market because they will be more protected from reductions in sugarcane production levels than their competitors. If the price of oil falls at the same time, encouraging Brazil to reduce the amount of fuel alcohol required in gasoline, even larger amounts of Brazilian sugar would be unleashed on the world market, suppressing the world market price but leading to greater market-share gains for Brazilian producers. Given that Brazil is already by far the world's largest producer of sugar, further market-share gains would have a disruptive effect on the world market price and export markets.

Brazil notified domestic support commitments for sugarcane in the WTO, stood at US$16 million in 1996–97. However, the Proalcool Program was not notified to the WTO because Brazil believes its costs do not represent internal support measures for sugarcane, sugar or alcohol producers (WTO, 1999a). In response to UR commitments, government intervention in domestic marketing has ceased and in 1998, the government removed a 40 per cent tax on exports of sugar beyond a set quota.

The liberalization of both sugar and fuel alcohol prices has had a profound effect on its regional and world competitors. The OECD (2000a) reported that Brazil's sugar policy reforms and its 1999 devaluation were key factors in the fundamental shifts witnessed in world sugar markets in 2000. Brazil's low-cost producers have more than quadrupled their share of exports from just 6 per cent in 1990 to a forecasted 27 per cent in 2001. The effects of these recent events have been felt far beyond Mercosur and seemed at first to entrench both the Argentine and Brazilian governments' positions *vis-à-vis* the issue of liberalization of sugar tariffs.

The asymmetries in the sugar sector indicate that Argentine abandonment of its tariff on Brazilian imports would result in further rural unemployment and widespread social unrest. However, failure to proceed on the sugar issue may have consequences far beyond Mercosur. As the world's largest producer and exporter of sugar, Brazil holds a strategic position in multilateral negotiations. So long as the issue remains unresolved within Mercosur, countries that either subsidize sugar exports, such as the EU, or protect their domestic markets through tariff quotas, such as the US, may feel less inclined to further liberalize trade in sugar at the multilateral level.

4.5   WTO multilateral negotiations in agricultural trade

Since Mercosur accounts for a significant share of world agricultural exports and enjoys comparative advantage in many products, it stands to gain from any substantial agricultural liberalization that arises from the ongoing multilateral negotiations. It is estimated that if the sugar markets of the EU, US and Japan were all liberalized, exports from Brazil would increase by 21 per cent (Abare, 1995). Mercosur countries negotiate individually at the WTO but there is close collaboration among government officials. Additionally, they share goals of liberalizing agricultural trade with other Cairns Group countries. While the Cairns Group has helped shape the agenda and has advanced proposals for the negotiations, as in the UR, developing countries have also seemed to find a stronger voice with issues of particular relevance to them, such as S&D, having become more central to WTO discussions (see Abreu, Chapter 1). Both state and market actors of Mercosur have had input in the ongoing multilateral negotiating process. Mercosur farmers' associations have, in conjunction with farmers' associations of other Cairns Group countries, lobbied ministers at Cairns Group Ministerial meetings as in the case of services (see Narlikar and Woods, Chapter 2). Alliances also sometimes run along sectoral rather than regional or sub-regional lines. For example, Brazilian sugar producers are the only Mercosur members of the Global Alliance for Sugar Trade Reform and Liberalization, a group that raises issues of relevance to sugar exporters.

Mercosur regional integration and the multilateral liberalization processes feed upon each other. In certain areas, clearly shared objectives will allow the regional partners to present a united front at the multilateral level. In other areas, the multilateral negotiating process itself will serve to bring about the necessary coordination of policies within the regional bloc. Members of the bloc look to the multilateral rules to adjust their national domestic policies. Therefore, the main issues discussed in negotiations are of particular relevance.

Market access

The UR brought agreement concerning the conversion of quotas and non-tariff barriers (NTBs) into tariffs (that is, tariffication), the provision of minimum access commitments (that is, tariff rate quotas) and the arrangement for special safeguard clauses as a form of transitional protection. Enforcement of these market access commitments has been elusive, and the tariffication process resulted in a considerable degree of protection. In this regard, tariff rate quotas have actually served as quantity limitations insofar as almost all international trade in agricultural products has taken place within the tariff quotas.

Post-UR simple bound mean tariff rates for agriculture are high in various countries including Colombia (88.3 per cent), Iceland (48.4 per cent), Korea (62.2 per cent), and Switzerland (51.1 per cent) (OECD, 1999). Not only are Mercosur bound tariffs lower than in the countries above, their applied tariff levels are even lower (see Table 4.2).

The levels of bound tariff rates provide Mercosur countries with ample leeway to negotiate further tariff reductions without threatening the margin of preference they give each other. Market access negotiations, however, are

Table 4.2   Mercosur mean tariff rates on agriculture

	Simple average ad valorem legal (1999 applied) (%)	Simple average final bound tariff rates (%)
Argentina	12.90	32.7
Brazil	13.25	36.0
Paraguay	12.67	33.1
Uruguay	13.00	33.4

Source: Calculations based on FTAA database (chs 1–24 of the Harmonized Commodity Description and Coding System, except ch. 3). Argentina and Paraguay include around 847 tariff lines, Brazil 1076 and Uruguay 113.

concerned with various other variables that need to be taken into account. That is to say, improvements in market access will involve programming the tariff measure package to include reductions in tariffs, tariff quota enlargement, reforms of tariff quota administration and the consideration of a safeguard mechanism. An example of how these variables would work can be shown in the case of sugar, which is largely dependent on tariffs, particularly the industry in OECD countries with an estimated average tariff rate of 60 per cent compared with 15 per cent in developing countries.

Since much of this access is preferential, Mercosur countries have called for increases in tariff quota volumes and the improvement of tariff quota administration methods.[11] They have also questioned whether there is a real need to continue with the special safeguard in the URA on Agriculture,[12] pointing out that it disregards whether imports are having an effect on the domestic market and is thus quite arbitrary, leaving negligible room for improved market access. Between 1995–2000, of the eight WTO members that used the special safeguards, four cases concerned sugar. Both the EU and the US have set trigger prices for the additional import levy at levels higher than the external reference price used to establish the tariffs. The issue of import safeguards is important to some parts of the sugar industry and it will thus remain on the trade reform agenda as the industry moves towards a more liberal multilateral trade regime.

By expressing concerns over the allocation of quota rent as well as the issues of transparency and non-discrimination, Mercosur countries reveal their willingness to strike a balance between the desire to compete for the distribution of benefits and a recognition of the need for increased access. Market access negotiations at the multilateral level can offer Mercosur opportunities to coordinate regionally, particularly on safeguard mechanisms.

Domestic support

The domestic support commitments of the URA on Agriculture were delicately balanced and closely linked to domestic political structures in the agricultural sector. Thus it allowed members flexibility to institutionalize their embedded trade policies. Analysis of the domestic support provisions negotiated during the UR reveals that patterns of compromise between farm lobbies and their respective governments were sieved into the international negotiations through the intervention of state agencies. Since then, during the meetings of the WTO Committee on Agriculture, Mercosur countries have been monitoring the implementation of the UR commitments and working to identify problems with the current disciplines.[13] One of the main concerns raised has been the lack of transparency to ensure that subsidies achieve their goals without having trade-distorting impacts, and consequently there have been calls for clearer and tighter definitions of permitted subsidies. Cairns Group members have also called for the elimination of the 'temporary' exemption from reduction commitments of direct payments granted under production limiting programs (WTO, 2000b). Also of concern is the use of Total Aggregate Measure of Support as a basis for reduction rather than the individual commodity AMS, as it enables members to increase support for some products while still meeting annual aggregate reduction commitments.

The sugar sector crystallizes the problem with domestic support. Most sugar support policies consist of price support based on relatively high tariffs or direct payments to producers. As previously mentioned, Brazil is the only Mercosur country that supports sugarcane through non-exempt direct payments and production and marketing credits. The WTO negotiations could aid Mercosur countries in better adjusting some imbalances. Since the general framework for regulating domestic subsidies within Mercosur is the WTO, the multilateral negotiations take on an added responsibility. Given that disparities in domestic support are a serious bone of contention, advances in the WTO will allow the closing of loopholes in the Mercosur agreement and thus limit the room to tinker with commitments. Insofar as multilateral negotiations provide an anchor to domestic support policies and the room for regional disagreements is reduced, the present and future health of Mercosur can be returned to a stable condition. Differences in negotiation positions will be played out but a WTO anchor to policies will bring about an improved environment for regional coordination.

Export subsidies

The URA on Agriculture had little effect on the farm export subsidies of developed countries, with the end results only 21 per cent lower by volume than their volume in the 1980s and 36 per cent lower on budgetary expenditure. However, given the trade-distorting effects from prior US and EU export subsidies, the agreed disciplines represent a substantial achievement.

On export subsidies Mercosur presents a united front. Only Brazil and Uruguay made commitments on export subsidies during the UR, but thus far neither have granted subsidies to agricultural products. It is apparent from debates on export subsidies that there is widespread agreement that further substantial reductions in these subsidies are required. Cairns Group countries, along with most competitive agricultural exporters, have called for the total elimination of export subsidies, which the EU resists. Both Cairns and Mercosur countries may be frustrated in their ambition to open up the markets of developed countries. But the internal cohesion of Mercosur is strong on this issue and countries will be bound to coordinate negotiation positions without difficulty and feed upon the positive dynamics allowed by this opportunity.

4.6   Conclusions

Much internal bargaining remains within the confines of Mercosur, as the resolution of fundamental day-to-day issues will involve striking a balance between minimizing the disruptive effects of trade and encouraging producers to take advantage of the opportunities that a more liberal trade regime has provided. Integration has brought about substantial liberalization of agriculture and there is evidence that the sector is becoming more efficient as emerging patterns of specialization seem to further comparative advantage. However, the liberalization of trade has occurred in the absence of coordination of domestic support policies, leading to social and intergovernmental tensions. The main beneficiaries have tended to be large, modern farms while poorer, smaller farms have struggled to survive in the context of growing social unrest. Intergovernmental tensions flare up in issues in which countries have divergent paths, mainly centered on the nature and the depth of domestic support to specific commodities, crystallized in the sugar sector.

The URA on Agriculture offered a good start but it has brought limited benefits to Mercosur countries. Progress needs to be made in securing better market access; outstanding issues also remain in domestic support and export subsidies. Mercosur is well positioned to take advantage of any further opening of international markets; land abundance, improving productivity, low costs and recent improvements in infrastructure all suggest that the sector will be able to respond swiftly and effectively. Considerable regional liberalization already carried out provides a platform for becoming a global player. Regional integration and multilateral liberalization have fed upon each other in complex two-way relationships that unfold differently for different issues. On issues of export subsidies and taming developed countries' export subsidies Mercosur speaks with a single, potentially more resonant voice. However, domestic support policies have caused sporadic friction between members. The laxity of WTO commitments on this issue was a detriment to regional relations, which were unable to single-handedly rein in their use significantly. These regional and domestic constraints are brought to bear in the multilateral arena, as flaring conflicts tend to be played out in the WTO. In these areas, further multilateral liberalization will serve to bring about some degree of coordination of agricultural policies within Mercosur. Thus the limitations of a relatively small regional association to go much beyond what is affordable multilaterally are evidenced in constrained regional progress on domestic support policies. The paucity of worldwide liberalization caps the amount of liberalization possible, with sugar as a case in point.

Notes

1. Calculated using the latest FAO data available.
2. In order to include the agricultural products as defined by the URA on Agriculture (Annex 1, Product Coverage), total agricultural exports for each country have been calculated including chs 1–24 of the Harmonized System (with the exception of ch. 3) and other tariff lines of chs 29, 33, 35, 41, 51, 52 and 53. Calculated using the latest data available from the FTAA database.
3. Latest official figure notified by Paraguay to the WTO (G/AG/N/PRY/6).
4. These subsidies are partial refunds of costs to small and medium-sized fruit and wine growers. In 1999, the government expenditure on this program was US$3.2 million (A/AG/N/URY/13.Rev.1).
5. Inputs from Mercosur countries pay a tariff of 0 per cent. The subsidy, which in 1999 was US$6.58, is calculated by taking into account the fiscal loss from not applying the Mercosur CET to imports of inputs from non-Mercosur countries (A/AG/N/URY/13.Rev.1).
6. The de minimis provision of the URA on Agriculture allowed countries not to include in the calculation of the Total Aggregate Measurement of Support trade-distorting subsidies which made up only a low proportion (5 per cent in the case of developed countries and 10 per cent in developing countries) of the value of production of individual products or, in the case of non-product-specific support, the value of total agricultural production.
7. Latest official figure notified by Argentina to the WTO (G/AG/N/ARG/9).
8. Latest official figure notified by Brazil to the WTO (G/AG/N/BRA/18).
9. With the exception of cotton and wheat, budgetary expenditures for these amber box measures were below de minimis levels at US$400 in 1998.
10. During the WTO Ministerial Conference in Seattle in 1999 and the preparations for the Fourth Ministerial Conference in 2001, buyers of sugar for the beverage and food manufacturing industry, including the Coalition for Sugar Reform (US) and farmers' associations of Australia, Brazil Canada, Chile, Colombia, Costa Rica, El Salvador, Guatemala, Honduras, India, Nicaragua, Panama and Thailand lobbied delegates in favor of freer world trade in sugar. Argentina, Uruguay and Paraguay have not joined this sectoral coalition, thus showing the tension between regional and sectoral forms of association to shape trade policy (see Tussie, Introduction, and Narlikar and Woods, Chapter 9).
11. A relevant example of the tariff rate quotas is the US raw sugar tariff rate quotas. Quota allocation for each of the Mercosur countries for the period 2000–01, was 152,700 metric tons to Brazil, 45,283 metric tons to Argentina and 7258 metric tons each for Uruguay and Paraguay.
12. Article 5 provides for the temporary application of an additional duty on top of applied tariffs in cases of import volume surges or import price reductions.

The special safeguard is a laxer alternative to the normal safeguard mechanisms provided through Article XIX of GATT 1994 and the Agreement on Safeguards. In contrast to these, the special safeguard can be activated under a volume-based trigger or a price-based trigger, although not both concurrently.

13. Of Mercosur countries, only Brazil and Argentina have assumed domestic support reduction commitments.

5
Liberalization of Trade in Services: Options and Implications

Luis Abugattas Majluf and Sherry M. Stephenson

5.1 Introduction

Latin American and Caribbean countries face a far-reaching and complex agenda of negotiations in the area of trade in services. First, periodic rounds of negotiations under the General Agreement on Trade in Services (GATS) in the World Trade Organization (WTO) will lead to further commitments and reformed multilateral norms and disciplines. Second, at the hemispheric level, countries are discussing a draft text of the Free Trade Area of the Americas (FTAA) that includes liberalization of trade in services. Furthermore, trade in services is dealt with at the sub-regional level by various integration agreements, such as the Mercosur Protocol of Montevideo, Decision 439 of the Andean Community (AC) and Protocol II of the Caribbean Community (Caricom) countries, as well as in bilateral free trade agreements covering services signed by several Latin American countries. Finally, this issue is ever present in trade initiatives being advanced at other levels, such as in the EU–Mexico Trade Agreement and in the framework for an EU–Mercosur agreement.

Liberalization of trade in services is proceeding in independent forums, according to different calendars, and with distinct objectives and procedures, weaving a complex web of negotiations. Nevertheless, these diverse processes are intimately related. GATS norms and disciplines constitute the foundation or least common denominator of other agreements. Consequently, the introduction of new disciplines and commitments in the GATS will impact other trade in services liberalization initiatives and reduce the space for preferential trade liberalization at the hemispheric, regional, sub-regional and bilateral levels. Moreover, agreements not only have to be compatible with current and future GATS provisions but must go above and beyond GATS. Liberalization of trade in services in the FTAA must therefore be 'GATS-plus' just as the sub-regional groupings in the hemisphere must venture into 'FTAA-plus' territory.

Management of this complex web poses challenging questions to Latin American and Caribbean countries. What politically viable spaces are available for introduction of that 'bonus' over other agreements at each level of negotiation? How can norms and disciplines incorporated in different agreements be made compatible? At what level can different commitments and disciplines be optimally dealt with? First, this chapter discusses the negotiations in the WTO, providing an assessment of the current situation and identifying the main elements of the agenda that will be confronted during the process. Section 3 highlights the main issues within the FTAA process and Section 4 discusses the interplay between the different levels of negotiation in terms of liberalization options.

5.2   Issues in GATS negotiations

Article XIX of GATS calls for periodic successive rounds of negotiations in order to push ahead with progressive liberalization of trade in services. Negotiations seek to eliminate or reduce adverse effects of measures on trade in services, promoting the interests of all the participants and assuring a balance of rights and obligations. As provided by Paragraph 2 of Article XIX, negotiations should be carried out respecting national policy objectives and taking into consideration the level of development of WTO members. Developing countries should have flexibility to liberalize fewer sectors and transaction types and, when granting market access, set conditions that promote the development of efficient and competitive domestic supply of services. The negotiations take place in Special Sessions of the Council for Trade in Services, while the normal business of the Council continues in ordinary meetings. Work on 'unfinished business' and other issues, continued in subsidiary bodies including the Working Party on GATS Rules (WPGR), the Committee on Specific Commitments (CSC), the Committee on Financial Services (CFS) and the Working Party on Domestic Regulation (WPDR). All subsidiary bodies report to the Council whether in Special Sessions or in regular meetings.

Two clear stages have transpired since the launching of a new round of negotiations in the first Special Session of the Council for Trade in Services held on 25 February 2000. During a first stage, work in the Special Sessions was devoted to discussing possible guidelines and procedures to undertake the mandate of Article XIX. Members analyzed different alternatives in order to build the required consensus for a comprehensive round of negotiations on specific commitments and other issues, agreeing upon a 'roadmap' at the Special Session on 26 May 2000. The roadmap was not intended as a substitute for guidelines; it was to guide work until March 2001 when stock was to be taken of the progress achieved to that date, and decisions were adopted on how to proceed. The second stage of the negotiations started with the adoption of negotiating guidelines and procedures at the Special Session held on 28 March 2001. The guidelines were the result of a complex process of negotiations including four draft versions, and reflect the precarious consensus achieved between developing and developed countries. Largely echoing mandates of Articles IV and XIX of the GATS, the guidelines fail to provide strong guidance for the negotiating process and leave some crucial issues unresolved. Contrary to expectations that political guidance would be provided to set the negotiations on a clearer track, the Doha Ministerial Declaration of November 2001 merely reaffirmed the negotiating guidelines and procedures adopted by the Special Session as the basis for continued negotiations. The Ministers agreed that participants should submit initial requests for specific commitments by June 2002 and initial offers by March 2003. Negotiations are to be concluded by January 2005.

The negotiation guidelines and procedures reaffirmed by the Doha Ministerial Declaration fail to resolve a number of issues pending since the Seattle Ministerial Conference including the assessment process, unfinished and current business, technical review, economic integration agreements, competition, negotiating modalities, recognition of autonomous liberalization, and developing country participation.

Assessment of trade in services

Article XIX, Paragraph 3 mandates an assessment of trade in services with reference to the objectives of the GATS, in particular to those established by Article IV.1, before proceeding with agreement on guidelines and procedures for the successive rounds of negotiations. The Council carried out the Process of Analysis and Exchange of Information between December 1998 and October 1999 and addressed the assessment mandate, but failed to produce concrete results. After negotiations were launched, the Council moved the assessment issue to the Special Session agenda, thereby linking it directly to the negotiations. Assessment was set as a standing item on the agenda, and the issue was discussed in all the meetings. However, no real progress was possible, as a lack of adequate statistics on trade in services and a limited response by members to the questionnaire have not provided an appropriate basis for the exercise.

During the first stage of the negotiations there was disaccord over the extension of the assessment into a continuous process rather than a comprehensive evaluation to be concluded prior to the launch of negotiations. There were two distinct positions regarding the mandate of Article XIX.3: India and Pakistan, for example, stressed that assessment was needed for the establishment of negotiating guidelines and procedures, therefore considering it a prerequisite of the process, and the EU, for example, considered assessment as a parallel process to negotiations, providing a mechanism by which to identify priorities for individual members during the process. Strict compliance with Article XIX.3 would have required that the assessment be a prerequisite to establishment of negotiating guidelines and procedures.

The guidelines and procedures adopted in March 2001 deemed the assessment an ongoing process and directed the Council for Trade in Services to continue its overall and sector-specific assessment of trade in services. Results of the ongoing assessment are to be used in readjusting the negotiations. Two issues needing attention have surfaced. First, what 'the negotiations shall be adjusted in light of the result of the assessment' exactly implies needs to be clarified early on. There are vastly disparate interpretations: specific commitments could be conditioned to the assessment's results, negotiating guidelines could be modified in light of the results, and different timeframes could be implemented. Second, there is disaccord over the ideal nature of the assessment. The assessment mandated by Article XIX.3 must concretely address the effects of trade in services and investment flows in relation to members' specific commitments. Moreover, it must determine to what extent those commitments have improved developing countries' participation in trade in services, domestic services capacity, and access to distribution channels and information networks. The benefits of services in trade liberalization and deregulation for developing countries have been stressed, assuming *a priori* that the rationale for liberalization of trade in services is the same as that of goods. Furthermore, it has been assumed that GATS liberalization measures would have produced the same impact as the developing countries' autonomous liberalization analyzed in most empirical studies. Moreover, the overall conclusions presented as general patterns are strongly biased by the empirical analysis of a very limited number of services sectors. Future efforts should be geared towards a comprehensive country-by-country review of developing country commitments and restrictions facing their exports to analyze whether Article IV obligations are met. In the meantime, Latin American and Caribbean countries should work towards their own comprehensive evaluation of the effects of the GATS commitments on their economies and their development prospects.

Unfinished and current business

The relationship between Article XIX negotiations and unfinished and current business in the Council and the Subsidiary bodies has been an issue of contention, as both involve highly sensitive issues that could profoundly impact members' development prospects. Some of the unfinished business involves touchy issues, like the WPGR agenda of safeguards, subsidies and government procurement. Other complex agenda items include the reviews being undertaken by the Council, Article II (MFN) Exemptions and the Annex on Air Transport.

The sequencing of Article XIX negotiations and unfinished and current business was discussed during the first stage of the negotiations, as the roadmap failed to provide definite directions on the sequence in which issues are to be addressed. A Brazilian proposal suggested that the negotiations be carried out in two successive and separate phases: an initial phase of rule-making in the GATS, and a second stage of adoption of specific commitments (WTO, 1999b). Other members proposed that current work and unfinished business proceed in parallel with the negotiations. The inclusion of the Council's and Subsidiary Bodies' work in the Special Session's agenda during the first stage of the negotiations eliminated any clear distinction between 'unfinished business' and the new round of negotiations. The distinction between unfinished business and negotiations was clarified by the negotiations guidelines' decision to not incorporate the work of the Council and subsidiary bodies in the Special Session agenda. Nevertheless, these issues prove difficult to separate in practice, as they constitute integral parts of the same process. Thus the negotiating guidelines and procedures reconfirmed what had already been agreed in the roadmap, without introducing specific guidance or concrete reference to the particular work being undertaken in the Council or subsidiary bodies.

For Article II MFN exemptions, however, the guidelines strayed from mere affirmation of roadmap mandates. After some debate, the guidelines established that MFN exemptions will be subject to negotiations according to paragraph 6 of the Annex of Article II MFN exemptions. Flexibility will be accorded to individual developing countries not as blanket special and differential (S&D) treatment, but rather case-by-case according to unspecified conditions. Elimination or significant reduction of exemptions to the MFN Clause would significantly contribute to strengthening the multilateral framework.

Safeguard negotiations under Article X are mandated by the negotiating guidelines and procedures. Some members have insisted on a timely conclusion of negotiations, but there is still no consensus on the feasibility and convenience of a safeguard mechanism in the GATS. Discussion has centered on the following: whether safeguards should be general or only for specific commitments; whether they should benefit all service providers or only those companies controlled by nationals; which emergency situations justify a safeguard; the viability of defining injury and causality criteria; and whether suspension of market access should be preferred over other measures. Members have agreed to focus on feasibility issues and, accordingly, discussions are addressing nine basic themes: definition of domestic industry, the issue of acquired rights, the concept of like services, compensation, indicators and criteria, applicable measures, modal application, and the issue of 'unforeseen circumstances'. Negotiations will face hurdles to conclude on time given resistance to the introduction of safeguard disciplines in the GATS.

Article XIII negotiations on government procurement and Article XV negotiations on subsidies are to be completed prior to the conclusion of negotiations on specific commitments. The work on these issues within the WPGR has failed to make headway and would have benefited from a formal timeframe. Discussions on government procurement have been limited to conceptual issues like the relevance of GATT definitions and the distinction between government purchases and concessions in national regimes. Clarified and further developed norms and disciplines in these areas would engender deeper specific commitments. In particular, clear disciplines on subsidies are required to evaluate trade distortions and their particularly negative impact on developing countries. Members are logjammed in a discussion on the necessary scope of subsidy disciplines, notwithstanding evidence of the distortion created by their prevalent use in trade in services (UNCTAD, 1993). The incorporation of a timeframe for work on subsidies linking the definition of subsidy disciplines to the presentation of specific commitments should be considered. Such a proposal would provide guidance on how to proceed with the work mandated in Article XV on subsidies, as well as provide an impulse to the definition of subsidy disciplines, which has been lingering for more than five years. Because of the fundamental role subsidies can play in the development of a domestic supply of services, disciplines on subsidies of services should incorporate special provisions for developing countries that allow for the maintenance and introduction of new programs to foster the domestic services capacity as provided by Article IV.

The CSC is focusing its work on two major areas: classification and scheduling guidelines. Classification work seeks to improve the classification structure that was used for scheduling specific commitments on services during the Uruguay Round (UR). In order to address nomenclature and classification problems identified in the Information Exchange Program, technical work has begun on a number of services sectors. Though classification is a technical issue, it could impact the outcome of the negotiations. For example, the general classification and level of aggregation can increase or reduce how flexible developing countries are to liberalize fewer sectors and transactions. Furthermore, Latin American and Caribbean countries should identify the sectors whose classification it is in their interests to revise. Most of the sectors on which current work focuses – environmental, energy, legal, postal and courier, and construction services – are not of particular importance to the region. Attention should be turned to 'labor services' provided in the country of origin which are later exported embodied in physical goods and comprehensive revision of tourism services. Further classification of those services typically provided through the temporary movement of service providers (GATS mode 4 of supply) may also be necessary. Reorganizing the Services Sector Classification List by skill level or employment-type could facilitate the adoption of specific commitments on mode 4 more than the current sector and sub-sector classification (Young, 1999). The CSC scheduling work will have to be completed prior to the end of the negotiations in order for the schedules of specific commitments to be adequately prepared.

The Preamble of the GATS recognizes the right of members to regulate services with the purpose of attaining national policy objectives. Likewise, Article XIX.2 explicitly states that liberalization will be carried out respecting national policy objectives. Thus, domestic regulation that does not discriminate between national and foreign service providers is subject only to provisions in Article VI on domestic regulation, even in sectors subject to specific commitments. However, authorization to provide services via economic need tests and other regulations can affect market access, even if it is not discriminatory. The negotiating guidelines and procedures were silent on this issue. Article VI states that domestic regulation must be transparent, administered with due process, and only as restrictive as is necessary to fulfill a legitimate policy objective, that is, the necessity test. The WPDR has been considering further development of disciplines on qualification requirements and procedures, technical standards, licensing requirements and transparency. Disagreement persists on whether the disciplines are to constitute a general obligation or only apply to those sectors in which members have made specific commitments. In the case of accounting services, it was decided that domestic regulation disciplines would only affect members that had adopted specific commitments. Proposals on domestic regulation disciplines, dating even from the pre-Seattle stage, seek to constrain flexibility in the implementation of national policy objectives, in pursuance of US objectives of transparency and 'good governance' in regulation of services (Van Gresstek, 1999a). Proposed linkage of domestic regulation and 'effective market access' could curtail the degree of freedom to regulate services in pursuit of national objectives to unprecedented limits. Proposals seek to expand the scope of Article VI to sectors and measures not included in the article according to new doctrines of 'market accountability'. Some proposals seek to establish disciplines that would guarantee that domestic regulations affecting services clearly respond to the proportionality and necessity criteria, requiring the least trade restrictive regulations that contribute to the execution of 'legitimate' policy objectives (WTO, 1999c). This would inhibit flexibility to undertake autonomous definition of regulatory frameworks to meet public policy objectives, and would lead to the harmonization of regulation based on developed countries' policies, objectives and standards. As has been the case with the Agreement on Agriculture and the Agreement on Subsidies (see Tortora and Tussie, Chapter 9), the establishment of what should be considered a legitimate measure under the GATS could generate a built-in asymmetry against developing countries. 'Legitimate' measures could require institutional capabilities beyond the reach of developing countries, which will confront serious difficulties in implementation. Any discussion on domestic regulation must take into consideration developing countries' institutional capabilities, since in many cases they are only capable of applying regulations with trade-restricting effects. Adoption of disciplines that support market access and national treatment commitments while maintaining the normative agencies' capacity to reach legitimate policy objectives is one of the major challenges that WTO members are confronting in the services negotiations.

Technical review

As evidenced by work in the Council on Trade and Services and the CSC, GATS norms and disciplines are in dire need of technical clarification.

Some members proposed that technical revision be included as an agenda issue in the negotiations, in order to correct imperfections and ambiguities in the structure and principles of GATS. The roadmap included the technical review of the clarity and logical consistency of the GATS text as an issue to be addressed by the Special Sessions. The negotiating guidelines and procedures skirted around the issue, merely stating that negotiations shall respect the existing GATS structure and principles.

Three basic technical revision issues raised in drafts of the negotiating guidelines, but not included in the final version, are sure to resurface in the course of negotiations:

- CSC operational considerations including the methodology for scheduling commitments, nomenclature and classification of services, and facilitation of the private sector's understanding and use of national schedules;
- clarification of concepts such as 'like service' and 'economic necessity', and of specific commitments' coverage of newly classified services; and,
- clarification of the agreement's norms and disciplines and the text's legal consistency.

Some proposals implicate substantive modifications in the structure of the GATS (see for example Prieto, 1999). For example, fusion of modes 1 and 2 of supply has been proposed, based on the confusion between cross-border supply and consumption abroad (WTO, 1999d). The inclusion of a fifth mode of supply to account for e-commerce has also been proposed. Some authors and OECD officials have proposed a complete switch to negative lists or the use of negotiation formulas that subtly introduce their use, either of which would implicate a substantial modification of the agreement. Interpretations of 'technological neutrality' could also implicate changes to the agreement, thus necessitating clarification of the term. The notion of technological neutrality was introduced in the basic telecom negotiations, suggesting that unless otherwise specified, all means of technology would be automatically covered by the specific commitment (see Bastos Tigre, Chapter 6). This notion should not be mistaken as applicable to all sectors of GATS, but rather should be explicitly included as a specific commitment in a negotiation through positive listing. Restrictions affecting a mode of supply should be registered horizontally or as a restriction to national treatment. Finally, some issues have been raised in relation to the definition of 'commercial presence', and attempts might be made, for example, to expand this concept from an enterprise-based definition to an asset-based one which would have serious implications for developing countries.

A final issue suggested for technical revision is the relationship between market access (Article XVI) and national treatment (Article XVII). Article XX.2 was created to clarify those specific commitments that fall into both types of limitations, establishing that the measures should be registered in the column to market access (Article XVI) with the understanding that the measures also qualify under Article XVII. The relationship between Articles XVI, XVII and XX.2 should be clarified to avoid ambiguities in specific commitments, in particular in the case of national treatment commitments.

Economic integration

One of the two allowances for MFN exemptions in the GATS is preferential treatment afforded by Article V on Economic Integration. Preferential agreements liberalizing trade in services must be compatible with the provisions of Article V, and should be notified to the Council for Trade in Services. In order to be GATS-compatible an agreement must fulfill two basic conditions: (i) it must have 'substantial' coverage of sectors, volume of trade, and modes of supply, and (ii) it must provide for national treatment for members' service providers, 'substantially' eliminating all discrimination. These conditions should be met either at the agreement's outset or within a 'reasonable' timeframe. Article V provides flexibility on these two requirements in two cases: when developing countries are parties to the agreement and when such agreement is part of a wider process of economic integration or trade liberalization.

Several countries have proposed revision and, if necessary, clarification and reinforcement of Article V.[1] Ambiguities surrounding crucial provisions leave the compatibility of preferential trade agreements largely uncertain (see Stephenson, 2000, for an analysis of Article V). The issue of regional trade agreements was included in the Doha Ministerial Declaration, so that negotiations will be carried out to clarify and improve disciplines and procedures under existing WTO provisions, including Article V of GATS. Some of the necessary revisions and clarifications follow.

- Definition of 'substantial sectoral coverage'. This criterion will be very difficult, if not impossible, to nail down because of limited statistics available.
- Definition of a 'reasonable timeframe'. Unlike trade in goods, for which Article XXIV set a reasonable timeframe of up to ten years, Article V left services liberalization timeframes subject to interpretation.
- Clarification of evaluation guidelines for restriction levels before and after an agreement.
- Clarification of restriction commitments implicated by Article V.4. It should be clarified if a binding of the applied measures in the moment of the agreement's signing is called for, which would affect both committed sectors and those in which commitments have not been assumed within the preferential agreement. Reference to the overall level of trade barriers within the respective sectors can be understood as deeming the agreement GATS-compatible as long as the net effect does not increase the level of restrictions. Hence restrictions on some items could increase as long as reductions in other items compensate for the difference.
- Clarification of flexibility granted by Article V to developing countries in preferential trade agreements. Sector coverage requirements on volume

of affected trade and modes of supply committed under Article V.1.b and maintenance or introduction of discriminatory measures is eased for developing countries in preferential trade agreements under Article V.3.a. The Council for Trade in Services is to evaluate agreements case-by-case on the merits of their provisions. The lack of clarity generates great uncertainty.[2]

Competition

In recognition of the need for remedy against anti-competitive measures in order to ensure effective market access, some countries and many analysts have proposed the extension of Articles VII and IX, either through general disciplines or sector-specific disciplines like the Reference Paper on Telecommunications (see Bastos Tigre, Chapter 6).[3] GATS provisions are clearly insufficient in remedying the anti-competitive behavior of firms. Article IX on Business Practices acknowledges that certain business practices may restrain competition and thereby restrict trade in services, but it merely calls countries to enter into consultation to eliminate such practices. Unlike other GATS articles, there is no commitment to establish multilateral disciplines in this area.

The Doha Ministerial Declaration calls for trade and competition negotiations on the basis of modality decisions to be made at the Fifth Session of the Ministerial Conference. Latin American and Caribbean countries should consider proposing negotiations directed towards the strengthening of pro-competitive rules in services through Articles VIII and IX and sector-specific pro-competitive disciplines, counterbalancing proposals on strict domestic regulation rules beyond the Article VI mandate. Some developed countries insist on restricting the state's actions, but resist any attempt to regulate private business behavior that could restrict trade in services.

Negotiating modality

Article XIX.4 leaves negotiation modalities for future rounds fairly open-ended. It establishes that the progressive liberation can be propelled by means of bilateral, plurilateral or multilateral negotiations, as long as they are oriented to increase specific commitments. Four approaches were proposed based on previous services negotiations: the request–offer approach, the sector-specific approach, the cluster approach and the formula approach. Developing countries favor the request–offer approach as a general rule, as it allows all participants to directly promote their specific interests by sector, by mode of supply and by target market. It also expedites the evaluation of the possible impact of the specific commitments and facilitates the evaluation of the value of the concessions granted and received during the process. Moreover, because negotiations are clearly focused, they require less information on overall limitations and restrictions maintained by other members than formula negotiations do. However, it has been suggested that limiting negotiations to this approach backtracks on progress achieved in prior negotiations. Instead, countries proposed the use of the sector-specific approach, the cluster approach or a formula approach.

The Sector-Specific Approach was forged in negotiations on maritime transport, telecommunications and financial services. A first issue is the scope and sectors to be involved. Some countries have proposed a special approach for 'high economic value' services sectors in which they expect significant specific commitments from all participants. During the pre-Seattle stage, environmental, energy, architectural, legal, audiovisual, financial and telecommunications services were identified as important to some members. Energy, environmental, and legal services sectors were incorporated in the classification exercise in the Committee on Specific Commitments, and will therefore most likely play an important role in the negotiations. Latin American and Caribbean countries should give priority to the analysis of those sectors in their economies and of the possible costs and benefits of liberalization.

Past experience with sector-specific negotiations offers up inconclusive results. In the case of financial services and basic telecommunications, sectors of interest for developed countries, significant results were achieved in terms of the number of participant countries and the level of the specific commitments. In the telecommunications negotiations 59 members adopted enhanced commitments, and in the financial sector 15 of 74 members upgraded their commitments (see Qian, 2000, for an analysis of the improvement of commitments on financial services). Quite to the contrary, the negotiations on maritime transport and mobility of natural persons, which are sectors of interest for developing countries, were a flop.

Under a sector-specific approach, Latin American and Caribbean countries must vie for due attention to sectors of their interest. El Salvador, Honduras and the Dominican Republic have taken the first step with a proposal on an Annex on Tourism aiming to clarify classification of this activity and achieve commitments on the domestic regulation. Reintroduction of the sector-specific approach in negotiations on maritime transport with competition disciplines may also be in the interest of Latin American and Caribbean countries. Most developed countries have not adopted commitments in this sector of particular importance for island countries, with the notable exceptions of Australia, Iceland and New Zealand.

The Cluster Approach, formally proposed by the EU, involves the identification of a group of sectors or sub-sectors that are commercially or technically interrelated, for which all members adopt a harmonized and coherent set of commitments during the negotiations. The rationale is that certain services are so commercially interrelated that restrictions on one service can prevent or curtail the supply of the others and thus render commitments meaningless. Furthermore, this approach would permit the appropriate recognition of the existing intersectoral connections without requiring a fundamental reorganization of the GATS Services Sector Classification List (OECD, 2000). It has been suggested that this approach could be used for environmental, energy and tourism services. However, it should be clear that the cluster approach would tend to disproportionately benefit developed countries since the countries with more highly integrated services supply chains in the cluster will receive more commercially meaningful concessions.

Consideration of the cluster approach has raised several issues that Latin American and Caribbean countries should evaluate. Classification of sectors and activities should be included as an integral part of the negotiations if a cluster approach is used. Second, there is a risk that the process evolve into a plurilateral approach in which only a few members adopt commitments if acceptance of the cluster is voluntary. Finally, the cluster concept must be clarified, designating whether the clusters are to be used as 'checklists' of interrelated sectors for negotiating purposes to ensure coherence in the final outcome of the request–offer process, or as draft model schedules which would presuppose acceptance of a pre-established set of commitments.

The Formula Approach has been advanced in three separate forms. First, proposals have suggested use of a general formula under which members eliminate the discrepancy between bound and effective level of restriction if specific commitments during the UR bound a higher level of restriction than was effectively applied. It is argued that this would enhance the transparency of national schedules. If this formula is applied, the binding of the current level of restriction should count as a member's contribution to the round of negotiations, and not as a preparatory step for the request–offer approach. Second, formulas of generic commitments outlawing certain types of restrictions have been put on the table. For example, nationality or residence requirements, 'economic needs tests', limits to foreign equity participation, or any other type of restrictive measure could be prohibited. Lastly, Mattoo offers up a proposal that merits further analysis. He suggests the application of a formula that calculates the level of concessions in terms of temporary movement of persons that would be required in exchange for concessions obtained with respect to other modes of supply. This formula approach could achieve reciprocity through which developing countries' commitments in mode 3 would be exchanged for developed countries with commitments on mode 4. Mattoo suggests that the concessions in terms of movement of persons could be implemented through 'foreign labor content entitlements' (Mattoo and Olarreaga, n.y.).

A final issue of contention in selecting a modality is the negotiation's 'starting point'. Ground zero from which negotiations were to grow was never set in the UR, leaving countries free to record their specific commitments at levels higher than the existing regulatory restrictions. The US proposed that the starting point be the current restrictions to market access and national treatment, sector by sector, which would bring serious difficulties to developing countries. The binding of the existing barriers to trade is in and of itself a significant commitment, and as such should be understood in terms of Article IV as a step forward in developing countries' progressive liberalization. Establishing the current level of restrictions as the starting point, in practice, implies an approximation to a negative list approach to liberalization. If this were to be complemented by a 'standstill' commitment, as proposed by some members, the negative listing approach will be completed, modifying the basic structure of GATS. Moreover, some of the restrictions applied by developing countries can not be removed without first introducing effective regulatory mechanisms. In those sectors requiring regulatory reform, the binding of the current regime should be considered a sufficient contribution towards increased transparency and progressive liberalization. Precommitments to future liberalization could offer stability and, in the end, if refused, reveal hidden protectionist intentions, but the risk that regulatory reforms not be in place at the time of committed liberalization is entirely too high in financially and institutionally constrained developing countries.

The guidelines and procedures agreed to in March 2001 selected the request–offer approach as the main method with which negotiations would advance. However, the door has been left open for alternative approaches to be utilized during the negotiation of specific commitments. It has been agreed that no sector would be *a priori* excluded from the negotiations. Additionally, the guidelines resolved other contentions with the selection of the current national schedules as the starting point for the new round of negotiations. Nevertheless, a Pandora's box was opened to extreme demands from some members, because the starting point was established without prejudice to the content of the requests.

Recognition of autonomous liberalization

Article XIX.3 of the GATS establishes that members' autonomous liberalization should be recognized in the negotiations. However, defining the mechanisms for such accreditation is far from simple. The recognition of autonomous liberalization in the next negotiations is in developing countries' interests. However, no member submitted a concrete proposal in the pre-Seattle stage on how the recognition could operate during the negotiations. The US has proposed that members that had undertaken autonomous liberalization between the UR and the end of the current round receive credit for this by notifying the other members. However, the proposal did not solve the question of whether the member should be requested to undertake further commitments or determine how autonomous liberalization should be valued. The application of formulas to recognize autonomous liberalization is hindered by discrepancies between the bound regulatory framework and the applied regulation. Elimination of the discrepancy would deeply modify the structure of GATS and thus allow members to consider their autonomous liberalization as a concession in the next negotiations.

Increased participation of developing countries

Increasing participation of developing countries in world trade in services is a basic objective of the GATS as delineated in Article IV. This objective is to be attained through specific commitments that strengthen the domestic services capacity of developing countries, improving access to distribution channels and information networks, and liberalizing market access in sectors and modes of supply of interest to them. The negotiating guidelines and procedures of each round of negotiations should specify the means by which participation is to be increased. Evidence suggests that Article IV objectives were not achieved during the UR (UNCTAD, 1995a). As an UNCTAD study points out, developing countries have not benefited from the GATS because commitments adopted by developed countries simply bound the status quo treatment without providing meaningful market access. Benefits reaped from GATS were limited for various reasons: mode 4 commitments were scarce; developing countries do not have the capacity to take advantage of the improved market access; and developing countries' competition in foreign markets is prevented by anti-competitive behavior, market dominance, subsidies, and other factors (UNCTAD, 1999a).

The major challenge for developing countries is how to implement mechanisms with which to increase their participation and to ensure that those mechanisms agreed upon are respected during the negotiation of specific commitments. Member submissions during the pre-Seattle stage and afterwards simply restated the content of Articles IV and XIX.3. The absence of specific proposals on how to make Article IV operational in the negotiating guidelines and procedures is noteworthy. The US submission completely ignored Article IV and limited the issue of developing country participation to a matter of technical assistance. Submissions by Hong Kong and the EU similarly minimized the special treatment for developing countries (WTO, 2000c, and EU, 2000 respectively). Hong Kong, for example, stated that flexibility for developing countries should be attained by postponing implementation deadlines rather than by excluding some sectors from specific commitments. The African Group submission, on the contrary, proposed specific measures to encourage developed countries to import services from developing countries. It proposed reserving part of the services imported by governments for developing countries and relaxing entry conditions for service providers from developing countries (WTO, 2000d).

The Article IV mandate could be implemented in various forms. First, sectors in which developed countries will make comprehensive specific commitments could be identified for developing countries. Latin American and Caribbean countries should identify those sectors in which they have export potential that could benefit from the dismantling of barriers in foreign markets. Second, the application of a non-reciprocal formula approach on commitments adopted by developing countries on the movement of natural persons (mode 4 of supply) should be considered. For example, a job category and skill level quota of service providers from developing countries could be established that would allow temporary entry for the provision of a specified service. Third, negotiations on the Annex on the Movement of Natural Persons could be reestablished. This will require prior work on classifying service suppliers per occupation and skills, limiting the scope of economic needs tests, improving transparency in regulating the movement of persons, facilitating the movement of business visitors, and additional commitments on recognition of qualifications, licensing and certification (Butkeviciene, 2000). Finally, any initial offer by a developing country could be conditional on verification of its fulfillment of Article IV mandates.

5.3 Options and implications for Latin America in the FTAA

The progress achieved in the new round of GATS negotiations will parallel but not necessarily determine the fate of trade in services in the FTAA. The FTAA agreement will be structured around three major elements common to all agreements on trade in services: coverage, related disciplines, and liberalization approach.

Coverage

Coverage of the liberalizing commitments must be compatible with Article V of the GATS. The agreement should have substantial coverage in terms of sectors, modes of supply and volume of trade involved. However, GATS Article V.3.a introduces a margin of flexibility within which to introduce exceptions, albeit with blurry bounds. All existing agreements in the Western Hemisphere exclude some sectors from their substantive obligations (OAS, 1996). Governments must determine the extent of the coverage and whether exclusions from the commitments will be permanent or temporary. The need for temporary exclusions will depend on the liberalization approach as well as each country's interests. Countries may face constitutional constraints and political or cultural considerations in highly sensitive sectors as well as fear of seriously jeopardizing domestic development by exposure to foreign competition (see Bastos Tigre, Chapter 6, for the case of telecommunications). As in the GATS, most agreements exclude government procurement from coverage, though North American Free Trade Area (NAFTA) and NAFTA-type agreements include it for both goods and services in the respective Chapter.[4] The level of governmental measures included under the agreement must be set as well, defining if central, provincial, and/or local government measures will be subject to the agreement. Furthermore, particular measures may be excluded from the coverage, like the explicit exclusion of subsidies or grants provided by a government or a state enterprise including government-supported loans, guarantees and insurance.

Related disciplines

Several disciplines related to trade in services will provide the building blocks to the normative structure of a hemispheric agreement. Related disciplines form part of the GATS as well as of various sub-regional agreements and include transparency, domestic regulation, recognition, monopolies and competition, safeguards, subsidies, rules of origin, preferential treatment for least developed members, technical cooperation and dispute settlement.

The principle of transparency is introduced in Article III of GATS. It requires that members publish all regulations and administrative practices that pertain to the GATS. Also, it introduces a notification mechanism for any measure affecting trade in services covered by the specific commitments under the GATS. Transparency can range from a low-level commitment of making information available to a high-level commitment of notifying proposed measures before they take effect. A moderate agreement could require publication of all measures or their notification to the other parties to the agreement.[5] Some agreements, like NAFTA, vary the level of transparency commitments based on the measure at stake. Others, like the GATS, NAFTA, the Group of Three (G-3), and Chile–Canada, establish 'inquiry points' at which other parties may easily access information.

Recognition of experience, qualifications, education, licenses or certifications constitutes the basis for the liberalization of trade in services of regulated activities. Some agreements introduce automatic recognition as a general obligation. However, most agreements incorporate limited provisions similar to Article VII of the GATS, by which if a member unilaterally or by agreement recognizes qualifications of another member, it must offer other members an adequate opportunity to demonstrate that their qualifications should also be recognized. First, recognition of education and qualification could be automatic if equivalencies are agreed upon. Second, the required certification or license that will allow the service provider to participate in the market must be granted, either by automatic recognition or by the commitment to allow access to the certification procedures on the basis of national treatment. For instance, the AC is working towards providing automatic recognition of licenses and certifications.

The issue of monopolies and competition has been introduced in some of the agreements to liberalize trade in services, but requires further development. GATS Article IX recognizes the potentially restrictive nature of certain business practices and calls for cooperation, exchange of information and consultations to eliminate such practices. However, the GATS does not provide for future work on business practices. Article VIII obliges members to ensure that monopoly suppliers behave consistent with obligations and commitments and do not act abusively when supplying services outside the scope of their monopoly. Members are asked to give prior notification when granting new monopoly rights. Article VIII also applies in instances when a member authorizes or establishes a small number of service providers and substantially prevents competition among those suppliers. No agreement has developed supranational norms or disciplines to control anti-competitive behavior. Provisions that have been introduced into trade in services liberalization agreements are of two basic forms. First, like in the case of Decision 439 of the AC, control of anti-competitive behavior can be delegated to national legislation until a common discipline can be established. Alternatively, as is the case of NAFTA, agreements can establish general guidelines similar to provisions in the Understanding on the Interpretation of Article XVII of the GATT 1994 related to State Trading Enterprises and of Article VIII of GATS. Despite these first steps towards an effective discipline on competition, further norms and disciplines to remedy cross-border anti-competitive behavior are required to guarantee that the benefits of liberalization not be jeopardized by business practices.

Safeguard provisions are designed to address two types of situations: balance of payment problems and import influxes that threaten national service providers. Agreements range from not specifying any safeguard mechanisms, as in Mercosur, to considering safeguards only as a remedy for balance of payment problems, as is the case of NAFTA, the AC and Caricom. Further conceptual development is needed in the GATS to define the type of corrective emergency measures to be applied to trade in services.

Subsidies require attentive disciplines given the distortions their use may create. The GATS acknowledges the potentially distorting effect of subsidies and calls for negotiations to develop multilateral disciplines though no timeframe has been set. However, sympathetic consideration is to be accorded to consultation requests by any member who considers itself to have been adversely affected by another member's subsidy (GATS, Article XV.2). Most agreements, in particular the top-down ones, are silent on subsidies. Agreements to liberalize trade in services can deal with this matter in two basic ways: following the lead of provisions for trade in goods, which prohibit subsidies with trade-distorting effects, as Mercosur has done, or establishing provisions that call for harmonization of export promotion measures and subsidies, as the AC has done.

The notion of special treatment for developing countries is introduced in Article IV of the GATS and enshrined in the Preamble. In order to facilitate and increase developing countries' participation, Article IV requires members to negotiate specific commitments to strengthen developing economies' domestic services capacity, improve access to distribution channels and information networks, and liberalize access in areas of export interest to developing country members. Furthermore, Article XIX provides that liberalization must take place with due respect for members' national policy objectives and level of development. Developing countries are flexible to open fewer sectors, liberalize fewer types of transactions, and progressively extend market access according to their development situation. Most agreements in the Western Hemisphere have not introduced any provisions related to S&D treatment for less developed countries in the agreement, though the AC is the exception. A major challenge will be to define specific provisions through which more favorable treatment can be granted to less developed members. S&D possibilities are closely related to the overall architecture of the agreement. In the case of a bottom-up agreement, allowing less developed countries to adopt lesser commitments and comply within longer time periods can accord preferential treatment. In these cases, S&D is reduced to 'best endeavor' clauses plus technical cooperation commitments to developing members. In the case of a top-down approach, there is no margin to grant more favorable treatment other than technical cooperation commitments.

Liberalization approach

Liberalization of trade in services is primarily attained through three principles that form the backbone of the GATS: MFN treatment, national treatment and market access. Other agreements to liberalize trade in services have introduced additional liberalizing principles: the right of non-establishment and the freedom to choose the mode of supply, the right to free transit and temporary presence, automatic recognition of degrees, certifications or licenses, and the elimination of nationality and residency requirements.

- *The Most Favored Nation Principle* is fundamental to securing non-discrimination among countries in international trade. MFN can be unconditional or subject to certain conditions. The GATS incorporates an automatic and unconditional MFN clause. However, some agreements on services condition MFN application to reciprocity or define it differently; in the case of NAFTA, MFN is applicable to 'like circumstances' for providers from different countries.
- *The National Treatment Principle*, incorporated in GATS Article XVII, guarantees that no differentiation be made between foreign and national providers. This principle can be formulated in degrees varying from identical treatment to limited discrimination. In moderation, agreements may introduce notions of national treatment such as 'different treatment of equivalent effect' or 'comparable competitive opportunities' for foreign providers (see CEPAL, 1996). However, most agreements incorporate the GATS strict notion of national treatment. An important issue is the identification of non-conforming measures. Article XVI of GATS presents a list of measures limiting market access, but not national treatment. Efforts could be undertaken in the FTAA to develop this issue since it would facilitate the adoption of specific commitments or registration of reservations, depending on the negotiating modality.
- *The Market Access Principle* allots foreign providers the right to access the market and provide services. Market access is addressed under disciplines related to non-discriminatory quantitative restrictions as well as through

national treatment provisions. While market access for trade in goods is enhanced and secured by the national treatment rule of GATT 1994, the principle for trade in services is only complete when commitments are made to provide national treatment (Butkeviciene and Diaz, 1998).

- *The Right of Non-Establishment and Freedom to Choose the Mode of Supply* are not a part of the GATS, but have been incorporated into regional agreements for services trade, particularly NAFTA-type agreements. These liberalization principles enhance market access by allowing service providers to select with which mode of supply to function, thus lowering foreign service suppliers' costs and allowing them to adopt the most efficient means by which to render a service.

- *The Right to Free Transit and Temporary Presence* allows for the liberalization of modes 2 and 4 of supply (foreign purchase and movement of natural persons, respectively). For countries with export potential in services embodied in persons, this type of provision would be highly beneficial.

- *Automatic Recognition* of Licenses, Degrees, and Certifications has been introduced as a general obligation in some agreements, complementing the right to free transit and temporary presence for those services requiring a license or certification. This general obligation is subject to agreement on mechanisms that will permit automatic recognition, achieved either by harmonization or definition of equivalencies. The AC incorporated this general obligation under Decision 439.

- *Elimination of nationality or residency requirements.*

Selective incorporation of these seven principles and the nature of the commitments will give rise to different liberalization approaches that, in turn, can be subject to different negotiating modalities. Two general approaches can be identified based on analysis of agreements already in force: GATS-type bottom-up agreements or NAFTA-type top-down agreements. In the bottom-up approach, liberalization principles only apply to those sectors and modes of supply for which members have adopted specific commitments. In contrast, in the top-down approach the liberalization principles are general obligations covering all modes of supply and sectors, except those explicitly excluded from coverage in members' lists of reservations. Thus, in the top-down approach all non-conforming measures for which no explicit reservations have been made must be eliminated, known as the 'list it or lose it' obligation.

Latin American and Caribbean countries must evaluate what combination of these liberalizing principles and approaches best serves their interests. It may be useful to progressively liberalize some sectors or modes of supply with the bottom-up approach while reserving the top-down approach for other sectors. Within these two general categories, different models can be drafted depending on the liberalization principles incorporated, their particular formulation, and the type of commitments adopted. These approaches can be supplemented with *status quo, standstill,* or *ratcheting* provisions.[6] Though neither approach necessarily guarantees full liberalization of trade in services, either approach is capable of achieving it while sustaining compatibility with Article V of the GATS. The major difference between the two approaches, however, lies in the transparency that each provides to service operators.

Bottom-up approach

The 'bottom-up' liberalizing approach, as set out in the GATS, defines only the MFN principle as a general obligation. Each WTO member schedules the level of commitments for a given sector, sub-sector, or activity according to the different modes of supply. No commitment is adopted with respect to those sectors or supply modes not included in the country's schedule, freeing them to introduce non-conforming measures in those sectors. The bottom-up approach can be supplemented with 'stand still' provisions that suspend those sectors without specific commitments from increases in non-conformity.

The bottom-up approach modeled on the GATS has been followed in the Western Hemisphere by Mercosur. The Mercosur Framework Agreement on Services, adopted in December 1997 in the Protocol of Montevideo, is essentially the translation of the GATS to a regional forum. It incorporates the GATS' structure, general obligations and gradual liberalization approach of sector-specific positive lists, though it one-ups the GATS by seeking full liberalization of trade in services within a period of ten years. The Mercosur agreement provides for universal coverage including all sectors, modes of supply and measures, as well as for mutual recognition of qualifications and licenses. It covers government procurement for services in a separate agreement. However, it does not incorporate provisions on monopolies, competition, subsidies or safeguards. Subsidies are to be dealt with by a general subsidies agreement within Mercosur.

The lists of positive commitments offer significant flexibility in defining the bounds of services liberalization. First, limited general obligations may be assumed, thus introducing opportunities for gradual and progressive liberalization. Second, members can avoid adopting strong initial commitments. Moreover, committing to ceiling bindings allows members to buffer their prevailing regulatory situation from constricting bound ceilings with a gap between bound and applied levels. This approach also allows for introduction of future regulatory modifications in those sectors for which there is no current clear definition of objectives and policies, which may be advantageous in cases where countries do not have regulations or defined objectives for the bulk of service sectors. Finally, it should make evaluating the value of concessions in the negotiating process much more feasible through the request–offer process followed, in terms of evaluating reciprocity in concessions in terms of commercial value.

Nevertheless, this approach also carries several drawbacks and limitations. The potential benefits accrued from the evaluation of concessions under the bottom-up approach are limited by the lack of adequate disaggregated statistics. Similarly, interpreting and documenting the tangible liberalization achieved under the agreements is difficult; in the absence of an adequate services sector classification list, there is rarely homogeneity in how commitments are recorded. Two final and perhaps more detrimental limitations of the bottom-up approach are its hindrance of timely, meaningful commitments and its lack of transparency. Because this approach promotes the binding of existing restrictions in the early stages of negotiation, acceleration of prompt and deep liberalization is unlikely. Such has been the experience in the GATS, under which the majority of the specific commitments are limited to binding the prevailing regulatory situation. Secondly, economic operators in the market may be negatively affected by its insufficient transparency. No information is available on restrictions in sectors not included in the lists of specific commitments, and even in those sectors bound by specific commitments ceiling binding may limit available information. Nevertheless, desired transparency can be pursued in other provisions, as is the case of the GATS.

Top-down approach

'Top-down' agreements based on negative listing require liberalization of all forms of discriminatory treatment for all service sectors, except for those measures listed in members' reservations. A top-down liberalization approach is best illustrated by two agreements in the Western Hemisphere: NAFTA and Decision 439 of the AC. Though the agreements share a common approach, significant differences exist between them.

NAFTA has been a model for a number of trade agreements in the Western Hemisphere, including Chile–Canada, Mexico–Bolivia, the G-3, and Mexico–Costa Rica.[7] NAFTA employs a mixed approach of general obligations together with specific treatment for certain service sectors. The following liberalization principles are incorporated as general obligations: (i) unconditional MFN treatment, (ii) national treatment, and, (iii) freedom over modes of supply. Non-discriminatory quantitative restrictions (QRs) are subject to transparency requirements and must be registered in the respective annex, subject to further liberalization negotiations at least every two years. Both national treatment and MFN are to be accorded in 'like circumstances' to services providers of the other parties, thus introducing a degree of conditionality. Members can register sector-specific reservations and non-conforming measures in the annexes. This negative list approach is also introduced in the chapters on investment (Chapter XI), financial services (Chapter XIV) and telecommunications (Chapter XIII). Further liberalization is to be attained through the progressive lifting of the reservations and non-conforming measures registered in members' reservations. A special annex addresses professional services, while temporary movement of businesspersons is subject to Chapter XVI, which governs this issue for all economic activities. Unlike GATS, NAFTA does not allow for modification or withdrawal of a commitment.

Trade in services is dealt with in NAFTA Chapter XII, which applies to 'cross-border trade in services', that is, modes of supply 1, 2 and 4 in GATS terms. Trade in services under mode 3 or commercial presence (establishment) is dealt with in Chapter XIII on Investment. NAFTA aims for universal sectoral coverage, particularly for cross-border trade. However, air transport services are excluded from the agreement. Similarly, although NAFTA aimed originally for coverage of measures affecting services at all levels of government, only measures enacted by the federal government are effectively covered by the agreement while those at other levels of government have been excluded from services disciplines. NAFTA does not incorporate provisions on subsidies or safeguards. Though automatic recognition of regulatory regimes is not a general obligation, disciplines do oblige the abolishment of nationality or permanent residence requirements for the recognition of diplomas and the granting of licenses for professional service providers. The agreement also calls for the development of a blueprint of procedures to assist professions in the achievement of mutual recognition of licenses and certifications. Disciplines on monopoly practices and state enterprises are found in NAFTA, strengthening and further developing the coverage of Article VIII of GATS.

The AC framework for the liberalization of trade in services in Decision 439 of June 1998 anticipates the creation of a common market through the elimination of all measures restricting trade in services. The framework applies to all sectors except air transport services and those services provided in the exercise of governmental authority. Some service sectors, including maritime and road transport, were subject to sub-regional regulations prior to Decision 439, and will therefore only be affected in those issues not covered by the common regimes.

Though the AC agreement does implement a top-down approach, it differs from NAFTA in three fundamental ways: (i) it does not exclude any sector from the agreement; and (ii) it incorporates five of the six liberalizing principles as general obligations (MFN, national treatment, market access, right to free transit and temporary presence, and automatic recognition of qualifications and licenses); and (iii) it posits the complete elimination of all restrictions to services trade among members. The liberalization approach or modality is similar to NAFTA: negative lists with registration of reservations and non-conforming measures have been established and made publicly available. However, full liberalization is to be achieved by 2005 through annual negotiations in which these reservations and non-conforming measures are to be progressively lifted. Notably, the AC agreement introduces the possibility that fast-movers of the bloc proceed with liberalization at their own pace, thus precluding the possibility that a slow member drag the process down. This provision introduces a certain notion of reciprocity at the sub-regional level, and engenders the undertaking of sector-specific negotiations in the annual rounds. Another difference between the AC and NAFTA is the number of related disciplines incorporated into the agreement; Decision 439 additionally provides for disciplines on safeguards, subsidies, and S&D for least developed members.

A top-down negotiating approach based on negative listing offers possibilities for more complete and more timely liberalization than does a positive list approach and is particularly beneficial in terms of the transparency it offers for service operators. An initial liberalization incorporates the bulk of service sectors and binds all registered non-conforming measures in a standstill. Future liberalization is then achieved by negotiations on progressive elimination of the reservations registered by each member. This approach sends clear messages to other member countries and the international community in general about countries' objectives and commitments. Since the core obligations enter into force at the outset, member countries must make a clear commitment to both the depth of commitments and the pace of liberalization. The obligation to provide comprehensive information on all outstanding measures that do not conform to the basic obligations of MFN, national treatment and non-discriminatory quantitative restrictions, as set out in the annexes of lists reservations to liberalization thus generates an entirely transparent environment.

Latin American and Caribbean countries have expressed concerns about the top-down approach. It may favor those countries with a more developed regulatory framework since those with less regulation cannot register reservations (of a discriminatory nature) in sectors without regulatory regimes. It is important to emphasize that the right to regulate remains intact under either negotiating approach, but the right to introduce new discriminatory regulation is lost under a top-down approach unless such sectors are specified in an annex of existing or future measures. However, the ability to take such steps is also lost under a positive list approach once commitments have been included in schedules. Latin American countries also fear disadvantages under the negative list approach due to unilateral liberalization asymmetries. It is felt that the automatic binding of 'status quo' regulations at the outset under this approach may give rise to an unequal exchange of concessions favoring more regulated or less liberalized countries. Finally, the requirement under the top-down approach to automatically liberalize new or future services creates considerable concern. Without a clear understanding of possible market developments or their economic implications, disciplines under this approach will automatically bind new service activities. The warp speed of technological change in services makes the pre-commitment of liberalization of new services an issue demanding attention in order to introduce greater flexibility.

Extensive preparation is needed to successfully comply with the 'list it or lose it' requirement under the top-down approach including the establishment of comprehensive inventories of measures or restrictions affecting trade in services. However, this preparation is a part of all services negotiations, including those under the GATS or positive list approach, as it is impossible to undertake commitments or register reservations without comprehensive knowledge of the national services regime and regulatory practices. The top-down approach presents the same difficulty as the bottom-up approach in assessing the commercial value of the sectors contained in the lists of reservations due to the absence of disaggregated services trade data or a common classification list in the recording of either commitments or reservations.

5.4 Overlapping negotiations and the relevant ambit of liberalization

Simultaneous negotiations at several different levels will continue to progress: the multilateral level under GATS, the hemispheric level under the FTAA process, and the sub-regional level among various groups of countries. These concurrent and overlapping levels of negotiation have different objectives, may have different approaches, and often contain different disciplines. And the members of all of these agreements intend to maintain them in permanent coexistence, despite problems of overlap including compatibility with respect to normative frameworks or disciplines and the depth of liberalization to be carried out in competing fora.

Normative compatibility

Regional agreements offering preferential liberalization of services concluded among a sub-set of WTO members must be compatible with Article V of the GATS, must be GATS-plus in the scope of its liberalization, and must remove substantially all discrimination to trade among members. Thus all preferential agreements, whether they include two members (as in bilateral agreements) or 34 members (as in the FTAA), must comply with these common denominators and must therefore be judged against the same yardstick. Complexity arises through the varying extents of GATS-plus in preferential integration agreements.

By definition, preferential agreements that form customs unions will strive for a deeper level of integration than will free trade area agreements, which may take two forms: more harmonized normative disciplines or more liberalized market access. The former is an extremely important aspect of customs unions. For example, countries in Mercosur, the AC and Caricom are working towards harmonization of regulations governing key service sectors as well as regulations governing the movement of qualified skilled personnel and the recognition of diplomas and licenses.

Sub-regional agreements whose members carry out truly deep integration making their regulations identical or compatible go beyond the GATS and thus should not hinder the coexistence of other preferential agreements or the GATS. They clearly serve to facilitate trade among members and do not raise discriminatory barriers to third countries, assuming the harmonized regulations do not represent disguised restrictions to trade under the criteria of GATS Article VI on Domestic Regulation. Clashes between competing services agreements are possible in the case of considerably varied disciplines contained in the normative frameworks. For example, a services agreement at the hemispheric level incorporating a safeguard clause in coexistence with sub-regional agreements without such a clause could send mixed signals to service suppliers as to which discipline applies, even in the absence of legal conflicts. Thus it would be desirable for the regional agreement with the largest sub-set of members (such as the FTAA) to contain as comprehensive a set of disciplines as possible, in order to extend the level ground within which service operators may function to the largest economic space other than the multilateral one.

Depth of liberalization and competing fora

Article V of the GATS evaluates all preferential agreements, whether customs unions or free trade agreements, by the same criteria, based solely on their coverage and market access liberalization. Market access liberalization of services requires the removal of discriminatory treatment among members. Changes in national laws or regulations are required in order to implement national treatment whereby foreign service providers are offered the same market access conditions as their domestic counterparts. Such changes require lengthy processes of garnering consensus among policy-makers, service operators, regulators and consumers and implementing new regimes. Applying one set of laws and regulations to suppliers within a given preferential agreement and a different set to those within another preferential agreement, and possibly still another set to members of the GATS is a daunting task, and almost an impossibility in certain sectors.

Thus the question of which is the most appropriate forum in which to liberalize services and remove discrimination gains importance, as governments may not wish to undertake this involved process several times on the one hand, and may not be able to differentiate their treatment among service suppliers on the other. Article V of the GATS only specifies that all regional agreements must liberalize market access further than the multilateral system does. How far regional liberalization is to go and how competing service liberalization initiatives are to be comparatively assessed is left undefined. Thus the question really boils down to the practicality of applying different laws and regulations to different suppliers. Does it make economic sense to carry out the liberalization of services trade on a fragmented basis?

Service sectors and products vary widely in terms of characteristics, efficient scale of output, and sensitivity in national economies. In order to better analyze the economic rationale underlying their liberalization, it is possible to consider services in the following four categories.

- *Infrastructure services*, including financial, telecom, energy, distribution, and transport services, are critical to the efficient operation of all economies and provide critical inputs into all economic activities, including other service activities. To be efficiently supplied, these infrastructure or network services require large amounts of capital to operate and large economies of scale to produce. The optimum level for liberalization of such services is therefore the largest market possible, in order to attract and accommodate investment from the most efficient service operators. Thus a preferential liberalization of these particular activities might not make economic sense, as it would limit the ability of a country to draw upon the most efficient, least costly suppliers. The world or global market is the logical forum to target for the liberalization of these services. Nonetheless, regional negotiations and agreements may play an important role by binding liberalization commitments that have not yet been undertaken in the GATS. Such commitments could then be extended 'de facto' on an MFN basis, as has been done in the case of the NAFTA and the EU to other countries.
- *Commercially oriented services*, including tourism, business, construction, engineering, and professional services, or those services that are not produced on a network basis but respond to commercial criteria in their production, break down into two groups. Tourism and business services are already very open sectors in all countries of the hemisphere and thus it would make little sense to think of liberalization on a regional level or a restricted scale. However, regional agreements could still be useful in binding commitments in these sectors, which could then likewise be applied on an MFN basis. Construction, engineering and professional services are often highly restricted sectors subject to tightly regulated national standards for the determination of the equivalence of experience, qualifications, education, licenses or certifications. Regional agreements have a useful role to play in these sectors, as it should be easier to develop a common set of recognition criteria among a smaller number of countries. National educational and legal systems that are often similar in countries of the same region facilitate such recognition agreements. Therefore liberalization of these commercially oriented service sectors at the regional level might make economic sense and also be more feasible.
- *Socially oriented services*, including educational, health, and environmental services, are more sensitive to certain national concerns and have been subject to very few multilateral commitments. Such sectors may therefore be more easily liberalized on a smaller scale and among countries that are

more similar in levels of development, consumer preference and background. However, certain activities, such as computer training schools or specialized language schools, or private clinics for specialized health services or environmental services, might lend themselves to liberalization at a broader level in order to attract the most efficient suppliers available for these niche or specialized services. Regional agreements could again serve as a catalyst for the binding of commitments that could be transcribed to the multilateral level.

- *Other services* are a mixed basket without a clear indication of the most economically appropriate level of liberalization. Recreational services, including cultural services, represent differing levels of sensitivity for different countries, and therefore the question of how much and where to liberalize these sectors must be decided by the national interests of the countries participating in these various agreements.

5.5 Conclusion

Services negotiations were jump-started by the implementation of the GATS in January 1995, and have continued at a vigorous pace ever since. No fewer than 14 sub-regional agreements containing disciplines for services trade have been negotiated among countries of the Western Hemisphere since 1994, and FTAA negotiations among 34 countries in the hemisphere have been ongoing since 1998. The conclusion of FTAA negotiations in January 2005 is to coincide with the conclusion of the work program launched in Doha, creating an enormous challenge for Latin American and Caribbean countries that are simultaneously participating in both the FTAA and the GATS negotiations, as well as trying to complete their own sub-regional integration agreements.

In this limited timeframe, countries in the Western Hemisphere must complete the normative framework for the rules and disciplines of the future FTAA services chapter. They must define the negotiating modality for the FTAA market access negotiations on services and carry out these negotiations while simultaneously negotiating the additional market access commitments in the ongoing GATS round. Finally, they must consolidate their own sub-regional agreements and attempt to achieve the ambitious objectives in these agreements, namely the complete removal of all remaining restrictions to trade in services among members of Mercosur, the AC and Caricom. All three levels of negotiations will require considerable negotiating energy and a thorough canvassing of the actual restrictive measures affecting services trade at the national level of each participating economy.

These overlapping negotiations will require the definition of negotiating priorities and goals in each forum, including the critical determination of the most appropriate level of liberalization for the service sectors. Even for those sectors where the global market is the most appropriate and economically efficient ambit for liberalization, regional agreements could still be useful in generating commitments in these sectors, which could then be applied de facto on an MFN basis. In any case, regional negotiations will merit sustained attention on the part of Latin American and Caribbean countries. Where to focus efforts towards opening service markets will depend not only upon the economic nature of the service in question and the optimal scale of economic activity, but also upon the difficulty of carrying out liberalization, the sensitivity of the sector, and the definition of national interest, and will thus vary according to the sector in question. As Narlikar and Woods develop in Chapter 2, it may prove more effective for sub-sectors in services to form coalitions through which to pursue their interests, rather than focus attention on multilateral/regional divides.

Notes

1. See, for example, WTO (2000c) and WTO (1999d).
2. For example, the EU–Jordan agreement includes an objective of evolving towards Article V computability, although it establishes significant liberalization commitments among the members. This agreement could be considered Article V-compatible *a priori* according to the interpretation of Article V.3.a.
3. EU, Hong Kong, Indonesia, Singapore, Japan and Switzerland. For an analyst's view see Prieto (2000).
4. NAFTA-type agreements include the G-3, Bolivia–Mexico, Costa Rica–Mexico, Canada–Chile, Chile–Mexico, Central America–Dominican Republic, Caricom–Dominican Republic, Mexico–Nicaragua, Central America–Chile, Mexico–Northern Triangle.
5. For example, Article 10-03 in the G-3 and Decision 439 of the AC, introduce the obligation of notifying all new regulations or modification of existing measures. NAFTA limits the obligation to publication of measures or to making them available in any other manner.
6. Ratcheting refers to a moving floor of commitments. No backtracking is allowed for any unilateral liberalization implemented after the effective freeze date. See Prieto and Stephenson (1999).
7. For a description of the agreements covering trade in service in the Western Hemisphere, see OAS (1996) and Stephenson (2001).

6
The Interplay of Multilateral Agreements and Domestic Regulations in Telecommunications

*Paulo Bastos Tigre**

6.1 Introduction

Institutional changes in telecommunications services have revolutionized the way national governments and multilateral agencies treat the sector. In Latin America, changes have been especially dramatic since new regulation has given rise to a completely different group of actors and industry structure. This chapter looks at the impact of international telecommunications agreements on Latin America. First, a framework is developed in section 6.2 in order to analyze conflicts, challenges and local interests in the telecommunications services sector. Second, multilateral and regional agreements are reviewed, namely the General Agreement on Trade in Services (GATS), Mercosur and NAFTA. The effect these agreements have had on telecommunications regulations in Latin America is analyzed in section 6.3. Finally, the chapter investigates conflicts and reactions to the new agenda. These include convergence and divergence in Latin American national policies concerning competition, propriety, safeguards, countervailing duties and antidumping measures. The argument stems from proper identification of factors affecting national telecommunications policies, including the relationship between national regulation agencies and distinct lobbies: users, equipment and service suppliers, existing regulated firms, new entrants and international agreements.

6.2 A framework for analysis

The role information technology (IT) plays in development has come to absorb increasing attention. According to UN Secretary General Kofi Annan, 'communications and information technology have enormous potential, especially for developing countries, and in furthering sustainable development' (1997: 1).

In fact, the availability of good information and telecommunications infrastructure is a paramount issue. A more complex question, however, is how
to develop such infrastructure in a way that maximizes local interests.
International forums like GATS are becoming more influential on national
telecommunications strategies. However, there is no single regulation model
since each uniquely depends on existing resources, capabilities, interests and
influence of major economic and political agents.

Telecommunications play a dual role in economic development, as a necessary means of production and a profitable economic good. On one hand,
access to telecommunications services is becoming one of the minimum
conditions necessary for participation in domestic and international markets
in the 'information age'. As Castells puts it:

> networks constitute the new social morphology of our societies, and the dif-
> fusion of networking logic substantially modifies the operation and out-
> comes in process of production, experience, power, and culture. (1996: 469)

Mansell and Wehn (1998) similarly argue that although it is difficult to
establish links between investment in telecommunication and development, it is fairly clear that political and economic control is contingent
upon the electronic communication environment.

On the other hand, telecommunications has become a key product in and
of itself in the world economy. The production of telecommunications infrastructure and the information it carries are now highly valuable goods. The
IT industry is the fastest growing economic sector in the world and participation in hardware, software and value-added services forms a key development strategy. IT services create highly qualified and well-paid jobs and
provide opportunities for equipment, software and service firms to prosper.

Building networks linking the business sector, government institutions and
society is a major task for developing countries. National policies concerning
regulation of telecommunications services are affected by the nature of their
relationships with major players, including both suppliers and consumers,
which are usually recognized as 'local interests'. The interactions between
national regulation agencies and major players are shown in Figure 6.1. The
figure provides a framework for analyzing Latin American interests in the
telecommunications sector.

Equipment suppliers and users (Relationships 1 and 3)

Relationships 1 and 3 look at pressure groups – telecommunications users
and local equipment, software and service suppliers – directly affected by
decisions made by the institutional framework regulating incumbent firms.
According to Becker (1983), pressure groups search to influence the regulation activity in favor of their own self-interest. Therefore, regulations will
favor groups with political leverage.

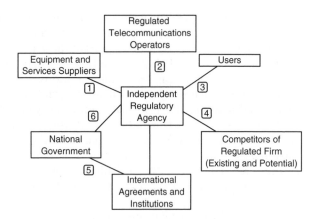

Figure 6.1 Actors influencing national telecommunications policies
Source: Adapted from Fiani (1998).

The telecommunications equipment supply industry is becoming an international oligopoly as governments are phasing out existing protectionist policies for local manufacturers. Support for locally owned firms has been shifting from procurement to research and development (R&D) financing. Many advanced countries see the telecommunications equipment industry as a key sector to promote exports and to create highly qualified jobs.

There is a basic distinction between the role played by large, multinational users and small, domestic users. Networks do not tend to focus on encouraging universal diffusion of public telecommunication services. So despite claims that the international public network is becoming more open and accessible to users, it is becoming more closely attuned to the needs of a specific segment of users; namely the locally operating firms (Mansell, 1993).

Regulated telecommunications operators (Relationship 2)

The regulated firm operates as a natural monopoly or a duopoly and they are the incumbent operators with universal service responsibilities. Their relationship with the regulatory agency is influenced by three main factors. First, the political environment, in which Vogel (1996) emphasizes the importance of the government's mindset as the filter through which decision-makers interpret market forces. In the United Kingdom the debate grew from an assumed connection between deregulation and international competitiveness: the more liberal the policy framework, the more easily technology and investment are attracted. This mindset helps explain liberal policies in Britain and Latin America. The second factor concerns the ownership of regulated firms, differentiating the roles played by state-owned and private operators. The third factor refers to the ability of regulated firms to 'capture' the regulation agency. Power conflicts are mediated by a number of issues and must be analyzed on a case-by-case basis. The generous timeframe given to newly privatized operators in Mexico and Argentina to act as transitional monopolies may be explained by the investing groups' political power.

From Mansell's point of view (1993), the notion of public interest is related to the influence of competing telecommunications users. There is a clear divergence between the interests of small business and domestic users and those of large multinational users, so that conflicts may exist between universal service and network segmentation to attend to the distinct demands of sophisticated large users. Mansell rejects the notion that rapid diffusion of advanced public network capabilities is in the interest of all users. This vision is relevant to the case of Latin America, where there is a striking trade-off between universal service and large users' competitiveness.

Competitors of regulated firms (Relationship 4)

It has been argued that regulation proves unnecessary in an environment of full competition. New technology has reduced sunk costs, thus changing the status of the public utility. Consequently, competition may be a substitute for regulation. However, the incumbent public utility has responsibilities that are not assumed by new entrants. These include charging fair tariffs without discriminating among users, expanding services towards universal service, giving open access to other service providers and securing interconnectivity.

According to Grieve and Levin, the regulator faces a mission impossible in dealing with public utilities:

> The public utility must undertake expensive investments so that it can serve all customers while its competitors can choose only certain customers. The regulator will be required to set just and reasonable rates. But if those rates must be sufficient to cover all of the public utility's costs, they may not be sustainable in a competitive market. If the regulator responds by allowing the public utility to lower its rates, the opportunity to recover the costs of the imposed obligations will not be provided. If the regulator attempts to ensure that the public utility's costs are covered through the imposition of any kind of policy, it faces the cries of competitors complaining that the utility is being granted protection from competition. The regulator simply cannot fulfill its obligation. (1996: 999)

Accessibility and interconnectivity also strain the relationship between the incumbent firm and its competitors. Some hold that the status of common carrier should be limited to only those firms that have access to final users (Fiani, 1998). It can be argued, however, that accessibility problems are more complex than the substitution of competition for regulation. In some cases accessibility may definitively influence the competition and efficiency of the whole telecommunications system. The ensuing controversy over interconnection terms and tariff rebalancing illustrates that regulation is often needed as a complement to, rather than a substitute for, competition.

Problems also abound concerning anti-competitive practices and management of scarce resources. In those areas, however, there is little discussion about the importance of national and international agreements and regulations.

Local and international policy issues (Relationships 5 and 6)

Supranational regulations are increasingly restructuring legal frameworks and pushing national governments to search for common ground concerning the liberalization of trade in telecommunications services. There are three basic elements in existing models for service trade liberalization: (i) coverage, which can be universal or sector-specific; (ii) basic principles and concepts; and (iii) type of commitments. The GATS is a global trend-setter, but in Latin America, Mercosur and NAFTA may eventually assume greater importance in shaping national policies. Negotiations between national regulatory agencies and multilateral institutions are usually mediated by the Ministries of Foreign Affairs and included in the general mantle of international relations. Thus, agreements are influenced not only by technical or local issues but also by general foreign policy issues.

6.3   International agreements

Telecommunications have become a major target of international regulatory agreements and a key issue for multilateral development organizations. Regulatory reforms were influenced by the neoliberal mindset, which viewed barriers to production and exchange of information and knowledge as hindering economic efficiency, technological rationalism and even the spread of democracy based on pioneer experiences in the early 1980s. As Ken puts it, 'under neoliberalism, knowledge has been defined as a commodity to be privately produced and exchanged according to competitive markets. The global regulation of telecommunications has come to mean minimizing barriers to the operation of such markets' (1996: 177). The main messages of the World Bank Development Report on Infrastructure are that the causes of past poor performance, and the source of improved performance, lie in the incentives facing providers. To ensure efficiency, it prescribed the application of three instruments: commercial management, competition, and stakeholder involvement. Also, government and private sector roles needed to be transformed, in order to offer users and private firms a larger role in the finance, operation and planning of the infrastructure system (World Bank, 1994).

Several international organizations are involved in the regulation of global communications, including the International Telecommunication Union (ITU), International Standards Organization (ISO), World Trade

Organization (WTO), World Intellectual Property Organization (WIPO), United Nations Educational Scientific and Cultural Organization (UNESCO) and the United Nations Committee for the Peaceful Uses of Outer Space (UNCOPUOS). The WTO, and particularly the GATS, play an increasingly important role in international telecommunications services liberalization and international network integration. Regional negotiations are also advancing liberalization of services.

The ITU deals with technical issues, primarily planning the radio frequency spectrum and setting international equipment and services standards. The ITU has enjoyed a strong reputation for its technical expertise and political neutrality as the oldest existing international organization, established in 1865 and restructured in 1947. It is an intergovernmental organization, but non-state actors, notably private sector interests, have played an important role in its various committees. Since the late 1970s, excess productive capacity of core capitalist states led telecommunications services firms to look increasingly to foreign markets. In this context the ITU has played a key role in the process of globalization, promoting widespread liberalization both nationally and internationally and increasing private sector participation in policy-making. Specifically, it has the following objectives:

- to maintain and extend international cooperation for the improvement and rational use of telecommunications;
- to promote the development of technical facilities and their most efficient operation in order to improve the efficiency of telecommunications services, increase their usefulness and make them, so far as possible, generally available to the public; and
- to harmonize nations' activities towards the achievement of those common ends.

The WTO extended its agenda to encompass trade in services under GATS. Though fairly new, GATS is recognized as the main multilateral institution that propels further liberalization of trade in services. The agreement's framework consists of three main elements: (i) a set of general concepts, principles and rules; (ii) specific commitments undertaken by WTO members on national treatment and market access; and (iii) several sector-specific annexes of both substantive and non-substantive natures. As explained by Abugattas and Stephenson in Chapter 5, GATS works toward liberalization of trade in services through specific commitments listed in national schedules, reflecting the so-called 'positive list approach'. These commitments are made within sectors, under four modes of supply: cross-border, commercial presence, consumer movement, or temporary presence of foreign service providers. Countries making binding commitments have no obligation to include all four or any number of the four modes of supply when considering specific sectors. The principle of 'positive list' allows for a choice of specific commitments in each particular sector or across sectors from a GATS 'menu' of measures. Each country 'offers' specific commitments on future liberalization plans. These binding commitments are further negotiated in the WTO in order to consolidate and promote liberalization of competition and trade in telecom services. In 1997, an Agreement on Basic Telecommunications was signed as an industry-specific protocol under GATS, which included a 'Reference Paper' on pro-competitive regulatory principles. The Reference Paper, which was attached to market access commitments offered by over sixty countries, made telecommunications the first sector to establish WTO standards for competition policies. Because only governments have rights and duties under the WTO, the Reference Paper focused its attention on achieving the core of pro-competitive regulation (universal access and independent regulation) through governmental obligations. It creates obligations concerning regulation of major dominant incumbent suppliers but does not extend its coverage to potential competitors in particular segments of the market. Since regulation of 'non-major suppliers' is a controversial issue, the approach adopted is considered rather cautious. As delineated in the following six principles of the Reference Paper, the driving force was to rein in the entrenched incumbent operators (Cowhey and Klimenko, 1999).

- Governments are committed to ensure that major suppliers do not engage in anti-competitive practices, such as anti-competitive cross-subsidies, misuse of information obtained from competitors or withholding information needed by competitors.
- Governments have committed to guarantee non-discriminatory interconnection with a major supplier for competitors at any technically feasible point in the networks.
- Governments have retained the right to maintain universal policy measures administered in transparent, non-discriminatory and competitively neutral ways.
- Governments are obligated to make licensing criteria publicly available and transparent.
- The independent regulatory body must employ impartial procedures towards all market participants.
- Governments will use timely, objective, transparent and non-discriminatory procedures for the allocation and use of scarce resources.

On the regional level, Mercosur and NAFTA are paving the road towards telecommunications liberalization. Although the Mercosur treaty does not specifically regulate telecommunications, references have been made in broader agreements. The 'Action Plan for Mercosur to 2000' issued in 1995 emphasized the will to define a common trade policy for the service sector and government procurement, and to present a joint position in multilateral negotiations. In 1997 the Montevideo Protocol on Trade in Services was signed as a Framework Agreement, and has been further supplemented through the addition of sector-specific chapters and national commitment schedules. The Protocol will come into effect as soon as three of the four member governments have ratified it. The Protocol includes a positive list of supplementary obligations in addition to those already in force, aspiring towards a service free-trade area in ten years through the reduction of internal market access obstacles. Mercosur's basic approach to the liberalization of trade in services is similar to that of the GATS; both call for a gradual market opening via the negotiation of service-specific commitments of either market access or national treatment. However, according to Stephenson:

> the Mercosur Protocol departs significantly from that of the GATS in the objectives it sets to achieve full liberalization of traded services within a ten-year period, culminating in an open regional market for services no later than 2007. This is to be achieved through annual rounds of negotiations, meant to progressively incorporate additional sectors and modes of supply within the orbit of liberalization through the expansion of the number of commitments in national schedules. (1998: 45)

The Mercosur Protocol contains many articles similar to those of the GATS, including those on MFN treatment, market access and national treatment. Detailed articles on transparency, information confidentiality, domestic regulation, recognition, denial of benefits, and exceptions (both for general and security purposes) follow the GATS very closely. The clause on competition policy makes reference to the provisions contained in Mercosur's Protocol for the Defense of Competition Policy. The clauses on government procurement and subsidies make reference to provisions that will be negotiated in these areas in the future. The Protocol provides for modification of schedules, but the withdrawal or alteration of any commitments cannot be retroactive. The dispute settlement provisions specify that conflicts in the area of trade in services will be settled under existing Mercosur mechanisms (see Weston and Delich, Chapter 10). The Mercosur approach to liberalization of trade in services is ambitious; although based on the GATS framework and negotiation modality, members have committed to a specific timetable (ten years) for the complete elimination of trade restrictions. Mercosur members have thus agreed to go far beyond the scope of liberalization at the multilateral level in order to realize a common market, much along the lines of the European Union (EU). The feasibility of this ambitious objective will only become apparent over time.

NAFTA disciplines on trade in services drastically part from WTO doctrine, based on their inclusion of both universal coverage applied to all sectors and sector-specific agreements such as telecommunications and financial services. NAFTA discipline also diverges from WTO doctrine in its adoption of the principle of cross-border trade, thus extending to services the rules applied to goods. It is not necessary to establish commercial presence to provide a service abroad, which would involve foreign direct investment, so firms may provide services in another country without local presence in that country. The key difference between GATS and NAFTA models is that negotiations in the first forum are based on a 'positive list' while in the latter they are based on a 'negative list'. In other words, the NAFTA model implicitly approves what is not included in the agreements while the GATS model only applies to what has been explicitly negotiated.

6.4   Regulations in Latin America

The GATS

Latin American telecommunications policies are converging towards the principles contained in the WTO Reference Paper for competition and independent regulation. Competition is assumed to give consumers choices to better meet their demands and to pressure suppliers to be efficient and accountable to users. In telecommunications, competition could be introduced directly, by liberalizing entry to activities that have no technological barriers, and indirectly, through competitive bidding for the right to provide exclusive service where natural monopoly conditions exist and liberalization of the supply of service substitutes. Out of six major principles included in the Reference Paper, four are designed to assure competition and one grants independence to the regulating agency *vis-à-vis* local governments. The remaining principle deals with the social problem of universal service provision. A preliminary evaluation of the WTO Reference Paper's six major principles applied to Latin America is shown in Table 6.1.

Privatization and competition

The privatization of Latin American telecom services began in 1988 in Chile, followed by Argentina and Mexico in 1990. Peru (1994) and Brazil (1998) followed suit. Dismantling monopolies and creating competition in telephone networks has been a very difficult task. The old telephone monopolies, now privatized, retain their competitive advantages of an established infrastructure, a large client base and privileged relationships with suppliers and regulators. In most countries, executives and directors of newly privatized firms came from the Ministries of Communications or from the former state-owned monopolies. They are still influential in policy issues and have vested interests against full competition. In some countries, such as Argentina, the temporary monopolies granted to bidders were extended for a longer period of time, reflecting the power of existing firms over government decisions. Telephone operators have run a highly effective cartel; they are closely bound to governments and control the final gate between the network and the user. Also, natural monopoly is still embedded in services provided by ex-monopolistic carriers. Hence the path to full competition may entail a long journey with many roadblocks.

Table 6.1 WTO reference paper and regulatory status in selected countries, 2000

Features	Mexico	Argentina	Chile	Brazil
Competition regulatory treatment	British model. Emphasis on negotiations rather than interventions.	10 years of private duopoly. Full competition since 2000.	Vigorous competition in long-distance.	Duopoly in regional, long-distance and celullar services. Full competition in 2002.
Prevention of anti-competitive practices	Many conflicts due to main incumbent's strength.	Monopoly extended for two years, showing existing player's strength.	Subtel controls tariffs of dominant incumbent since 1999.	Incumbents are testing regulator's strength in several practices.
Interconnect/ non-discriminatory, cost-oriented rates	Interconnection rates are still high and provisioning by major carrier difficult.	Based on incremental costs of unbundled services since 1999. Very high rates for long-distance.	Surcharge on incoming international traffic for interconnection.	Long-distance competition still in initial stages. Billing problems.
Transparent allocation of scarce resources	Yes – auctions for wireless spectrum	Yes – auctions for satellite	Yes – public competition and license charges	Yes, except for open signal TV
Independent regulatory body	Cofetel (1996)	CNC (1996)	Subtel (1977)	Anatel (1998)
Universal service	Teledensity* of 13.3. Competition in local services will increase subscribers.	Teledensity of 23.1.	Teledensity of 24.5. Subsidies for service provision in rural areas.	Teledensity of 19.8. Universal targets to be implemented based on special funds.

* Teledensity is the measure of telephone lines per 100 inhabitants in a region.

Source: Author's compilation.

Table 6.2 summarizes and compares privatization processes in four countries. A pragmatic approach was usually adopted, which transferred investment responsibilities from state-owned firms to the private sector. Granting a transition monopolistic period to operators boosted private capital, but it had the disadvantage of postponing competition. Reforms have included a change in the legal framework creating a role for independent regulators.

In Mexico, in addition to privatizing Telmex, the government has introduced competition and allowed foreign investors to participate in the market. The 1993 Foreign Investment Law permitted up to 100 per cent foreign ownership of many operations, including cellular telephony and value-added services. In 1996, the Zedillo administration ended the Telmex monopoly

Table 6.2 Comparative telecom privatization processes

	Chile	Argentina	Mexico	Brazil
Year of privatization	1988	1990	1990	1998
Privatization objectives	Not specified	Implicit, including: user-oriented quality, network expansion, and public debt reduction	Explicit, including: national sovereignty, quality, workers' rights, national ownership network expansion, and R&D	Explicit, including: network expansion, public debt reduction, foreign capital attraction, and competition
Nature of concession	Non-exclusive concession for local services	Exclusive license for local, long-distance and international services, during an initial period; non-exclusive license afterwards	Exclusive concession for local services; exclusive concession for long-distance services for 6 years	Non-exclusive
Concession period	Indeterminate	7 years with possible extension of 3 years of exclusive license; permanent for non-exclusive license	50 years automatically renewable for 15-year periods	Indeterminate
Foreign ownership limits	None	None	51% of the 20.4% control share must be Mexican-owned	Cellular (B band) up to 49%
Tariff rules	Tariff limits (5 years) for monopolistic services only, based on incremental costs compared with a benchmark enterprise	Tariffs fixed prior to privatization with increase of annual inflation less 2% (for productivity sharing)	Tariff fixed each 4 years, based on incremental costs compared with a benchmark enterprise; average tariff increase of annual inflation less 2%	Price cap system (a limit is set for a basket of services)
Expansion commitment	None	1.2 million new lines (5.6% annual growth)	12% annual growth	Quantitative goals for universalization
Local services	Open	Open after 7 or 10 years	Monopoly	Duopoly for 3 years, then open
Long-distance services market	Dominant position of ENTEL, former state-owned firm	Open after 7 or 10 years	Open after 6 years	Duopoly for 3 years, open afterwards

Source: Author's compilation.

on long-distance and authorized several competitive carriers including Alestra (affiliated with AT&T), Avantel (MCI), Iusatel (Bell Atlantic), and Amaritel (US Global Telecommunications). In Venezuela, the domestic fixed-line market was opened to competition in November 2000 when monopoly on domestic service expired. The main operator, Venezuelan National Telephone Company (CANTV), was privatized in 1991. US-based firms already operate cellular phone companies and are expected to enter the fixed-line market. Peru privatized the fixed-line operator in the mid-1990s, granting a five-year monopoly on fixed-line services. In 1999 it formally opened its fixed-line local and long-distance market, publishing a series of decrees confirming changes in its telecommunications law. In January 1999, former President Alberto Fujimori said that four tele-communications companies were likely to be granted licenses to provide domestic and international long-distance services in several provincial cities. Cepri Telecom, a commission for privatizing telecom services, has issued a series of auctions for authorizing new competitors to enter the market in several services, including wireless local loop (WLL), long distance and fixed lines. Uruguay decided in a public referendum not to privatize its state-owned telecommunications operator ANTEL. The country is rela-tively well served in terms of main lines per inhabitant and users did not favor privatization.

Impact of new technologies on competition

New technologies are changing the advantages of existing services suppliers. Wireless communications, including mobile cellular and WLL, are enabling new firms to supply voice service to customers. WLL, also known as 'fixed wireless', is a new technology that provides telephone services via station-ary phones that communicate to a wireless network antenna via a wireless transmitter-receiver. It has the advantage of requiring lower investment than traditional fixed telephone lines since it does not require cabling. While mobile cellular phone service usually constitutes a separate market, WLL competes directly with existing domestic fixed telephone services sup-pliers. In Brazil WLL was temporarily reserved (until 2002) to new entrants in the local service market, known as 'mirror firms' of incumbent fixed-line service suppliers, in a policy designed to encourage new competition. This policy was heralded as a way to provide universal phone service in places with inadequate or nonexistent networks, since WLL technology requires less investment and provides an opportunity to reduce entry barriers in existing fixed local telephony monopolies.

Technological convergence with cable TV and Internet also provides opportunities to introduce competition. Strategic convergence among TV, Internet and telephone markets still depends on regulation changes. However, cable TV firms are already authorized to provide Internet services in Brazil and Argentina. The entry of Internet and cable TV into the voice market will take more time, since it requires new investments in equipment as well as regulatory authorization.

The debate over accounting rates and competition

When one operator connects its equipment, networks, services, or customers to those of another operator, a compensatory 'interconnection' payment is usually made by the first operator to the second according to bilaterally negotiated 'accounting rates'. Since the 'last mile' connecting these providers to the final users is often a monopoly, interconnection charges may be arbitrarily high. Interconnection administration has become strategically important to telecommunication operators, as the industry becomes more complex and competitive. Interconnection is the fastest growing section of telecom traffic after the Internet. In Latin America, as elsewhere, the interconnection market is being forced into early maturity, especially as costs often determine whether a new entrant sinks or swims. There is now a massive wholesale market dealing in billions of minutes of voice or data traffic. In the UK, it is estimated that 10 per cent of British Telecom's revenues come from interconnection fees collected from other fixed operators, mobile and paging companies and Internet service providers (ISPs). For firms buying interconnection, like cable and wireless, charges represent 40 per cent of their operating costs, or 30 per cent of total turnover.

With a growing number of networks, it is no longer just a case of the incumbent putting through the 'last mile' traffic of alternative long-distance operators. A new class of network operators is springing up and entering the 'carriers' carrier' market. Interconnection agreements used to apply for the long term, but rates are changing so rapidly as the market becomes more competitive, that agreements are now fixed monthly, weekly or even daily. There is no general agreement on billing systems for interconnection. Legislation in most countries requires companies to ensure that retail-billing systems are secure and properly audited, and that interconnection systems have to play a 'catch-up game' towards universal high quality. Nevertheless, setting up billing systems is no easy task, given the difficulties of calculating the prices that should be unbundled and charged for interconnection. In some countries, such as Sweden, interconnection is held to be a commercial matter and the regulator does not intervene. But elsewhere the regulator can often play an important role in defining the structure of the incumbent's interconnection billing. For example, in the UK, the regulator has determined in great detail the price that British Telecom can charge for the use of 'elements' of the network, resulting in an arcane and somewhat arbitrary system. In the US, an already complex situation is exacerbated by the requirement that incumbents provide unbundled access to the local loop. The EU is now assessing whether it will force incumbents to unbundle their local loops as well.

The Secretary of the ITU General Pekka Tarjanne warned that the global telecom market would face 'chaos and anarchy' if the ongoing row over reforming the accounting rate system is not resolved. He argues that market forces, if left unfettered, could prevent developing countries' access to telecom services, leaving them and their citizens out of the global information infrastructure. For more than seven years, the existing system of bilaterally negotiated accounting rates has been discussed without a solution. The ITU has endorsed the WTO's recommendation to open markets and set cost-based tariffs calculated from the actual cost of supporting the network that delivers the call. But according to Scott-Joynt (1998), two events have galvanized discussions surrounding accounting rates. The first was the implementation in February 1998 of the WTO's Basic Telecom Services Agreement, signed by 72 countries representing 93 per cent of the world telecom market and designed to open markets to competition. The second was a US Federal Communications Commission (FCC) decision in 1999 to unilaterally impose its own 'benchmark' rates, ranging from 15 to 23 cents a minute according to the level of development, on all carriers doing business with the US. These figures undercut developing world accounting rates by 80 per cent in some cases, and have been met by a storm of disapproval from those who accuse the US of trying to force its own law on the rest of the world.

Call-back international services are also putting an increasingly large strain on the network, as the international accounting rate system does not adequately deal with the problem. Call-back is a long distance telephone service that bypasses locally authorized service providers by changing the origin of the call. For example, a call from Argentina to the US can benefit from lower rates in the US by using call-back. The existing ITU rule is a 50–50 accounting rate mechanism, designed to share long-distance tariffs between local and international operators. However, the US and newly liberalized countries in Europe are anxious to protect call-back revenues and the enormous cost savings from refiling of international traffic through third countries. Call-back operations bypass existing rules, since no taxes are paid to local operators. Latin American countries, headed by Mexico, want the accounting rate system issue to be interlinked to call-back and refiling. The WTO Basic Telecom Services Agreement of 1998 would forge a multilateral agreement on accounting rates if the ITU Study Group failed in its mission. Study group recommendations set out cost elements for termination fees, arguing that if all rates and tariffs were cost-based there would be no room for refiling, call-back and other arbitrage opportunities that are distorting the market. Further delay in resolving the dispute could lead to the ITU losing its authority to the WTO on this crucial international trade issue.

The allocation of scarce resources, like orbital slots and radio frequencies, represents a challenging demand on the regulatory apparatus. Its capacity to respond depends upon building technical and political capacity to deal with incumbent firms. Brazil, Argentina and Mexico have opened their satellite services markets and orbital slots to competition and private investment in the wake of the WTO telecom agreement. In 1998, Brazil invited bids for several of the country's 13 orbital slots to compete with Embratel, the privatized satellite operator. In Argentina, the sole satellite operator, NahuelSat SA, wants to be allowed to sell services in the US, while companies such as PanAmSat want better access in Argentina. The two governments have been negotiating a bilateral agreement to allow the exchange of services on a reciprocal basis. The privatization process is farthest along in Mexico, where the government's three-satellite system was sold in late 1997. Argentina and Brazil have approached the FCC to ask for a redistribution of slots in the US 'domestic arc' – the band of slots designated for satellites serving the US. The two South American countries argue that US operators currently have the best slots. Observers worry that those new commercial operators – or newly commercialized old operators – will cause a wave of interference problems as they attempt to beam into lucrative markets in the Americas. They expect an increase in interference and satellite spacing problems in the region. Satellite operators are increasingly using big hemispheric beams expecting to gain broader market access. At present, operators and regulatory authorities ensure that adjacent satellites avoid interfering with each other by 'coordinating' beams – pointing them in different directions so that they don't overlap – and reusing frequencies efficiently. But the use of broad hemispheric beams, which give operators broader geographic coverage, may complicate such coordination.

6.5 Impact of international regulations and challenges for local interests

Local equipment and services industry (Relationship 1)

Most developed countries have subscribed to the WTO's International Technology Agreement, which eliminates tariffs and other barriers to trade of IT products. Latin American countries, with the exception of Costa Rica, have not signed on. Although few Latin American countries have a telecommunications equipment industry, most countries are able to add value to the IT service network by providing software, system integration and information contents. To the extent that equipment and services are produced locally, more qualified jobs are created and hard currency is saved. Also, close user–producer relations are essential to the diffusion of telecom services when local needs are idiosyncratic. Contrary to theory, there is plenty of evidence to show that no country has become an important player in the global IT industry without some level of government intervention (for example, Evans, 1995; Dedrick and Kraemer, 1998; Tigre, 1992; and Amsden, 1989).

Policies adopted in most Latin American countries exempted telecom equipment, software and tradable services from import taxes, a policy designed to attract investment. But local firms complain that they face unfair competition in most segments of the market. In fact, the market share of local IT equipment and services is decreasing in Latin America, due to two factors.

First, privatization projects have dramatically increased dependence on imports since new owners are usually transnational corporations (TNCs) with global supply sources. Second, neoliberal policies adopted in Latin American countries substantially reduced or eliminated tariffs and non-tariff barriers on IT imports. Few countries, namely Brazil and Mexico, retain incentives for local IT equipment and services production at all. US and multilateral pressure to open IT markets have usually succeeded in wiping out local industry.

Mercosur countries have tried to negotiate a common external policy for IT. The agreement includes the establishment of rules of origin, unified product codes and a common external tariff (CET) based on a basic production process (BPP). The BPP rule defines a minimum assembly process for each class of products, for which local undertaking is considered essential. In 1995 a tariff convergence agreement established a gradual harmonization of import tariffs for IT products from outside the bloc, to average 16 per cent in 2006. However, Argentina unilaterally dropped import tariffs for capital goods to ground zero in 2001. Brazil has raised complaints over its subsequent loss of preference in supplying the Argentine market, which had previously absorbed most Brazilian exports of telecommunication equipment. Brazil is the largest Latin American telecom equipment producer and has local technological capability. Since the 70s Brazil has developed a telecommunications equipment industry based on a state-owned operators procurement policy, which encouraged local technology development. A research center at Telebras developed a digital switching system, Tropico, which responds to nearly 40 per cent of Brazil's installed base. The availability of inexpensive, locally developed equipment forced down the price of TNCs and allowed Telebras to save US$2.2 billion in equipment costs from 1990 to 1996. However, the opening of the equipment market with the privatization of telecom services in the late 1990s created a challenge for both local technological development and locally owned telecommunications equipment manufacturers. Imports increased six-fold from US$392 million in 1992 to US$2.7 billion in 1998, creating a trade deficit in electronic goods of US$7.5 billion in 2000. The survival of Brazilian industry depends on congressional support for R&D and local manufacturing. Argentine IT imports also increased substantially after privatization and reduction of tariffs and non-tariff barriers. The equipment market was estimated at US$1.7 billion in 1996, one-third of which was supplied by imports from the US. As availability of basic telephone services grows, demand for specific equipment is expected to increase. The continuing effects of privatization, liberal trade policies, user demand for state-of-the-art equipment, and an expanding local market will result in increasing imports.

In Mexico, import duties were eliminated for on-line equipment, private branch exchange switches, cellular phones and modems when NAFTA took effect in 1994. Tariffs on central office switches and telephone sets were eliminated in 1998. Many TNCs are establishing IT equipment manufacturing facilities in Mexico because proximity to the US market gives Mexico a transportation cost advantage that may exceed Asia's labor cost advantage. The comparison between Mexico on one hand, and Brazil and Argentina on the other, shows that liberalization must be a two-way street. Mexico opened up its market but gained access to the US market and attracted TNCs to carry out local production. Brazil and Argentina, in contrast, opened their markets unilaterally with the results of fewer local manufacturing activities and increased imports.

Regulated operators (Relationships 2 and 4)

Since the 1960s and 1970s the telecommunications services industry in Latin America has evolved as a system of nationally or regionally based public monopolies sanctioned either by law or by the common consent of the state. Since operators were predominantly state-owned, there was no need to develop a separate regulatory body to contend with private business. Since privatization, however, government and public interests have been mediated by regulatory agencies. These agencies must deal with several companies operating in different regions and segments of the market. Most operators in Latin America are now foreign-owned and follow a global strategy.

While the market is close to saturation in developed countries, in Latin America there is potential for infrastructure expansion and, in some cases, there is still unsatisfied demand for telephone lines. This may explain the explosive growth in demand for cellular telephones. The telecommunications market in Latin America is relatively small in world terms but is growing quickly. From 1995 to 1999 the average geometric annual growth of fixed lines was 11.1 per cent while cellular grew 76.6 per cent a year (Wohlers and Plaza, 2000). From 1992 to 1997 the region's share in total world spending rose from 5.4 to 7.0 per cent. The three largest markets – Brazil, Mexico and Argentina – accounted for 65 per cent of total spending (US$55 billion) in 1997.

In the 1980s and early 1990s the development of telecommunications infrastructure in Latin America was negatively affected by economic stagnation. In the late 60s Brazil had a higher ratio of telephone lines per person than either the Republic of Korea or Taiwan, which now have three times as many as Brazil and other Latin American countries. Beginning in the mid-1990s, however, privatization boosted the supply-side, both by increasing the availability of new main lines and by digitalizing networks and switching systems. Foreign investments in telecommunications services were equivalent to US$7 billion in 1995, compared to US$9 billion in Southeast Asia and only US$2.5 billion in Central and Eastern Europe. In most countries, privatization agreements included a minimum level of investment by private operators that agreed to comply with ambitious investment and quality goals. In Mexico, the impact of deregulation and privatization on the telecommunications network has been generally positive. Ninety per cent of switches are now digital compared to 29 per cent in 1990, and fiber optic cables are replacing many copper lines (Dedrick *et al.*, 1999).

Mexico is also the most visible case of interconnection problems that are plaguing the entry of new firms. Competitors of the incumbent firm Telmex have pursued redress for anti-competitive practices.[1] Telmex set its fee structure after the government established guidelines for interconnection costs in April 1996. Those guidelines, which were protested by seven long-distance operators, left some issues unanswered and gave Telmex the opportunity to charge the highest interconnection fee possible. In July 2000, the US Trade Representative (USTR) requested WTO consultations with Mexico regarding alleged barriers to competition including lack of effective disciplines over the former monopoly, Telmex; failure to ensure timely, cost-oriented interconnection; and failure to permit alternatives to an outmoded system of charging US carriers above-cost rates for completing international calls into Mexico. USTR argues that even though the market has theoretically been open to competition for several years, Telmex has increased its market share and engaged in anti-competitive practices like denying competitors phone lines, predatory pricing, and refusing to interconnect or charging excessive fees to do so. Moreover, the USTR is concerned with enforcement, pointing out that the current rates for international calls are too high (US$0.19 per minute compared to US$0.06 per minute for calls into Canada and the UK), and the dominant carrier, which has incentives to keep rates high, is the sole negotiator of the international rate (USTR, 2000). Telmex said that the US FCC unfairly accused it of charging high rates for connecting calls that originate from rival companies, claiming the decision did not take into account advances made in Mexico in interconnection tariff reduction during the 1990s. Telmex, citing the need to recoup large capital investments in its telephone infrastructure, has been allowed to only slowly reduce these rates by the Mexican government.[2] Rival providers of long-distance services have suspended planned investments in Mexico, arguing that they are not prepared to risk more capital until there is fair competition. In addition to settlement fees, the FCC voiced concern over other anti-competitive issues in Mexico, including the lack of progress in opening the phone market to competitors wanting to resell Telmex services under their own brand name and the continuation of a 58 per cent surcharge on inbound international calls.

Challenges for users: universalization, fair tariffs, and new services (Relationship 3)

The WTO Reference Paper states that any member has the right to define the kind of universal service obligation it wishes to maintain, leaving its definition open to a variety of distinct interpretations ranging from universal geographical availability to non-discriminatory access or the equal treatment of all users in terms of service price and/or quality. Privatization and new regulations have had a positive impact on universal geographical availability in Latin America. Teledensity almost tripled from 1990 to 2000 in the region (see Table 6.1 for teledensity rates in various countries). Line density in Peru stood at about 7.9 in 2000, compared with 23.1 in Argentina, 24.5 in Chile, and over 80 in the US (Bonisteel, 2001). If projections are confirmed, telephone density in Latin America will soon be similar to less developed European countries. However, the penetration of basic telephone services in Latin America is very uneven. Scarcely populated areas and uneven income distribution are major factors behind the relatively unbalanced diffusion rates. Areas where services are inaccessible and/or unaffordable abound. Brazil and smaller Latin American countries still have a telephone density of less than one line for each three households. But in general, the number of main lines has increased sharply, while the waiting list for new telephone lines has been shortened.

The absence of effective policies and regulations supporting the supply of telephone services for low-income populations and remote regions will jeopardize universalization. In the privatized telecommunications system, services and networks were redefined mainly in light of large user demands. Hence universal diffusion of public services is not a primary objective of the new network. Instead the network is becoming more closely attuned to the needs of a specific segment of the user community; namely, global firms.

For the corporations that the network caters to, the quality of telecommunications is essential to enabling decision-making, resource management, and e-commerce purchase and sales. Since the supply chain is becoming more international, corporations are increasing their dependency on state-of-the art and enhanced service. The availability of advanced and reliable services is becoming a key issue for location decisions. Firms' data processing services have been relocated to regions or countries endowed with more advanced telecom infrastructures. In Latin America, transnational firms are adopting the so-called concept of 'Panlatino Americanization', regionalizing their activities by function and geographical areas. Hence, an integrated regional infrastructure is essential. As telecommunications services firms become increasingly international, firms in Europe and the US engage in several acquisitions, joint ventures and strategic alliances worldwide, focusing on building a world infoway that can offer large international clients one-stop shopping.

Inclusion of advanced services like Internet in the discussion poses additional challenges to universalization. Latin America's share in world Internet hosts increased from about 0.2 per cent in 1992 to about 1 per cent in 1997. Brazil leads Latin America among worldwide hosts, ranking eleventh with 876,596 hosts in January 2001, followed by Mexico ranked fifteenth with 559,165 hosts and Argentina twenty-fifth with 270,275 (Network Wizards, 2001).

A final challenge to users and universalization are the rising costs of local telecommunications. New policies eliminated cross-subsidies and established a ceiling for tariff increases. Tariffs in Latin America are now comparable to those of Asian countries for international calls, but may be higher on local calls. International telecommunications are a more competitive market since call-back and Internet can bypass existing operators and can thereby force prices down. Tariffs are becoming more flexible as a result of increasing competition. Volume discounts for large users can shift the cost burden to the bulk of its smaller business and residential customers. There is, therefore, a need for effective policy intervention, through the public regulatory process, to remedy the disparities in access.

6.6   Conclusions

International agreements are corralling Latin America telecommunications regulations towards convergence on liberalization policies. Countries in the region have signed the WTO Reference Paper designed to curb anticompetitive practices, assure interconnectivity, provide universal service and allocate scarce resources objectively, transparently and non-discriminatorily. But multilateral agreements usually involve general concepts and principles that can be implemented in different ways, according to sector-specific commitments undertaken by each individual country. The agenda is now moving to more specific issues like interconnection fees, call-back services, allocation of scarce resources, propriety and safeguards. However, the new agenda is being negotiated bilaterally rather than multilaterally. The liberalization of the international telecommunications markets is a driving force in US trade negotiations, propelled by authorities like the FCC and USTR that push Latin American countries to comply with demands. The unequal bargaining power does not lend itself favorably towards ad hoc negotiations. It is more convenient for weaker countries to deal with multilateral agreements, where rules are more transparent, than to get involved in bilateral disputes. Touchy principles like national sovereignty may be better respected in international forums than in bilateral struggles.

The impact of liberalization in Latin American telecommunications must be analyzed according to the vested interests of different participating agents. Users in most countries benefited from the modernization wave of the 90s. Privatization and new regulation have had a positive impact on telephone line availability, and fostered technological advances. Despite the economic stagnation that is affecting most countries in the region, the telecommunications market in Latin America is growing at a faster pace than in the rest of the world. Investment has skyrocketed, as operators look for new expansion opportunities. In contrast, equipment and services producers have been negatively affected by reductions in both existing technological activities and future prospects for local participation in the global

IT industry. New operators have cut existing links with local IT technology suppliers. The decline of local participation in hardware, software, and value-added services is particularly dramatic in larger countries like Brazil and Argentina, where opportunities to create highly qualified and well-paid jobs in equipment, software and local service firms are disappearing. As a result of increasing imports, the trade balance in goods and services has deteriorated sharply. The new regulation and privatization policies have fallen short of providing adequate incentives for local technological development. Mexico strove to retain local ownership. The policy was costly, since competition in local services is still limited and tariffs are high, but it also engendered positive long-term perspectives. Telmex is now the only privately owned Latin American operator that competes in the world telecommunications market and invests in other Latin American countries. In South American countries, in contrast, privatization policies implicitly discriminated against local investors in order to attract foreign capital for short-term macro reasons.

Ownership in the hands of global players has in turn made it difficult to boost competition in local markets. The preservation of local ownership of privatized operators, as most European and Asian countries have maintained, could have been a more positive force in providing alternatives to global oligopolies. International agreements promoted liberalization, but left windows of opportunity that only a select number of countries have been able to use in a competitive fashion. In most Latin American countries, however, the local market was left in the hands of global, interlaced firms whose power at the national level is, to say the least, difficult to check. Local non-monopoly ownership in fixed lines could provide closer links with local industry and technology. Locally owned agents could play a role in global networks by expanding operations to foreign countries while containing employment generation and value-adding to the domestic market, as exemplified by Telmex. In a sector often referred to as the cutting edge of the new information economy, developing both supply and demand may prove fundamental to sustainable economic development.

Notes

* The author would like to thank Diana Tussie, Bernard Hoekman, Miguel Lengyel, Ronaldo Fiani and Alejandra Herrera for their comments and valuable suggestions and Simone Pacheco Amaral for her competent assistantship. LATN would like to acknowledge the financial support of the World Bank.

1. Avantel SA, a MCI joint-venture start-up long-distance operator in Mexico, filed a court complaint in 1998 to force the government to decide whether rival Telmex can charge fees that cost up to 70 per cent of its revenue. It is seeking to speed up an answer to petitions that have been sitting before the Federal Telecommunications Commission, two of them for more than a year. Avantel wants to know if Telmex can charge other carriers for occupying space at its switching centers where calls from

one company to another are connected. The company also questioned whether the government's rules apply to certain satellite telephone link-ups. The goal was to clarify with Mexican regulators the fees Telmex charges for 'interconnection'.

2. The FCC approved Telmex's proposal to reduce the settlement rates to 19 ¢/min from 39.5 ¢ by 2000. However, the agency rejected interim settlement rates of 37.5 ¢ for 1998 and 34.5 ¢ for 1999.

Part III

The Management of Competition and Conflict

7
Policy Competition for Foreign Direct Investment

*Daniel Chudnovsky and Andrés López**

7.1 Introduction

Fierce competition has arisen among developing as well as developed countries to attract increasing volumes of foreign direct investment (FDI). This new attitude in developing countries is part of the broad change towards market-friendly policies, as barriers and regulations are dismantled and intense competition for FDI is taking place at national as well as sub-national levels. This chapter addresses the global and regional dimensions of such competition. Section 7.1 addresses the main issues regarding policy competition for FDI. Section 7.2 describes the logic of the competition and the existing empirical evidence on its effects. Section 7.3 deals with the existing multilateral disciplines on investments. Section 7.4 considers the regional dimension of FDI policy competition, analyzing the cases of the European Union and Mercosur. Section 7.5 presents concluding remarks.

7.2 Policy competition for FDI: empirical evidence and policy debates

The inflow of market-seeking investments is largely determined by the size, growth rate and perspectives of the host market. Natural resources and/ or labor force are relevant in resource-seeking, export-oriented investments. However, multinational corporations (MNCs) seem to be increasingly involved in so-called 'strategic-asset' seeking investments, in which the relevant locational advantages are related to the physical, communications and technological infrastructure, the skills of the labor force, and so on. Economic and political stability and a sound regulatory framework seem to be necessary but not sufficient preconditions to guarantee a steady flow of FDI when the above-mentioned locational advantages are lacking (see UNCTAD, 1992, and Jun and Singh, 1996).

There is a broad consensus that incentives do not rank high among the main determinants of FDI inflows, as they are essentially unable to attract investments to regions or countries which lack other location advantages such as an attractive domestic market, natural resources, or a skilled labor force. Nonetheless, when potential locations share common 'fundamental' attributes, incentives may influence investment decisions. Thus, incentives attract investment to specific sectors, regions or countries where it otherwise might not have occurred (Aranda and Sauvant, 1996, and UNCTAD, 1994).

The main theoretical rationale for investment incentives is to correct the failure of markets to reflect spillovers. If an investment creates spillovers that cannot be fully captured by the investing firm, a gap emerges between private and social returns. Incentives venture to close that gap. Incentives can also be granted to offset the effects of other policy interventions such as performance requirements (PRs) which MNCs must accept as a gateway to invest in a certain host country. Moreover, for countries in which there is a dearth of FDI, incentives can be a way to attract 'pioneer' investors. If this policy succeeds, a sort of 'demonstration effect' could arise, fostering additional, self-sustaining FDI flows. PRs such as local content, export commitments, research and development (R&D) expenditures, and job creation have been extensively, though not exclusively, used by developing country governments. In principle, they are designed to ensure that the operations of foreign firms are in tune with the policy objectives of the host country.

Incentives as well as PRs are primarily defended by those who consider that market forces do not lead to the socially desirable amount or composition of FDI, do not prevent FDI from having deleterious effects on host countries' development objectives, and/or fail to align private and social returns of investments. In turn, orthodoxy questions the efficacy of incentives and is generally hostile towards PRs. Incentives could be useful to promote regional development, to correct market failures, or to realize positive externalities, but in most cases they are seen by the orthodoxy as a 'second best' solution. The orthodox criticism is even more virulent regarding sector- or firm-specific incentives policies, as these entail a 'distortion' of the resource allocation that 'free market forces' would produce. The World Trade Organization (WTO) has accepted incentives only under very stringent conditions to correct market failures, such as when a country is trying to deal with structural problems in a certain region. Incentives are also seen as an important source of distortions in the international allocation of investment resources. In this regard, the orthodox view argues that developing countries are at a disadvantage when investment incentives are in place, as they skew investment and trade in favor of countries with 'deep pockets' to afford such incentives. Even if an adequate incentive could be granted, its costs would surely surpass potential benefits due to the lack of detailed knowledge, the burden of monitoring tasks and the scope of rent-seeking activities. In turn, PRs are seen as 'second best' solutions, whose outcome is uncertain and which lead to rent-seeking behavior. In general, orthodox models tend to underline that PRs are welfare-reducing. It has also been stated that the effectiveness of PRs has declined. As foreign affiliates of MNCs become more oriented towards global or regional markets and as the number of countries eager to attract FDI grows, MNCs are less tolerant of requirements. In this scenario, PRs may be at best ineffective and at worst counter-productive, since FDI would prefer countries in which such requirements are not pushed (OECD, 1998b).

These arguments assume 'perfect competition'. When imperfect competition assumptions are introduced, the outcome of policy measures such as incentives or PRs is indeterminate: 'the prospect of capturing a share of the rents and externalities from the operations of international investors... raises the stakes for those who are successful in attracting (or holding) them and imposes large opportunity costs on those who are not successful or do not take part in the competition' (Moran, 1998: 3). In light of this, developing countries' inability to design and enforce activist FDI-related policies and the real threat posed by rent-seeking activities call for the strengthening of checks and balances rather than a ban on public intervention. The empirical evidence remains inconclusive. There have been failures as well as successes, which suggests that the outcome depends on a set of institutional, political and economic conditions. Once perfect competition assumptions are lifted and the lessons of experience are taken into account, there are circumstances that may justify investment incentive programs:

- in the presence of underdeveloped or backward regions or regions that have high unemployment rates and which, by themselves, are not able to attract the investment flows that are needed to foster development;
- when governments are interested in promoting investments in specific sectors, or export-oriented investments or when they need to increase the spillovers of the investments; and
- in the presence of a discrepancy between investors and host country development objectives.

Risk of political capture of the incentives programs deserves special attention. The difficulties of monitoring and enforcing incentives are well known, especially in Latin American countries. Governments seldom perform detailed studies on the costs and benefits of incentive packages. Reasons are politically motivated, as governments tend to search for investments to bring new jobs to their countries/regions that would otherwise go to other countries/regions if incentives were absent. In this scenario, the danger of bidding wars in which the costs of incentives exceed the social benefits for host countries must be seriously evaluated.

The global scenario as well as the pattern of trade and investment flows must also be considered. Geographic mobility makes regulation more difficult than in the past. In turn, the technological gap between domestic firms and MNCs, especially in high-tech activities, seems to have expanded. Except for the few countries that have unique location advantages like the domestic Chinese market, stringent PRs could be innocuous or even have a counter-productive effect by diverting investments to countries without such requirements.

Policy competition for FDI: the issues

All told, most governments appear to be persuaded that incentives have a role to play. Furthermore, the evidence clearly shows that a greater number of governments are involved in investment competition than in the 1980s and that the overall 'cost-per-job' of the typical incentive package has risen (see Aranda and Sauvant, 1996; OECD, 1998a, and Oman, 1999).[1] This competition is mostly intra-regional, since governments seek to compete with neighboring countries for investments that are already, in principle, destined for their region. It occurs not only among national governments but also among sub-national governments, which now play an increasingly central role.

Investors often define a 'short-list' of locations and negotiate conditions and possible incentives with each of the competing governments. Investors may openly foster competition among authorities, or even 'ask for their best offers' before making the final site selection (Oman, 1999), feeding the bidding wars. There are three major classifications of incentives: financial, fiscal and indirect.

- *Financial incentives* including transfer of funds directly to foreign investors by the host government such as investment grants, subsidized credits and loan guarantees.
- *Fiscal incentives* including tax holidays, tax rebates, accelerated depreciation allowances, exemptions from import duties or duty drawbacks, specific deductions from gross earnings for income-tax purposes and deductions from social security contributions.
- *Indirect incentives* including subsidized land and dedicated infrastructure, preferential access to government contracts, special regulatory treatment and granting of monopolistic positions (Aranda and Sauvant, 1996, and WTO, 1996).

A large and growing number of countries target incentives to attract investment into specific types of activities or areas. These targets include:

- specific sectors such as high-tech and high-value-added manufacturing and infrastructure;
- specific regions with low GDP per capita and high unemployment;
- export-oriented investments;
- attraction of MNC regional headquarters; and
- specific MNC activities that generate spillovers or contribute to solve certain social problems like R&D, labor training and job creation.

Though governments do not tend to differentiate between domestic and foreign investment in the design of incentives, there are important exceptions to this rule. Moreover, foreign investors tend to make more extensive use of incentives designed to attract 'mobile' investment projects. Consequently, any debate on FDI-related policies must take into account that incentives exist, that most governments apply them, and that they are here to stay, at least in the foreseeable future. Moreover, contrary to presumptions, developed countries' resistance to abandoning incentives is at least as strong as that of developing countries.

Oman (1999) suggests two possible outcomes regarding policy competition for FDI. The first is based on a 'positive-sum game', according to which competition produces net benefits for investors and host economies alike. The reasoning is that governments know the high priority investors attach to the 'fundamentals' and thus seek to improve domestic supplies of human capital and infrastructure as well as to ensure political and macroeconomic stability. A corollary to this hypothesis is that intensified competition to attract FDI leads governments to 'do a better job on the fundamentals'. Hence, in addition to inducing governments to take actions that enhance growth and productivity levels (even in the absence of additional FDI), those actions are likely to increase the global supply of FDI. The opposite scenario is the 'negative-sum-game' in which benefits tend to be offset by a sort of 'prisoner's dilemma'. Hence, as competition heats up, governments engage in costly bidding wars that drive the level of public subsidies offered to investors to socially unjustifiable levels. There are many other potentially negative consequences of bidding wars:

- public funds dedicated to incentives could be used more productively to finance public goods such as human capital formation and infrastructure;
- incentives programs place already established investors at a competitive disadvantage *vis-à-vis* the 'newcomers' receiving the incentives. This may even induce 'round-tripping' whereby investments are made abroad in order to return as a 'new' foreign investment;
- potential investors may perceive extensive incentives as unsustainable, reducing rather than enhancing their propensity to invest in the economy; and
- competition may negatively affect environmental and labor standards.

In sum, investors would be the immediate beneficiaries of bidding wars, at the expense of governments and host economies. While governments have a collective interest in refraining from such bidding wars, they get entangled out of fear that FDI will be diverted to more generous countries.

A distinction can be drawn between 'incentives-based' and 'rules-based' competition. The former refers mainly to the fiscal, financial and indirect incentives already mentioned, which may be granted automatically or discretionally. Discretion may be seen as a necessary condition for a successful negotiation with investors that ensures an efficient targeting of incentives; yet, it also reduces transparency. In the case that incentives are linked directly to PRs, they may be seen as a compensation for their disincentive effect. Some instruments not originally designed to influence investment flows may have significant effects on investor decisions. This is the case of antidumping measures, rules of origin, national standards, and so on, and the so-called investment-related trade measures which include tariffs, quotas, and export programs. In turn, rules-based competition may range from changes in environmental and labor standards to the signing of regional-integration treaties, the tightening of intellectual property rights protection, the strengthening of judicial systems, the establishment of Export Processing Zones (EPZs), the privatization of state-owned enterprises and the wholesale liberalization of trade and investment policies.

Empirical evidence

The evidence from the OECD Development Center multicountry study (Oman, 1999) does not support the extreme hypotheses of either the positive-sum or negative-sum game. Regarding the former, policy competition for FDI has not been found to be a primary determinant of positive government actions such as investing in education and infrastructure. Nonetheless, some evidence exists that competition for FDI has helped to foster 'better government' in many developing countries. It also has, in some cases, contributed to enhancing the local supply of infrastructure and education.

Moreover, the evidence does not lend strong support to the view that competition for FDI is unleashing uncontrolled worldwide bidding wars that drive investment incentives above socially justifiable levels. In addition, 'races to the bottom' have not been found in environmental or labor standards, though the danger of such 'races' does exist. In fact, the evidence shows that competition for FDI may exert some upward pressure on those standards, especially in the case of investments in relatively 'clean' and knowledge or skill-intensive manufacturing and service industries. This statement must be qualified given the difficulty of properly assessing the costs of incentives and the benefits of investments as governments are generally reluctant to give information on these issues.

Still, bidding wars obviously take place and it is fairly probable that policy competition has allowed investors to increase their share of the benefits accruing from their investments. Some incentive regimes designed to stimulate the social and economic development of poorer or disadvantaged regions have fallen short of this objective. For example, in OECD countries regional-development policies may have been co-opted for the pursuit of policy competition that does not principally benefit the poorest segments of the population or those most hit by unemployment. In contrast, in developing and emerging economies some evidence of policy competition benefiting poorer areas may be found, as in the northeast of Brazil. There is also evidence of policy competition favoring large firms at the expense of smaller firms. At the same time, the lack of transparency of many deals has created possibilities for corruption and rent seeking.

Competition for FDI is intense and still growing; however, new peaks are not expected for three reasons:

- the upsurge in global FDI flows has been a stimulus for, rather than an effect of, competition;
- most countries have already completed the shift away from inward-oriented and often FDI-hostile strategies; and
- incentives-based competition tends to be highly concentrated in the auto industry. It is unlikely that in the near future investment levels in this industry will match those experienced in the last two decades, since there is a significant worldwide productive over-capacity in this sector.

Caution is required, nonetheless, on three fronts. The first one is transparency. Concretely, the question is how to ensure the accountability of government officials involved in the negotiation of incentives. The issue of transparency also points to the need to monitor the incentives. The second front is what Oman defines as 'bounded competition', which means that policy competition is disciplined by a regulatory framework which sets rules for the granting of aid and establishes procedures and sanctions in order to guarantee their enforcement. According to Oman (1999), bounded competition should be the objective of any regional or multilateral arrangement on FDI, since an outright suppression of competition is not feasible. Finally, developing countries, whose financial resources are often scarce, should move from incentives-based towards rules-based means of attracting FDI, while maintaining or strengthening their defense of labor rights and the environment. In this context, 'rules-based' competition may have some advantages over incentives:

- benefits may extend not only to investors but to the society at large except when environmental or labor standards are lowered;
- more stable, predictable and transparent rules for investors and governments alike are established; and
- room for bribery and corruption is minimized.

7.3   Multilateral efforts

Investment incentives have scarcely been touched by the 'patchwork' of international rules regarding investment except for selected PRs covered by the WTO. The main international rules on investments are the so-called bilateral investment treaties (BITs), which are mostly limited to the protection of investments once they are made. The number of BITs reached 1513 by the end of 1997, of which 249 were between developing countries. Apart from BITs, there are numerous bilateral treaties aimed at avoiding double taxation (UNCTAD, 1998). Some follow the US matrix guaranteeing the application of national treatment (NT) and most favored nation (MFN) at both pre- and post-establishment stages. Others are similar to the European model, which adopts the more traditional criterion of granting NT and MFN rights only at the post-establishment stage. The US matrix usually contains other 'high-level' disciplines not covered by the European model, such as PRs and entry of key personnel.

The proliferation of BITs does not lead to a multilateral framework on investments *per se*, since coverage and discipline levels are very heterogeneous. In the multilateral realm, various Uruguay Round Agreements (URAs) addressed the issue and WTO Working Groups have been established to deal with trade, investments, and competition policy. The OECD has also pursued some multilateral investment disciplines, but these instruments have not introduced 'high-level' disciplines, as some are non-binding and most lack effective dispute settlement procedures. These deficits led to an OECD initiative to launch the Multilateral Agreement on Investments (MAI).

The URAs and the WTO

Five of the URAs contain provisions on investments: the Agreement on Trade-Related Investment Measures (TRIMs), the General Agreement on Trade in Services (GATS), the Agreement on Trade-Related Aspects on Intellectual Property Rights (TRIPs), the Agreement on Subsidies and Countervailing Measures (ASCMs) and the Understanding on Rules and Procedures Governing the Settlement of Disputes (DSU). The basic telecommunications agreement and the financial service agreement signed in 1997 extended multilateral rules on investment to two sectors of considerable economic significance.

Since investment was seen as a means of delivering services, GATS covers a wide range of investment issues in the service sectors. With the exception of the prohibition of measures 'which restrict or require specific types of legal entity or joint venture through which a service supplier may supply a service' (Article XVI.2.e), GATS does not include any provisions regarding incentives or PRs. Though TRIPs does not contain provisions regarding investment incentives or PRs, it was supposed to create an environment conducive to investment by enhancing the protection of intellectual property rights.

The TRIMs agreement does not deal with investment *per se* but only with those PRs directly related to trade. The list of prohibited measures includes: (i) local content requirements; (ii) trade-balancing requirements; (iii) foreign exchange-balancing requirements; and (iv) those which restrict the export of products, whether specified in terms of the particular type, volume or value of products or of a proportion of volume or value of local production. Prohibited practices include those that are mandatory in nature and those with which compliance is necessary in order to obtain an advantage. A five-year transition period ending in December 2000 was established in order to eliminate prohibited TRIMs in developing countries, which can be extended if developing countries find difficulties. Nevertheless, some TRIMs remained untouched by the agreement's prohibitions. The deadline has in fact been extended in many Latin American countries, to benefit the automobile sector (see case studies in Vol. II). Non-prohibited TRIMs include, for example, export requirements, product mandating requirements, foreign exchange restrictions, technology transfer requirements, licensing requirements, remittance restrictions and local equity requirements (Low and Subramanian, 1995).

Finally, the ASCMs deems some financial and fiscal incentives inconsistent with WTO rules (see Tortora and Tussie, Chapter 9). Fiscal incentives would generally be considered subsidies, since they fall within the definition of government revenue otherwise due that is forgone or not collected, such as fiscal incentives in the form of tax credits. Financial incentives would meet the ASCMs definition of a government practice involving a direct transfer of funds such as grants, loans and equity infusion. Furthermore, at least some kinds of indirect incentives would appear to be subsidies; for example, the provision of land and infrastructure at less than market prices would appear to fall within the definition of a government providing goods or services other than general infrastructure, or purchasing goods (WTO, 1996). Nonetheless, the thrust of the ASCMs is toward trade in goods and, as such, may not be easily applied to investment incentives.

Although the ASCMs requires WTO members to notify their subsidy programs, in practice there have been delays and some countries have failed with the notification obligation or have claimed to have no subsidy programs. A bigger problem is that outside the EU, many countries (including the US and Canada) have provided little or no information for sub-national governments. Moreover, it is not clear how rules are going to work in practice with sub-national incentives, especially regarding who should be the complaining party. A case of subsidies for Mercedes Benz investment in Alabama in 1993, as analyzed by Thomas (1998), exemplifies the ambiguity over which party should raise a complaint. In this particular case, the US would not complain about its own subsidy, and the individual US states do not have the standing to do so. The EU would presumably not complain since an EU firm is the beneficiary. Finally, Japan might not complain because many Japanese firms have benefited from similar subsidies in the US. It is easy to think of a similar situation happening within Mercosur, since Argentina and Brazil are both federal countries.

In addition to the above multilateral provisions, the Singapore Ministerial Conference in December 1996 established a Working Group to examine the relationship between trade and investment and another which would study the interaction between trade and competition policy and anti-competitive practices, the latter being of special interest for developing countries. Both Working Groups are conducting an 'educational' project, but the issue of investment will probably be included in the WTO agenda. The advantages of the WTO over other fora such as the OECD lie in its global coverage and its dispute settlement system. Nonetheless, some developing countries fear that the dispute-settlement mechanisms of WTO will tilt the balance in favor of MNCs.

The Multilateral Agreement on Investments

The OECD Ministers decided to launch negotiations on an MAI in May 1995 in order to set high standards for the treatment and protection of investments. The rationale for doing so was that regional agreements were necessarily partial in their geographic coverage and that existing instruments were neither binding nor comprehensive and lacked effective dispute settlement procedures. The MAI was a comprehensive agreement, covering all economic sectors, with a broad definition of 'investment', including FDI, portfolio investments, real estate investments and rights under contract. Unlike most of the existing BITs, the MAI was to provide guarantees at the pre-establishment stage and sought to cover measures taken at all levels of government (central, state, provincial and local). The MAI adopted the principles of NT and of MFN and was to include provisions dealing with issues such as transparency, free transfer of investment-related payments, entry and stay of key personnel, expropriations and dispute resolutions. It applied a 'top-down' approach under which the only exceptions permitted were to be those enumerated in 'negative lists' subject to progressive liberalization.

The MAI sought to go further than existing rules on PRs by extending disciplines first to services and then to requirements that distort investment flows even if the investment in question is unrelated to international trade. Some PRs would be allowed, subject to the condition of NT, in connection with: the location of production, the provision of particular services, the training or employment of workers, the construction of particular facilities and the conduct of R&D.

Despite these inroads, investment incentives did not feature prominently. Even if the MAI had been signed, it would not have contained more than an exhortation for transparency, NT and MFN clauses, consultation procedures and a 'built-in' agenda. According to one of its negotiators, key OECD countries argued that MAI should not seek to discipline investment incentives, while others were proposing the creation of new rules (Ahnlid, 1997). Since a requirement to extend incentives to all eligible foreign investors might increase the cost of incentive programs, some members of the OECD argued that the application of non-discrimination principles would probably lead to indirect discipline on investment incentives. However, other countries completely opposed the introduction of rules, arguing that investment incentives were a legitimate and useful policy tool. Some countries in this group sought country-specific reservations from MFN and NT. Even countries that promoted disciplines acknowledged that incentives could be relevant in certain circumstances, such as in the promotion of regional, social, environmental and R&D objectives. The fact that incentives are often granted sub-nationally also seems to have contributed to the reluctance of some participants. In addition, a number of countries argued that tax incentives should be excluded from MAI. Some countries were also concerned with the fact that any additional disciplines on investment incentives in the MAI could divert FDI to non-members and place MAI members at a disadvantage in their ability to retain or attract investment. In fact, although a number of possible options for disciplines were proposed, including a ban on so-called positive discrimination (that is, better treatment for foreign investors than for domestic investors) and an agreement on caps for certain investment incentives, they were not seriously discussed (Ahnlid, 1997).

Though the MAI was negotiated among OECD countries, it was conceived as an open agreement which many developing countries were expected to join. In fact, five non-OECD countries – Argentina, Brazil, Chile, Hong Kong and the Slovak Republic – joined the negotiations as observers, and expressed their intention to eventually join the agreement. However, there is no clear-cut position among developing countries on if (and how) investment incentives should be disciplined. On one hand, some influential developing countries are reluctant to yield their right to PRs and to incentives geared to attract the specific types of FDI best suited for their development needs (see Ganesan, 1998). On the other hand, other developing countries are in favor of imposing international disciplines, especially taking into consideration the intensive use of incentives by developed countries, diverting flows that could go towards developing countries in a 'level playing field'.

These differences of opinion proved detrimental to the OECD MAI proposals, and negotiations were formally abandoned in April 1998. The failure of the WTO Seattle Ministerial Meeting has delayed but not necessarily eliminated the possibility of a multilateral agreement on investments. In any case, investment will surely be one of the key issues in any future multilateral negotiations.

7.4 The regional dimension

Most competition to attract investments occurs within regions, not between them (Oman, 1999). Thus, any international cooperation among governments to help limit the potential damage caused by competition to attract FDI would probably be best envisaged at the regional level rather than the global level. Nonetheless, this being true for most projects, globalization allows increased mobility of investments; high-tech activities are mostly footloose, as illustrated by the case of the Intel investment in Costa Rica, for which the original 'short-list' included 13 Asian and Latin American countries (Spar, 1998).

The European Union (EU) remains the regional agreement with the most comprehensive treatment of incentives, through provisions contained in the Treaty of Rome. These disciplines could provide a model for other regional arrangements, including Mercosur.

The case of the EU

Article 92 of the Treaty of Rome led to a general ban on subsidies, or 'state aids', in the EU common market. Within the EU legal framework, 'aid' means any advantage conferred to a firm by public authorities, without payment or against a payment which only minimally corresponds to the figure at which the advantage can be valued. State aid may consist of subsidies, interest-free loans, relief from taxes, supply of goods or services on preferential terms, and so on. State aid to be controlled by the European Commission (EC) must be distinguished from general economic support measures, which apply across the board to all firms in all sectors of economic activity. A contribution confined strictly to offsetting an objective disadvantage imposed on the recipient does not fall under Article 92 jurisdiction. Neither do state aids below ECU 100,000 over three years. Even above that threshold, the effect of the aid on competition must be shown (EC, 1997).

The general ban on 'competition-distorting' support notwithstanding, Article 92 states some circumstances in which aid is considered compatible with the common market. Support covered by exemptions provided by Article 92 are monitored and controlled by the EC through a vetting system. Member states are required to inform the EC of any plans to grant aid, and to obtain authorization before putting the plan into effect. Countries must apply for authorization to apply aid intended to promote the economic development in 'least-favored' regions (Article 93.3.a) and 'development areas' (Article 92.3.c). These exemptions only allow aid towards initial investment, except in backward regions where aid towards continued operation may be approved. 'Least-favored' areas are located in regions with an abnormally low standard of living (per capita GDP of 75 per cent or less of the EU average) and serious underemployment. To qualify for aid under 3.c, per capita GDP or gross value added at factor cost (GVA) of the 'developing area' must be at least 15 per cent below the respective member state's average, or structural unemployment must be at least 10 per cent above the member state's average. That figure is then adjusted by reference to an EU average, in such a way that the better the position of the region under consideration compared with the EU average, the greater disparity there must be between it and the national average in order to justify the granting of aid. At a second stage, results of the first phase are corrected, within limits, to take into account other relevant indicators such as unemployment trends and structures, employment development, net migration, geographic situation or population density.

There are quantitative limits to regional aid. For 'least-favored' regions aid cannot exceed 75 per cent net grant equivalent of initial investment. For 'development regions' it cannot exceed 30 per cent, and, depending on the category, it often must be lower. In fact, the quantitative ceilings vary from region to region, and the 75 and 30 per cent limits apply only to regions where development or employment problems are most serious. A single investment can only receive both regional aid and other regionally differentiated aid provided the sum of the regional aid and the regional component of the other aid do not exceed the above-mentioned ceilings. In turn, there is no threshold on national spending on state aid. In fact, data showed a decline in the average amount awarded in most EU countries in the 1990s. Notably, award rates are markedly below the ceilings, and government expenditures on incentives have been declining in most countries (Oman, 1999).

Direct financial incentives are the leading incentive in the EU, of which national authorities are mostly in charge. Indirect financial contributions are mostly granted at the local level. Local assistance plays a key role in the later stages of inward investment promotion (Bachtler, 1996), usually taking the form of training and employment assistance, property concessions and preparation of potential investment sites. Western European countries do not explicitly promote FDI over domestic projects, yet in practice most incentives are granted to foreign investors. For example, roughly half of all regional development aid in Great Britain went to FDI between 1984 and 1995 and nearly 80 per cent of all greenfield FDI in Ireland received regional aid according to data for the late 1980s.

The EC has taken a number of steps in order to tighten its controls (Aranda and Sauvant, 1996), leading towards greater homogeneity in the forms of assistance offered across the EU. Aid is largely directed towards initial investment or job creation throughout the region. Moreover, the poorer regions are authorized to offer higher levels of assistance than wealthier ones, which is reinforced by the EC's ability to forbid regional aid that would relocate an investment from a less prosperous to a more prosperous region.

All in all, the EU approach to disciplining incentives appears to have worked reasonably well. It provides a regulatory framework which grants some measure of autonomy to governments that wish to offer incentives, but it also confers some autonomy to the supervisory body and establishes procedures for enforcement and sanctions, backed by provisions for judicial review. However, the aid programs have actually reinforced rather than reduced existing differences in locational 'attractiveness', since countries authorized to offer the highest award rates tend to be those that most lack the resources to do so.[2] It has also been observed that the decrease in aid in less developed countries has been proportionately greater than in more prosperous states and that several advanced areas of the EU offer regional spending that is competitive (on a per-capita assisted basis) with that of poorer European regions (Thomas, 1998). This has led some authors to suggest that it is by no means clear that regional incentive policies have been able to achieve their basic objective of stimulating development in less developed regions, when considered at a European level. In fact, the evidence suggests that competition over incentives has favored the more prosperous countries (Oman, 1999).

One reason may be that the EC addresses its requests for information and its decisions on state aid to national governments, though regional and local authorities increasingly deal directly with investors. Since national authorities have little motivation to force sub-national governments to respond to EC inquiries and decisions, local and regional governments can evade scrutiny. Also the EC may ultimately lack the political independence and the administrative authority that it would need to impose its views on EU governments. France and Germany have been able to negotiate major increases in the population ceilings that the EC intended to set, and then designate the areas eligible for assistance largely on their own terms. These tensions have led to tighter aid guidelines to ensure both the reduction of regional disparities and genuine support for the less-favored regions. The reduction in aid size for large firms is of particular importance to offset the potential for regional aid to induce firms to relocate. Moreover, the guidelines stipulate that the aided investments and jobs must remain in the region for at least five years. An amendment to the method for choosing regions under Article 92 has also been introduced. Regarding large projects, the new framework introduces rules aimed at reducing any competition-distorting effects by lowering the aid ceiling compared with the maximum intensity ceiling authorized in the region. On the other hand, new rules on investment-linked employment aid have also been introduced to enable member states to provide more support for labor-intensive investments.

The case of Mercosur

Mercosur has been remarkably successful at increasing intra-regional trade and attracting FDI. The participation of Mercosur member countries in world FDI inflows increased from 1.4 per cent in 1984–89 to 5.9 per cent in 1997–99. Interest in attracting investment flows has engendered competition mostly at regional or sectoral levels. Controversial cases like the automobile industry have led to arguments in favor of disciplines on incentives.

The Mercosur legal framework for investment lies in two protocols signed in 1994: the Colonia Protocol for Reciprocal Protection and Promotion of Investments (called the 'intra-zone' protocol) and the Colonia Protocol on Promotion and Protection of Investments from Non-Member States (termed the 'extra-zone' protocol). The intra-zone protocol guarantees that member states will grant NT and MFN rights not only at the post-establishment stage, but also at the pre-establishment and establishment stages. PRs such as export commitments and local purchase of goods and services are forbidden, but investment incentives are not mentioned. The extra-zone protocol confers foreign investors NT and MFN rights only at the post-establishment stage. Discrimination in favor of investors from non-member states is prohibited. Despite a declaration of principles regarding the need to establish a basic framework to avoid the distortion of investment flows, nothing in this protocol effectively prevents member states from granting unilateral investment incentives.

There are wide disparities between the leading partners in Mercosur, Argentina and Brazil. Brazilian sub-national governments have significant autonomy in fiscal matters, while in Argentina the federal government has failed to apply ceilings (Motta Veiga and Iglesias, 1997, and Motta Veiga, 1999). In practice, a fiscal war among Brazilian states broke out. Significant fiscal decentralization took place during the 1980s, which allowed sub-national governments to develop programs to stimulate new investments that bore fruit when macroeconomic adjustment was achieved inducing a new cycle of productive investments. Brazil thus returned to its position as a key FDI host country.

In Argentina, a sort of 'rules-based' competition prevailed during 1991–2001, based on strict legal protection of property rights, predictability, and the adoption of market- and investor-friendly policies. Incentives-based competition only surfaced in an automobile regime established in 1991, which included investment incentives and PRs for local producers, and a mining regime adopted in 1993, including a 30-year guarantee of no tax increase for investors. Privatizations also had some specific features geared to attract foreign investors. FDI showed a strong response to these incentives, but was also attracted by macroeconomic stability and the growth of the domestic and regional market. Sub-national policy competition for investments remained relatively insignificant during the early 1990s. This situation changed by 1996–97, when the 'fiscal war' among the Brazilian states began to raise concerns that the lack of regulations was counter-productive. Buenos Aires, the most affluent Argentine province, announced a reduction in some provincial taxes for new investments in response to Brazilian incentives (De la Guardia, 1997). Though the limited fiscal attributions of the Argentine provinces kept sub-national 'fiscal wars' under relatively low ceilings, there is significant anecdotal evidence showing an increase in the use of investment incentives in the late 1990s. This tendency was reinforced after the Brazilian devaluation in February 1999. In that year, the governor of Córdoba, the second richest Argentine province, announced that he was ready to offer the best bid for an investment Volkswagen was to make within Mercosur.[3] By the end of 1999 widespread concern prevailed as a number of firms decided to relocate plants due to inviting incentives in Brazil.

Real bidding wars among Brazilian state governments have taken place.[4] Lack of transparency is the most questioned aspect of this phenomenon. There is also evidence that policy competition has led to the removal of laws or norms that companies considered too stringent. This regulatory derogation could explain the unequal application of national environmental and labor standards amongst regions and states. The federal government also took initiatives of its own as exemplified by the automobile regime in 1995, in order to compete with Argentina, which was blamed for diverting investments destined for Mercosur. The federal government has also avoided the control of policy competition at the sub-national level. In fact, when Rio Grande do Sul decided to reduce the incentives to Ford and General Motors, the federal government granted Ford incentives for a plant in Bahia and announced that fiscal incentives would be available for all firms wishing to produce in the backward zones of the north, north-east and middle-east of Brazil.

Federal incentives were aimed at obtaining a trade surplus while sub-national incentives were mostly concerned with 'demonstration effects' to attract further investments and with employment generation. Objectives such as fostering R&D activities or other 'spillover-generating' activities have been mostly absent both at national as well as sub-national levels (Laplane *et al.*, 2001). According to Motta Veiga and Iglesias (1997), for example, the sub-national dispute to attract automobile industry investments has wasted or misallocated funds and will lead to future idle capacity. Although no clear evidence exists, it seems that assemblers and their main suppliers made their investment decisions independent of subsidies. Nevertheless, the context has forced modernization within sub-national governments in order to enhance local competitiveness. Hence, state governments are learning not only how to negotiate incentives but also how to help investors identify investment opportunities (Motta Veiga and Iglesias, 1997).

A Working Group was established in 2000 to analyze investment incentives in place in Mercosur countries and evaluate feasible alternatives for harmonization. It can be expected that at least more transparency should result from these initiatives, which could be the first step in designing a framework to monitor and control policy competition for investments within Mercosur.

Studies about the impact of FDI on Argentina and Brazil have raised issues which call for more activist FDI-related policies (Chudnovsky and López, 1997, 1998, 2001; Laplane and Sarti, 1997, and Laplane *et al.*, 2001). First, not only have exports by foreign firms increased more than exports by domestic firms in Argentina and Brazil, but the import coefficient of foreign firms also seems generally larger than their export coefficients. Specifically, MNCs tend to have huge deficits in their trade relations with developed countries. The contribution of FDI to the growing merchandise trade deficit in both Argentina and Brazil has thus become a critical issue. While this situation may change in the future, so far only those MNCs engaged in resource-based investments are clearly net exporters. Second, technological spillovers seem to be minimal. MNCs do not devote significant resources to R&D activities, and have seldom created technological networks with suppliers, customers, competitors or research institutions. Moreover, in the 1990s MNC affiliates apparently destroyed links with domestic suppliers more often than they created new links, since trade liberalization allowed a higher foreign content of local production, *pari passu* with the trend towards a greater reliance on 'global suppliers' visible, for example, in the automobile industry (see case studies, Vol. II). Last but not least, the implications of investment incentives for competition policy have yet to be assessed. In the EU, the competition policy directorate decides whether a proposed incentive may or may not be granted under agreed disciplines. In turn, the necessary linkage of international investment and competition policy issues has been stressed especially by developing countries, which argue that an international agreement should cover international restrictive business practices.

Mercosur member states signed a Protocol for the Defense of Competition in 1996 but congressional approval is pending to make it enforceable. The Protocol provides mechanisms to curb business anti-competitive practices; calls for the convergence of domestic competition laws; and provides an agenda for surveying public policies that limit, restrict, falsify, or distort competition conditions and affect trade among member countries. The Protocol calls upon member countries to undertake preparations to set common standards and mechanisms (Tavares de Araujo, Chapter 8). Argentina's enactment of a new Defense of Competition Law in 1999, which aligns the Argentine competition policy regime with that of Brazil, may help harmonization in this area. Both the Protocol for the Defense of Competition and the mentioned working group could form a basis from which to build regional disciplines on investment incentives. Thus the task of introducing these disciplines should be closely related to the defense of competition, both at the national as well as the regional level, following the experience of the EU.

7.5   Concluding remarks and policy suggestions

Arguments against investment incentives can not be dismissed; still most countries are reluctant to give them up. Developed countries' interests are focused not on limiting policy competition, but rather on procuring higher protection standards and rights for their firms investing abroad. In fact, incentives-based competition for investments has been growing in recent years, and, contrary to what one might presume, developed countries are the main players. Without multilateral or regional disciplines, countries seeking higher inflows of FDI are thus obliged to engage in incentives-based competition, especially for investments in high-tech sectors or the automobile industry. Beyond this competition other arguments may justify the employment of incentives and PRs: FDI inflows may not always reach the socially desirable volume or composition and host countries may fail to reap potential spillovers from MNCs.

This is not to say that the social benefits of these policies always surpass their costs. Resulting bidding wars may be far from socially beneficial and incentives may open the door to rent seeking and bribery. These objections call for a better design, monitoring and enforcement of incentives and PRs and for a cautious approach that emphasizes reaping more externalities and attracting specific types of FDI, rather than restricting entry. More broadly, policy competition for FDI may have some positive externalities, especially when competition is rules-based. Countries have learned that investments are mostly attracted to countries with macroeconomic stability, high rates of economic growth, well-functioning legal systems, and so on. Moreover, a key element to attracting FDI is the magnitude and quality of what have been termed 'created assets', which are more prone to attract high-quality investments. Thus positive externalities will arise if governments are impelled to compete on the basis of the quality of their institutions, human resources, infrastructure and so on.

This does not suggest, however, that free-for-all competition should be unleashed. In the case of regional agreements, the need to harmonize FDI-related policies is compelling. Even if full harmonization should prove impossible, any attempt in that direction may contribute to avoiding diversion of regional investment flows, limiting resources devoted to bidding wars and increasing the spillovers to be reaped from MNCs.

Developing countries may very well lose the battle for investments if competition is left to run its course. Thus efforts should be made to increase transparency and limit location incentives at the multilateral level. Developing countries should also try to constrain the use of other instruments that, in a disguised fashion, are employed by developed countries to retain investments, such as rules of origin and antidumping regulations (see Tortora and Tussie, Chapter 9, for effects of antidumping on FDI). Although it could be demonstrated that the welfare of not only developing countries, but of perhaps the entire world, would be enhanced by creating a 'slightly sloped' playing field in favor of developing countries, global welfare would perhaps be better served if a 'level' playing field were achieved. In that scenario, developed countries would be forced to abandon or seriously restrict disguised protectionist practices and limit the use of locational incentives. This suggestion highlights the fact that at the multilateral level the issue of incentives cannot be treated separately from other dimensions. In light of the previous discussions on incentives and FDI-related policies, three main policy suggestions arise:

- *The Mercosur experience shows that investment-related regional disciplines need to be established to limit competition and redirect it towards socially desirable objectives.* Incentives-based and even rules-based competition will reinforce rather than reduce regional inequalities. Hence the adoption of rules similar to those of the EU should prove helpful in the limiting of bidding wars and the orientation of aid towards those areas with structural problems. Disciplines on investment incentives should be closely connected with those regarding competition policy. New regional initiatives should also take into account the EU disciplines' failure to consider the interests of the less developed regions within the region. Schemes similar to EU structural funds could help foster development in backward regions. At the same time, should further sector-specific regimes be implemented as has occurred in the automobile industry, common rules must be adopted and policies should be unified. Last but not least, disclosure of information and transparency could help limit incentives-based competition, as well as reduce the possibilities of bribery and corruption among government officials.

- *A more activist approach is needed to enhance the benefits that Mercosur countries reap from FDI.* The evidence shows that many countries have implemented successful proactive strategies including the targeting of priority sectors and the fostering of 'spillover-generating' activities, such as R&D, labor training and domestic linkages. Domestic absorption capability is a key factor in reaping benefits from FDI. Policy areas that prove important in increasing this capability include human resource training and education, institution building, creation or development of markets such as capital markets, fostering of domestic entrepreneurship, and enhancement of transportation, communications and science and technology infrastructure. Without significant improvements in these areas it will prove increasingly difficult not only to reap spillovers, but also to receive high-quality FDI inflows.

- *Participation as a single voice must be increasingly unified in regional and multilateral fora where investment issues are discussed.* The FTAA Working Group on Investment is first tackling a stocktaking of the existing BITs and national regimes on FDI in member countries and, second, recommendations on the different issues which could be addressed by an eventual agreement on investment in the FTAA. It must be taken into account that the issues at stake in multilateral negotiations on investments extend far beyond incentives and PRs. For example, both Argentine and Brazilian firms have made significant investments abroad, which could benefit from strengthening the guarantees brought about by a multilateral negotiation. Even accepting that a 'grand bargain' may arise if an eventual multilateral agreement is negotiated, Mercosur countries should try, as part of the group of developing countries, to preserve margins for implementing policies that contribute to aligning FDI with host-country development objectives and foster increasing high-quality FDI inflows.

In the case of regional agreements, there is room both for cooperation as well as for competition within the regional bloc. The challenge is to foster cooperation in order to attract high-quality inflows by creating a common foreign investment agency, for instance. Moreover, common investment projects such as infrastructure must be promoted. Finally, drawing on experiences of classification of subsidies as prohibited, actionable and non-actionable (Tussie and Lengyel, 1998), rules classifying competition as forbidden, restricted and allowed must be defined. In this way, countries could not only attract significant FDI inflows, but also reap more spillovers from those inflows.

Notes

* The authors are very grateful to Diana Tussie for her perceptive comments and suggestions on a previous draft and to Patricio Meller, Jaime Campos and Ted Moran

for their useful comments at LATN meetings. The usual caveat applies. Research assistance by Silvana Melitsko is gratefully acknowledged.

1. A survey from the early 1990s showed that among 103 countries surveyed only four did not have any type of fiscal incentives, only 24 out of 83 did not have financial incentives and only eight out of 67 did not have any type of 'indirect' incentives (UNCTAD, 1995b). In turn, a Deloitte and Touche survey on some 40 countries showed that nearly 85 per cent had fiscal incentives (UNCTAD, 1999b).
2. For example, Portugal spends per capita about one-tenth of Germany's expenditures.
3. See Chudnovsky and López (2001) for a description of the incentives package granted to Volkswagen, which included municipal and provincial tax exemption for a five- to ten-year period.
4. Brazilian sub-national governments' incentive packages typically include state and municipal fiscal and financial incentives and subsidies dedicated to infrastructure. State participation in the capital of major ventures, via direct injections or by means of a development fund and subsidized labor force training, are also present in many packages.

8
The Policy Implications of Schumpeterian Competition

Jose Tavares de Araujo Jr

8.1 Introduction

Latin American governments have been faced with the difficult task of maintaining a coherent stance throughout the process of economic reform. Stabilization, trade liberalization and privatization were meritorious goals of the new policies launched in the region beginning in the late 1980s. But in those cases where the government was unable to keep special interests at bay, the reforms turned into short-lived monetary anchors, erratic trade policies and badly regulated private monopolies. The end results were unemployment, increased social inequalities, decadent public services, low rates of economic growth and currency crisis.

Using the Schumpeterian notion of creative destruction, this chapter discusses the role of competition policy, here narrowly defined as antitrust, in the process of economic reform. As any public policy, antitrust is constantly submitted to several potential failures, especially related to regulatory capture. But it can render two important services to an open developing economy: a set of rules that guides the competition process toward efficiency and fairness, and a mechanism to protect the national interest from foreign anti-competitive practices. To set the stage for the discussion, section 8.2 briefly recapitulates the Schumpeterian approach to competition and indicates the core of the policy agenda derived from this approach, in which the antitrust authority is compelled to act as the regulator of last resort in the economy. Section 8.3 presents the domestic challenges faced by the newly created Latin American and Caribbean antitrust agencies, while section 8.4 deals with cross-border issues at four levels: bilateral, sub-regional, hemispheric and multilateral. Section 8.5 concludes.

8.2 On Schumpeter, contestability and antitrust

The most widely accepted economic approach to competition was proposed by Joseph Schumpeter, who defined competition as a dynamic process wherein firms strive to survive under an evolving set of rules that constantly produces winners and losers. In this process, the basic instrument that allows firms to advance beyond their competitors is the introduction of information asymmetries. Depending upon the momentary set of rules, such asymmetries may result from three types of entrepreneurial activities: technological innovation, rent seeking and organized crime (Baumol, 1990).

The above approach has a peculiar record in the history of economic thought, including various revisions by Schumpeter. His 1912 book on *The Theory of Economic Development* established the links between innovation and competition. His 1928 paper on *The Instability of Capitalism* highlighted the transient character of competition conditions. The influence exerted by innovations in the rhythm of economic activities was extensively documented in *Business Cycles* (1939). Finally, in *Capitalism, Socialism and Democracy* (1942), the random frequency of technical progress and its interplay with competition patterns were brilliantly synthesized under the notion of *creative destruction*, a process of industrial mutation 'that incessantly revolutionizes the economic structure *from within*, incessantly destroying the old one, incessantly creating a new one' (1976: 83).

Despite the heuristic power of these analytic tools, the Schumpeterian approach remained far from the mainstream of academic research for many decades. But this situation has changed rapidly since the late 1970s, due in part to the work of Nelson and Winter (1982), so that:

> Schumpeter's assertions inspired what has become the second largest body of empirical literature in the field of industrial organization, exceeded in volume only by the literature investigating the relationship between concentration and profitability. (Cohen and Levin, 1989: 1060)

The beginning of this new phase coincided with another important event: the debate engendered by the theory of contestable markets developed by Baumol, Panzar and Willig (1982), which argues that industry structure is determined endogenously and simultaneously with the vectors of industry outputs and prices.

Schumpeterian competition and contestability theory provide a broad view of issues related to industrial organization and a challenging agenda for public policy. According to this view, industrial growth results from the interaction among technology, market size and competition strategies. Efficiency can be compatible with any design of industry structure. In every industry, the available technologies will imply a certain degree of scope and scale economies, and a specific ratio between transaction costs and production costs, which in turn will define whether the most efficient structure is a diversified set of firms, an oligopoly or a monopoly. Due to the process of creative destruction, these industrial configurations are, in principle, temporary, including their entry barriers and the corresponding disciplinary power of potential competition.

The policy agenda derived from these theories contains two interconnected challenges. The first is to identify the situations that require intervention and the respective policy instruments to be applied. While the competition process generates technical change and economic growth, there is no guarantee that the public interest is being served, since entry barriers, asymmetric information and market power are natural ingredients of that process. Hence antitrust authorities are constantly on a borderline position, where the reasons for intervening are as attractive as are those for doing nothing. As Demsetz noted:

> In a world in which information is costly and the future is uncertain, a firm that seizes an opportunity to better serve customers does so because it expects to enjoy some protection from rivals because of their ignorance of this opportunity or because of their inability to imitate quickly. [...] To destroy such power when it arises may very well remove the incentive for progress. This is to be contrasted with a situation in which a high rate of return is obtained through a successful *collusion* to restrict output; here there is less danger to progress if the collusive agreement is penalized. (1973: 3)

This is a convincing point often made by the Chicago School. As Easterbrook argued in the same vein,

> the hallmark of the Chicago approach to antitrust is skepticism. Doubt that we know the optimal organization of industries and markets. Doubt that government could use that knowledge, if it existed, to improve things, given the ubiquitous private adjustments that so often defeat public plans, so that by the time knowledge had been put to use the world has moved on. (1992: 119)

However, a dominant position acquired through a cumulative sequence of successful innovations can be long-lasting, and if the antitrust authority is absent the firm may easily venture into abusive behavior whenever the opportunity arises. Hence, skepticism must be blended with a dose of cautious activism.

The second policy challenge is to ensure that innovation will be the only available instrument for creating information asymmetries, effectively removing rent seeking and organized crime from the menu of competition strategies.[1] In fact, if this task were fully accomplished the former challenge would turn into a rare event, and competition policy would probably lose its relevance. Rent-seeking opportunities may arise either from asymmetric information engendered by the competition process, whereby the public authorities are captured by special interests, or from policy priorities independently defined by the government. Similarly, the room for organized crime is directly related to the lack of market transparency and the amount of gaps in the regulatory framework. Therefore, antitrust authorities are not only supposed to be immune to regulatory capture but also to be strong enough to repress such practice elsewhere in the public sector whenever required, acting as a dependable regulator of last resort in the economy.

In this ambiguous environment, one usual prescription for antitrust action is the removal of entry barriers, especially those created by the government. According to Armentano, for instance,

> abusive monopoly is always to be associated with governmental interference in production or exchange, and such situations do injure consumers, exclude sellers, and result in an inefficient misallocation of resources. But more importantly for this discussion, such monopoly situations are legal, created and sanctioned by the political authority for its own purposes. All such legal restrictions on cooperation or rivalry should be repealed. Thus, ironically or intentionally, the bulk of the abusive monopoly in the business system has always been beyond the scope of antitrust law and antitrust policy. (1996: 3)

Likewise, Singleton suggested that competition policy should focus its efforts, 'first and foremost, on eliminating government-created entry barriers; second, on minimizing natural barriers; and third on prohibiting anti-competitive, entry deterrence by dominant firms' (1997: 4). Albeit important, removing entry barriers is just one topic among many others on the competition policy agenda and, evidently, is not a panacea. There are situations in which part of the problem is precisely the lack of entry barriers. As Rashid (1988) showed, quality has a clear tendency to deteriorate in industries with a large number of small firms and low entry barriers.

8.3   Trends in Latin America and the Caribbean

The promotion of economic development is a national priority in every Latin American and Caribbean country. The role of competition policy in this endeavor is to complement governmental actions in the areas of education, science and technology, by creating a market environment in which firms can only survive if they are following the international rhythm of technical progress. The region's experience with import substitution policies provides a good illustration of this point. A well-known feature of these growth strategies was the lack of research and development (R&D) investments by the private sector. Even in those countries that initiated ambitious public programs of science and technology in the 1960s and 1970s, such as Brazil, Colombia and Mexico, for instance, the private sector did not fulfil expectations.

Likewise, the innovative behavior of domestic firms can also be used as a benchmark to measure the success of a trade reform. If, after a certain period, import competition has only led to trade deficits, destruction of local supply, and no formation of endogenous sources of technical change, then the government has just replaced one group of inconsistent policies with another. Indeed, a normative prescription to be extracted from the analytical framework discussed in section 2 is that the provision of a coherent set of rules and incentives is a crucial assignment for the government in a world of volatile competition conditions.

The enactment of new laws and the creation of autonomous antitrust agencies in many Latin American countries during the 1990s have been important initial steps toward that set of rules and incentives. These new institutions are now forging their public image and preparing themselves to act as regulators of last resort in those economies. At present, their two principal challenges are, first, to introduce a clear-cut division of functions between the competition policy authority and the sectoral regulatory agencies; and, second, to curb rent-seeking opportunities within a domestic scenario of unfinished economic reforms.[2]

The identification and eventual removal of entry barriers would imply a major improvement in the competition conditions. However, in contrast with the US, Canada and the European economies, where any student can read an extensive theoretical and empirical literature on this subject (see Schmalensee and Willig, 1989; Geroski and Schwalbach, 1991; Sutton, 1991, and Caves, 1998), there does not appear to be a single economy-wide study on Latin American entry barriers. So, while the advice to promote market contestability became a platitude in the discussion about competition policy in developing countries, it has been useless thus far, at least in Latin America, because nobody has the relevant information about the existing entry barriers and their economic consequences.

The typologies suggested by Salop (1979) and Singleton (1997) are useful starting points for an assessment of these barriers. Salop distinguishes an *innocent* entry barrier, which is unintentionally erected as a side-effect of successful innovations, from those *strategic* obstacles purposely invented to avoid potential competition; while Singleton highlights the importance of government-generated entry barriers. In policy-oriented research, it is convenient to introduce two additional subdivisions: *temporary* versus *long-lasting* restrictions; and *regulatory* versus *protectionist* barriers. The former subdivision provides a time dimension for the competition policy agenda, and the latter separates the governmental measures that are imposed to protect the public interest from those actions that respond to special interests.

After identifying the relevant barriers across the economy, the next step is to analyze their consequences, which consists essentially of inquiring whether the affected sectors are following the international patterns of productivity, profitability and product differentiation. With the information gathered through this exercise the antitrust agency will be, at last, prepared to foster market contestability in some selected areas of the economy. The exercise may also include a cost-benefit analysis of each entry barrier, indicating the firms, social groups and geographic regions affected by that restriction. This would allow the development of a competition advocacy program at a national level, mobilizing other public and private institutions in a collective effort to overcome the existing market distortions.

One stimulating example of the results that can be obtained through this type of exercise is a paper by Djankov and Hoekman (1998). Although not using the above-mentioned typologies, they studied the current conditions of competition in the Slovak Republic by reviewing a set of indicators such as entry and exit, import competition, profitability, revealed comparative advantage, concentration indexes and size distribution of firms. They also presented a brief description of the policies implemented by the government since 1992 in the areas of antitrust, trade, foreign investment and privatization. This description highlights the fundamental role played by the competition office as a regulator of last resort in the Slovak experience:

> In 1995, the office issued over 200 comments on proposed and existing legislation and decrees; initiated 37 cases against government agencies (mostly provincial and municipal); reviewed 230 privatization deals; and investigated 141 cases dealing with potential anti-competitive practices. Of the latter, 39 dealt with horizontal practices (collusion, cartels, etc.), 77 involved allegations of the abuse of a dominant position, and 25 focused on proposed mergers. Most of these cases centered on the behavior of (public) utilities. (Djankov and Hoekman, 1998: 1111–12)

The common goal of these actions is to engender a coherent set of market incentives, avoiding those situations wherein the government fosters competition through one channel and creates market distortions through another, as has been so typical in Latin America for many decades. And the results have been well documented: nowadays, the conditions of competition across industries in Slovakia are, in most cases, similar to those prevailing in Belgium, while less than a decade ago the former country had a closed and highly concentrated industrial system. The average rate of profit is around ten per cent (Djankov and Hoekman, 1998).

Economic indicators are important competition policy instruments. In fact, establishment of a benchmark for changes in a given economy's conditions of competition may be guided by comparisons between industrial structures of similar countries, and the more countries compared, the more valuable the information. Djankov and Hoekman conclude that:

> incorporation of descriptive statistics on concentration, import penetration, or price-cost margins for all WTO members in trade policy review reports would provide policymakers and analysts with a better sense of differences in market structure across countries, as well as information on the evolution of trends across countries than is currently the case. (1998: 1126)

For Latin America and the Caribbean these data sources would be critical both to strengthen the existing antitrust agencies and, more importantly, to frame the public debate in countries that do not yet have such institutions, as the next section indicates.

8.4 Cross-border issues

In discussions of the Free Trade Area of the Americas (FTAA) the international aspects of competition policy are currently being treated at four overlapping levels: bilateral, sub-regional, hemispheric and multilateral. Bilateral cooperation among antitrust agencies has been pursued mainly by the US, which signed agreements with Canada, Australia, Germany and the European Union (EU). Typically these agreements cover the following procedures:

- Mutual notification of enforcement activities that may affect the interests of the other country, including both anti-competitive practices and mergers. Notifications shall be sufficiently detailed to enable the notified Party to make an initial evaluation of the effect of the enforcement activity on its own interests, and shall include the nature of the activities under investigation and the legal provisions concerned. Where possible, notifications shall include the names and locations of the persons involved.
- Officials may visit the other country in the course of conducting investigations.
- Either country may request that the other initiate an investigation in its territory on anti-competitive practices that adversely affect the interests of the former country.
- Mutual assistance in locating and securing evidence and witnesses in the territory of the other country.
- Regular meetings to discuss policy changes and exchange information on economic sectors of common interest.

Bilateral agreements constitute a partial attempt to cope with the growing number of antitrust cases with cross-border implications. In the US, for example, about 30 per cent of the investigations carried out in 1997 by the Department of Justice involved multinational firms that often had operations in over 20 countries, while in 1993 only ten per cent of the cases had international dimensions. In recent years, nearly 50 per cent of the merger cases reviewed by the Federal Trade Commission required contacts with foreign antitrust agencies (see US Government, 1998). Anti-competitive practices by multinational corporations usually imply significant damages to the public interest, as the two following cases illustrate. The citric acid cartel was controlled by four firms: Bayer, Hoffman-LaRoche, Jungbunzlauer and Archer Daniels Midland Co. In an operation involving annual sales of about US$1.2 billion worldwide, these firms pleaded guilty to price fixing and sharing the sales of citric acid in the US and elsewhere during the period July 1991–June 1995. As of March 1998, the US criminal fines imposed on this conspiracy were over US$140 million and other private actions were pending (see US Government, 1998). In the case of aluminum, Higgins *et al.* (1996) have estimated that the international cartel created in 1994 was able to extract over US$1 billion from US consumers in less than one year of transactions under that arrangement.

Bilateral agreements are the only existing binding mechanisms for dealing with cross-border anti-competitive behavior (see Lloyd and Vautier, 1999). The ongoing discussions in other forums such as the World Trade Organization (WTO), the FTAA, North American Free Trade Agreement (NAFTA), Mercosur, the Andean Community (AC), the EU and the Australia–New Zealand Closer Economic Relations Agreement (CER) may eventually lead to effective instruments in the near future, but they are not yet applicable, as discussed below. As they stand, bilateral agreements have two evident limitations: they do not curb anti-competitive actions originating in third countries and they ignore the interests of the rest of the world. As Falvey and Lloyd (1999) have argued, there are instances in which the maximization of global welfare is not compatible with the short-run interests of the nation in which the anti-competitive conduct originates, and resolving this conflict requires multilateral cooperation.

To start a debate on these issues, the WTO set up the Working Group on the Interaction between Trade and Competition Policy in December 1996. In the following two years about 170 governmental papers were presented to this working group, covering a substantive agenda that goes well beyond the relationship between trade and competition. Despite the active participation by practically all WTO members with antitrust laws, the debate has been limited by two constraints. The first is that any meaningful multilateral treaty on competition rules would only be enforceable if all, or at least the vast majority of, WTO members had national laws covering the relevant topics included in that treaty. The second is that the present design of the WTO is prepared to deal essentially with government conduct, whereas the major focus of competition policy is the behavior of firms. As Lloyd observed:

> A multilateral system with the WTO acting as an international competition authority would need to investigate private actions in markets. Competition law in this form, by comparison with international trade law, is extremely intensive in its requirement of facts relating to the nature of competition, market share and so on. These vary from case to case and require detailed investigations. When the markets concerned in a case are international, this investigation would require information from different countries. There must be doubts concerning the ability of a remote centralized multilateral authority to understand behavior in markets, and in markets located in different countries to boot. (1998: 1143–4)[3]

Several suggestions have been made in recent years to improve this situation (see Scherer, 1994; Fox and Ordover, 1997, and Jacquemin *et al.*, 1998). The development of a small and autonomous International Competition Policy Unit (ICPU) was proposed by Jacquemin *et al.* Located in Geneva and working in close coordination with the WTO, the ICPU would be focused on the long-term convergence of international competition policy standards. The preliminary steps toward multilateral negotiations on this subject would include the strengthening of the network among antitrust authorities, which has been initiated by the WTO working group; substantive discussions on how to deal with the global effects of anti-competitive behavior; identification of the points of convergence and divergence among the existing national laws; and a program of technical assistance to help those countries that do not currently have competition policy.

While a multilateral system is not in place, regional trade arrangements may provide an interim solution, since the harmonization of the competition conditions is a natural priority for member countries. Within the FTAA process NAFTA is the most advanced agreement in this direction, because all the members already have antitrust agencies. Although it does not include any formal commitment on policy harmonization, a natural development of the present situation would be the accession of Mexico into the 1995 US–Canada cooperation agreement. Moreover, the convergence in the area of merger regulation is already well advanced. The AC and Mercosur also have provisions on competition policy, but they still need some amendments to become operational (Jatar and Tineo, 1998, and Tavares and Tineo, 1998).

One typical issue in the inquiry about the international aspects of competition policy is the participation of small developing economies, which most often do not have antitrust agencies. In Latin America and the Caribbean some small countries such as Costa Rica, Jamaica, Panama and Peru already have these institutions, while others like the Dominican Republic, Trinidad & Tobago, Guatemala and El Salvador are preparing their respective laws. Considering the challenges impinged upon the antitrust authority by the Schumpeterian process of competition, the scant empirical knowledge on the contestability of markets in the region, and the precarious state of the contemporary policy instruments for dealing with cross-border issues, one attractive option for the other small FTAA economies would be to follow the attitude of Hong Kong and Singapore, which decided against the adoption of antitrust laws, under the argument that free trade is sufficient to promote competition in their domestic markets (see Lloyd, 1998).

However, this option is not convenient, for three reasons. First, as argued in section 2, anti-competitive behavior is not related to the size of the economy but to some characteristics of the competition process, especially asymmetric information, entry barriers and market dominance. Indeed, in the American experience of antitrust enforcement, most cases could have happened in any small, open economy, and, very likely, with greater damaging effects on the public interest (Tavares, 1998). There is no doubt that trade liberalization is a powerful instrument, but it is not sufficient to eliminate all the relevant market distortions. Second, large flows of monopoly rents can be extracted from small countries by international cartels, mergers and acquisitions through foreign direct investment and the growth strategies of transnational corporations. The available evidence shows that this is not just a theoretical possibility, but a growing trend in the world economy. In the absence of antitrust institutions these facts seldom become objects of public scrutiny. Third, nearly all Latin American and Caribbean countries belong to sub-regional projects of economic integration, which contain explicit commitments on the harmonization of the competition conditions. If these commitments were transformed into operational mechanisms they could provide a timely alternative for those countries that do not have antitrust laws. In the case of the AC and Mercosur, after necessary improvements in the Decision 285 and the 1996 Fortaleza Protocol, Bolivia, Ecuador, Paraguay and Uruguay could use these regional instruments as their antitrust agencies. Eventually, on a later stage, they might set up national agencies whenever the practical experience indicates that this would be the best option. If similar procedures were adopted by the Central American Common Market (CACM) and the Caribbean Community (Caricom), 17 countries would benefit.[4]

8.5   Conclusion

The Latin America and Caribbean agenda derived from the Schumpeterian approach to competition includes both complex assignments and simple tasks, ready to be implemented, which would pave the way to achieving the former goals. The enactment of a coherent set of market incentives that would lead to economic growth and less inequality in the region depends upon mature institutions that result from a collective learning process on the management of public resources. Removing trade barriers, selling state firms, and even fiscal reforms can be done over a couple of years, if there is political will. But setting up instruments to regulate a newly open economy is a cultural event that implies the development of subtle notions such as credibility, accountability and fairness. Without these notions the distinction between innovation, rent seeking and organized crime is meaningless, for example. And the same happens with the concept of regulator of last resort.

Two initial steps in this long-term endeavor were identified in this paper: the research on market contestability and the improvement of sub-regional antitrust mechanisms. If economic indicators like those used by Djankov and Hoekman (1998) were available for all countries in the Western Hemisphere they would meet several domestic demands – from competition advocacy to technology policy – and would be instrumental for multiple foreign policy goals – from bilateral cooperation to WTO negotiations. Promoting sub-regional mechanisms would yield complementary results, by strengthening the existing antitrust agencies, by filling an institutional gap in countries, and by highlighting the convergence among the different levels of international negotiations. Interestingly, in competition policy there is no room for dichotomies such as regionalism versus multilateralism, or FTAA versus sub-regional arrangements. All provide inputs to the present challenges.

Notes

1. The magnitude of this challenge has been well described by the US authorities: 'Our recent international cartel prosecutions have demonstrated that even a century of vigorous antitrust enforcement has not brought an end to cartel behavior on a grand scale. It is for this reason that the Department of Justice recently has asked Congress to increase maximum corporate fines for price-fixing, bid-rigging, and market allocation to $100 million' (US Government, 1998: 12).
2. For an illustration of these challenges in the case of Mercosur countries, see Tavares and Tineo (1998). For the case of the telecommunications industry, see Bastos Tigre, Chapter 6.
3. Antidumping similarly involves the behavior of firms, but the WTO has resolved the jurisdiction problem by establishing a system in which national authorities carry out the investigations subject to WTO monitoring. See Tavares, Macario and Steinfatt (2001) for a discussion on the differences between antidumping and competition policy.
4. Four countries of the CACM would be included: El Salvador, Guatemala, Honduras and Nicaragua; and 13 from Caricom: Antigua and Barbuda, The Bahamas, Barbados, Belize, Dominica, Grenada, Guyana, Haiti, St Kitts and Nevis, St Lucia, St Vincent and the Grenadines, Suriname, and Trinidad and Tobago.

9
Commercial Defense Policy: Issues at Stake

Manuela Tortora and Diana Tussie*

9.1 Implications of multilateral agreements: retaining discretionary power versus the search for transparency

Antidumping measures have been likened to the equivalent of a nuclear weapon in the armory of trade policy (Srinivasan, 1999). While globalization eliminates obstacles to trade, the vitality and sophistication of domestic defense policies explain why international trade is often viewed as a guerilla war. The use of antidumping and other commercial defense measures increased throughout the 1990s, hand-in-hand with trade liberalization. Indeed, any analysis of these measures demonstrates that defense measures are a by-product of the dilemma between economic policy prescriptions and political feasibility. The implementation of the Uruguay Round Agreements (URAs) on antidumping (AD), countervailing duties (CVDs) and safeguards sought to reduce discretionary powers and improve transparency in the application of commercial defense measures. Compared to previous General Agreement on Tariffs and Trade (GATT) rules, the URAs achieved an important international codification of principles, standards, definitions and basic procedures in these sensitive matters. Nevertheless, domestic laws and practices have had to fill in the loopholes left, allowing authorities to keep commercial defense alive, as a kind of compensation for the radical reduction of traditional trade barriers. The implementation of domestic laws has revealed the extent to which authorities may still use largely discretionary and minimally transparent policies.

Antidumping is the most commonly used commercial defense policy instrument. Targeted at specific imports, it is relatively easy to apply and fairly effective in increasing the prices of imports to follow the interest of local firms. The extent to which the measures protect local firms depends on two factors: how precisely targeted the AD instrument is and how timely its adoption is. National authorities are allowed discretionary power to determine both factors, unless the domestic law is so detailed and so tightly enforced that it leaves little flexibility. Similarly, the transparency of the investigation on foreign imports depends on two factors. One is the technical and legal capacity of the institution in charge of the investigation. The other is the institution's immunity from lobbying.

Six loopholes were left by the existing multilateral rules; they have been filled by domestic laws and procedures:

- Determination of which petitions merit investigation.
- Definition of 'domestic industry' that is allowed to apply for protection.
- Definition of 'like product' – that is, the product that might merit protection.
- Calculation of the margin of 'dumping'.
- Establishment of authorized AD protection measures.
- Determination of 'injury'.

Countries have overhauled their institutions to carry out investigations and enforce AD policy. Technical capacity has been stepped up, yet many quarters fear that, by initiating sensitive AD cases against a major trade partner, they run the risk of inviting retaliation. That may explain why, in Latin America, AD is used more often against other peer Latin American countries, or against less important trading partners, such as Russia or China, than against imports from the US or the European Union (EU).

Some of the AD loopholes are also found in the Agreement of Subsidies and Countervailing Measures (ASCM), particularly in terms of the classification of 'domestic industry', the determination of 'injury', and once again, the national authorities' accuracy, transparency and efficiency in dealing with cases. Discretionary elements and poor transparency may arise from the categorization of prohibited, non-actionable and actionable subsidies. Introduced in the Uruguay Round (UR), this method of categorization has allowed the EU to preserve its programs of regional aid (see Chudnovsky and López, Chapter 7). Developing countries, on the other hand, have not succeeded in using this tool or enforcing CVDs against subsidized imports.

Unlike other defense measures, safeguards or 'escape clauses' apply to fair rather than unfair imports, and are to be used under exceptional circumstances such as a major economic crisis or an unforeseen, sudden surge of imports. Similar to the domestic enforcement of multilateral rules on AD and CVDs, national authorities may exercise discretionary power in the case of safeguards through their interpretation of 'import surge' and 'serious injury'. They also determine what time limits and compensation to domestic industry are reasonable. Furthermore, the criteria taken into consideration in the national authorities' investigation are usually not publicly disclosed.

The UR ushered in major improvements in the so-called voluntary export restraints (VERs) frequently used by the US and EU to provide an adjustment plan for their steel and automobile industries. Despite these improvements, fair imports may still be restricted. Increasing interdependence of firms around the world may encourage private rather than governmental agreements as a new and easier form of commercial defense. Transnational firms, for instance, may find it easier and more efficient to obtain the protection they are looking for by reaching agreements with their competitors instead of using the cumbersome domestic safeguard mechanisms, whose results they perceive as unreliable (see Tavares de Araujo, Chapter 8).

All in all, since fair enforcement is more important than the rule itself, the use (or abuse) of the loopholes left by the new multilateral rules on AD, CVDs, and safeguards greatly depends on the capacity and intentions of the national authorities. In fact, manipulation of trade-remedy laws is a skeleton in everyone's closet, with misapplication of antidumping in cases more aptly classified as fair trade. Practice is often more decisive than the rule.

9.2   The practice in the Western Hemisphere

Latin American integration schemes had adopted specific provisions on antidumping, countervailing and safeguards well in advance of their corresponding domestic institutions. Through creation of a set of supranational rules, the Andean Community (AC) has achieved harmonization among its member states' trade-remedy and competition rules. Though not all Latin American integration schemes are regulated by such supranationality, all include at least some basic commercial defense provisions.

The URAs helped to reduce disparities in trade-remedy laws in Latin America. However, the significant common ground established is based solely on principles, leaving drastic differences in procedures. As a result, examination of the commercial defense policies must be undertaken at two levels of analysis. At the domestic level, it is necessary to address the introduction, for the most part during the 1990s, of new laws and institutions in the national legal framework. At the regional level, the multiplication of integration agreements must be considered. These two levels are in eternal interaction and modify national positions, concepts and instruments.

Still there is a commercial defense policy 'deficit' at the national level, easily explained by the legacy of import substitution, which made trade-remedy measures less relevant. In the 1990s, the combined effect of the unilateral openness, together with the UR tariff bindings, increased the need for commercial defense both for intra-regional and extra-regional trade. Quite to the contrary, very sophisticated domestic trade-remedy laws with appropriately trained institutions have existed in the US since the 1930s (see Table 9.1), long before the UR initiated Latin America's creation of similar institutions from scratch.

US trade-remedy laws[1]

US trade-remedy laws are global trendsetters. To a great extent the GATT–WTO regulations are the international extrapolation of US legislation (Tussie, 1987). Moreover, US trade-remedy laws dictate the terms of access for Latin American

Table 9.1 Principal US trade-remedy laws

Law	Purpose and process	Degree of political discretion
Antidumping duties (Sec. 731, Tariff Act of 1930)	If the International Trade Administration (USITA) of the Department of Commerce finds that imports are dumped (i.e., sold at less than fair value), and the International Trade Commission (USITC) finds that they cause or threaten material injury to industries, the products are subject to duties equal to the dumping rate.	Low: Investigations are mandatory when a valid petition is received; neither the president nor his subordinates can prevent orders when the statutory criteria are met.
Countervailing duties (Sec. 701, Tariff Act of 1930)	If the USITA finds that imports benefit from prohibited subsidies, and the USITC finds that they cause or threaten material injury to industry, the products are subject to duties equal to the subsidy rate.	Low: Investigations are mandatory when a valid petition is received, and neither the president nor his subordinates can prevent orders when the statutory criteria are met.
Unfair Trade Practices (Sec. 337, Tariff Act of 1930)	If the USITC finds that imports violate patents, trademarks, or copyrights, or are otherwise unfairly traded, it can issue a cease-and-desist order and/or exclude these products from the US market.	Medium: The president can veto USITC decisions within 60 days, but as a practical matter presidents are almost never involved in these cases.
Escape Clause, also known as Safeguards (Sec. 201, Trade Act of 1974)	The USITC can recommend to the president that duties, quotas, or other remedies be granted, to aid an industry that is found to suffer serious injury from increasing imports.	High: The president can accept, reject, or modify the USITC's recommendations, and Congress can override the president's decision by enacting a joint resolution (which can be vetoed by the president).
Market disruption by communist countries (Sec. 406, Trade Act of 1974)	The USITC can recommend to the president that duties, quotas, or other remedies be pursued, to aid an industry that is found to suffer serious injury from increasing imports from a non-market economy.	High: The president can accept, reject, or modify the USITC's recommendations, and Congress can override the president's decision by enacting a joint resolution (which can be vetoed by the president).

Table 9.1   cont.

Law	Purpose and process	Degree of political discretion
Agricultural imports (Sec. 22, Agricultural Adjustment Act of 1933)	The USITC can recommend to the president that duties or quotas be imposed on imports that threaten to interfere with farm price-support programs. This law can no longer be applied against WTO member countries since the UR.	High: The president can accept, reject, or modify the USITC recommendations, based on his/her consideration of economic and political factors.
National Security Clause (Sec. 232, Trade Expansion Act of 1962)	The secretaries of Commerce and Defense can recommend that limits be imposed on imports that impair national security (e.g., by suppressing US production of strategic goods).	Very High: The president can accept, reject, or modify plans, and – in cases involving oil – Congress can vote to block import restrictions.

Source: Van Grasstek (1999b).

manufactured goods to their largest export market. Hence the evolution of US legislation penetrates Latin American interests from two fronts.

These highly sophisticated and comprehensive laws relate to all the GATT provisions on dumping, subsidies, safeguards and even national security. Examination of the list of these laws reveals their variety and the degree of political discretion given to the Executive (see Table 9.1). In practice, domestic firms tend to use less discretionary laws, preferring to keep a 'low profile' in their petitions. Since the instruments requiring political decisions are more open to political debate, opponents of protectionism have a greater chance to intervene and block the protection. This results in an inverse hierarchy of laws wherein the more 'technical' and 'discreet' instruments, such as the AD and CVD laws, are used more often, and safeguards are used less.

The US initiated nearly 800 AD investigations in the 20 years between 1980 and 1999. About half of the 132 cases initiated post-UR led to the imposition of duties, while many others led to a VER agreement or a 'suspension agreement' with the exporting firm or country. Of the more than 300 CVD cases initiated in the same period, over 15 per cent of them began between 1995 and 1999, compared to 17 per cent of AD cases initiated in the same period. In fact, the rate at which CVD cases are being filed is declining more rapidly than the rate of AD cases (see Table 9.2).

Like AD and CVD laws, the 'escape clause' included in the US Trade Act of 1974 (Section 201) has responded more to domestic objectives than to multilateral commitments. This law was transformed from its original, limited purpose of granting temporary and compensated protection when injury is attributable to the unanticipated consequences of trade liberalization to a much broader statute used to protect virtually any industry suffering from import competition. This discretionary power was supplemented in the UR

Table 9.2   US antidumping and countervailing duty cases, 1980–99

	1980–84	1985–89	1990–94	1995–99	Total
AD cases Initiated	149	234	273	132	788
AD duties imposed	47	127	107	68	349
CVD cases initiated	136	97	52	30	315
CVD duties imposed	47	56	25	11	139

Source: USDC (2001).

amendments to GATT Article XIX by the elimination of compensation for trading partners whose exports are affected by safeguard measures. However, the President, whose decision is believed to be more politically motivated than the International Trade Commission's recommendation in safeguard cases, has granted import relief in just 15 of the 36 cases in which affirmative injury determinations were reached, out of the 67 investigations conducted from 1975 to 1998. As listed in Table 9.1, there are four additional US trade-remedy laws providing significant political discretion to the President, which remained unmodified by the UR: national security clause, market disruption by communist countries, agricultural imports, and unfair trade practices.

US trade-remedy laws provide domestic firms with a real opportunity to obtain the protection they deem necessary against both fair and unfair imports. The chief trade-remedy laws are seen by many industries as a menu of options from which they may choose restrictions to impose on imported competition. It is fairly common for matching AD and CVD petitions to be filed against the same product, and against multiple countries, so as to max-imize pressure on foreign competitors. In fact, the URAs do not prevent countries from such aggressive simultaneous filing. Moreover, firms can exert pressure by merely threatening to file a petition, thus incurring upon the exporter legal and accounting expenses. Defense against the average AD or CVD petition can cost millions of dollars in legal and accounting fees, which industries may prey upon to harass foreign competitors.

The steel industry is renowned for such practices. In 2001 it sought appli-cation of the general escape clause under Section 201 while simultaneously applying for AD duties against a multitude of origins. *In March 2002, President Bush caved into pressure and slapped a 30 per cent tariff on steel imports. Though developing countries are exempt from the temporary safeguard, the decision will surely increase global surpluses and drive down world prices.* During the UR, talks were initiated for a Multilateral Steel Agreement akin to the WTO-sanctioned system of quotas under the Agreement on Textiles and Clothing (ATC). However, failure on this front converged on the use of AD. Each time there is a 'surge' in steel imports, the US industry launches a campaign advocating trade-remedy protection. The context surrounding those measures is highly politicized. On the one hand, the Executive wants to avoid blatantly protectionist restrictions that would hurt key trade partners and entice other industries to solicit similar favors. On the other hand, the steel industry has tremendous clout in Congress thus making its support critical to winning passage of a new trade bill. Steel products from Argentina, Brazil, Venezuela and Mexico have appeared with increasing frequency on the list of investigations initiated in the aftermath of the Asian and Russian financial crises, as US firms have taken advantage of the discretion and flexibility of domestic laws. As usual when growth rates fall, the steel industry succumbs to the menu of protectionist temptations, and the US Congress and Executive respond in turn. The industry's success in attaining protection may be due to its hard-won experience of how best to file cases, but perhaps more directly, the protection may result from provisions that the industry was able to incorporate into the AD disciplines that solely protect steel. Blonigen and Prusa (2001) cite the example of the captive production provision, which allows steel mills to send their product downstream and thus remove it from the total products counted in a dumping investigation. Whether through sly use of the established rules or a heavy hand on the formulation of rules in their own interest, the US steel industry epitomizes many of the faults of the AD system.

There is a danger that, by taking advantage of the loopholes within the URAs, US legislation may be accommodated to make it easier to provide 'temporary' domestic protection through the use of trade-remedy instruments. Protectionist arguments used by steel and textile lobbies to obtain political support will be entangled in the discussion of the trade promotion authority needed by the Executive to move ahead with further trade negotiations and will remain at the forefront of negotiations in the Free Trade Area of the Americas (FTAA).

The Free Trade Area of the Americas

The significant differences between US trade-remedy laws and those of many other countries in the hemisphere will be pounded out within the framework of FTAA negotiations. The Ministerial Meeting held in Buenos Aires in April 2001 instructed the Negotiating Group on Subsidies, Antidumping and Countervailing Duties to intensify its work on identifying options for deepening subsidy disciplines contained in the ASCM. It also instructed the group to intensify efforts to reach a common understanding to improve the rules and procedures for enforcement. The mandate will bring to the forefront simmering disagreements on substantive issues of harmonizing, simplifying, accelerating and reducing the costs of trade-remedy procedures; improving WTO standards and their compliance; and improving the implementation of domestic laws, discretionary powers, and the use of such measures in a free trade area. Some countries are concerned that the examination of substantive issues may necessitate significant changes in domestic laws. The US is mindful of the significant differences between its domestic procedures and those of many other countries in the hemisphere, which may trigger the introduction of significant changes. Moreover, few hemispheric countries will agree to commitments before the Executive obtains trade promotion authority from Congress.

The FTAA Working Group will rely on the 'Compendium of Antidumping and Countervailing Duty Laws and Regulations' to carry out its work.[2] The main points arising from the comparison of national rules are the following:

- All but a few countries in the hemisphere (some Caribbean and Central American countries) have adopted domestic regulations in compliance with the URAs.
- Definitions such as 'like product', 'dumping' and 'domestic producer' are similar in countries that adopted UR standards, while there are some differences in the countries whose laws were adopted before 1995.
- Domestic regulations differ on room left for ad hoc interpretation, especially on definitions of 'injury' and 'threat of injury'.
- There are more similarities among the domestic laws of members of the regional and sub-regional agreements than there are between their laws and those of the US and Canada.
- The authority in charge of carrying out the investigation differs. In many countries it is a branch of the Ministry of Trade, while in others it is an autonomous body with, at least in theory, more political independence. The US and Argentina are the only countries with a 'bifurcated system', with participation by both an independent body and a ministerial body: the US International Trade Commission (USITC) and the Department of Commerce and the National Foreign Trade Commission (CNCE) and the Trade Ministry respectively.
- The requirements to initiate an investigation and to determine if a petition is filed by or on behalf of the domestic industry are quite similar. However, the US is unique in its allowance of 'labor support' considerations in determining if the 'domestic industry' is represented in the petition.

Chile takes a hard line, arguing that insofar as antidumping measures are antithetical to the notion of a free trade area, they should be eliminated. The US has already expressed that Chile's proposal is unacceptable. The debate is a 'dry run' for what could be a similar exercise in the WTO. The results of this debate, together with the work regarding the hemispheric competition laws and the establishment of a specific Disputes Settlement (DS) mechanism, may largely sculpt the FTAA. It should be kept in mind that neither Canada–US Free Trade Agreement (CUSFTA) (1989) nor NAFTA (1994) banned trade remedies, as Canada had originally proposed. However, they do provide a special panel that determines if the domestic authorities' decisions were in accordance with their own laws, as does the WTO (see Weston and Delich, Chapter 10). Hence the current common ground is scant and mainly concerns principles rather than domestic procedures or institutional mechanisms; it could be improved by FTAA negotiations. The US may find a strong interest in establishing clear and uniform 'WTO-plus' standards, since there is a looming danger that the Latin American countries may increase their use of commercial defense (see Abreu, Chapter 1). However, the US would run the risk of having to clarify (or modify) many of its own rules and procedures. Likewise, Latin American countries should see the FTAA negotiations as an opportunity to minimize the discretionary gaps within US legislation.

That a majority of countries in the Western Hemisphere have not proceeded to altogether abolish these measures in the context of ever multiplying free trade areas or even customs unions is an indication of the long and winding road that the FTAA will have to travel and of the economic and political costs associated with the initiative.

Latin American restraints and wrangles

Trade relief measures in Latin America peaked in the early 1990s. The case of Argentina is paradigmatic: between 1988 and 1994, 135 petitions were received and 50 investigations were initiated, while between 1995 and 1999 the CNCE received 74 petitions and initiated 64 investigations. In 1997, Argentina initiated 14 investigations and had 26 AD duties in force, which ranked Argentina at the top of the list of WTO members. The final adoption of AD duties followed a similar pattern, increasing in the first years of Argentine trade liberalization and the beginning of Mercosur, and then decreasing in the mid-1990s. Of previous petitions, 57 final duties were adopted in 1995–99 (CNCE, 1999).

This evolution is explained by the trade liberalization process and its relation to macroeconomic conditions and financial volatility. When the first wave of unilateral trade reforms was introduced in the region at the end of the 1980s, AD and safeguard policies became intensively used. Governments and the private sector saw them as appropriate 'compensation' for the lowering of tariffs and non-tariff barriers (NTBs). Subsequently, in the mid-1990s the pace of commercial defense policies leveled off, coinciding with higher rates of growth. Finally, defense policies peaked again in 1999 following the financial crises, particularly in countries such as Argentina, Venezuela and Peru, which did not devalue their currencies (Grilli, 2000). Real appreciation of the domestic currency and the fall in GDP increases petitions hand-in-hand with positive determinations of injury to domestic production.

The origin of investigated imports also follows distinct trends. In the first stage, defense measures were mostly applied against intra-regional imports. Subsequently, starting in 1998, mainly Asian, Russian and Brazilian products were targeted, which had become more competitive because of devaluation. These trends show how financial pressures can radically increase the use of defense measures and affect implementation. Latin America is not unique: since 1995, developing countries have outpaced industrialized countries, initiating almost two-thirds of these measures, most of which are directed against other developing countries.

The case of Chile deserves singling out. In contrast to the general trend, Chile resorted to exchange rate management and after significant unilateral lowering of tariffs and NTBs during the 1980s, trade-remedy laws were seen as more of a 'last resort' than a source of easy protection for domestic industries. In bilateral trade agreements signed in the 1990s, Chile introduced provisions geared towards the gradual elimination of AD and CVDs. For instance, the 1996 Chile–Canada trade agreement provides for a reciprocal exemption of domestic rules on dumping as soon as the tariffs applied to their bilateral trade have been eliminated, or by January 2003 at the latest. Special consultation mechanisms are designed to confront 'exceptional circumstances', to achieve improved subsidy disciplines and to eliminate the need for countervailing actions. The bilateral agreements signed by Chile in the Latin American Integration Association (LAIA) legal framework follow the same pattern: the 1998 Chile–Peru agreement provided that domestic laws, insofar as they were in accordance with WTO standards, would be applied. At the same time, both countries are committed to eliminating all incentives or export subsidies on the items included in the trade liberalization program before the year 2002. This innovative way to eliminate distortions is probably more effective than the use of trade sanctions and fosters the elimination of unfair practices. Similarly, the Chile–Mexico agreement negotiated in 1998 seeks to eliminate AD duties in reciprocal trade and provides for the elimination of all agricultural subsidies by January 2003.

In fact, use of trade remedy measures against partners of integration schemes has exposed the dangerous misuse of these measures and their deleterious effect on integration. To take Mercosur as a leading case, Argentines fearing an influx of Brazilian imports into their market argued that since Mercosur was merely an 'incomplete tariff union', safeguards were legitimate. However, the Treaty of Asunción (Article I, Annex IV) had only provided for the temporary use of safeguards against imports from other member countries to be applied during the transitional period, which had ended on 31 December 1994. It was argued that, in the absence of a specific code on safeguards, the LAIA resolution providing for safeguards among member countries was applicable, insofar as the LAIA Agreement of 1980 is the legal umbrella for Mercosur. Argentina imposed a safeguard on textile imports from Brazil in 1999, to which Brazil responded by taking Argentina to the WTO. The Textile Monitoring Body (TMB) recommended that Argentina lift the safeguards, but the TMB cannot make such a recommendation binding. The controversy was finally solved by arbitration under Mercosur's Third Ad-Hoc Tribunal (see Weston and Delich, Chapter 10, for a discussion on dispute settlement in Mercosur). The Tribunal concluded that Argentina must terminate the measure since the Treaty of Asunción contains a general prohibition on the application of safeguards on one hand, and, on the other hand, there is no special regime for textile products.

A similar legal wrangle could well emerge within the Andean Community (AC), where the customs union is also 'incomplete' and LAIA rules also provide the common legal framework. In practice, members have not faced a sudden increase in imports due to a major devaluation. However, at the end of 1998, after the devaluation of the Colombian peso, voices were heard in the Venezuelan import-competing sector in favor of safeguards. At the same time, Venezuelan agro-business lived in fear of Colombian safeguard measures. The decision on safeguards against third countries finally accelerated in the context of Ecuadorian import restrictions established in April 1999. Colombia threatened to retaliate by implementing safeguards against Ecuadorian imports, while clarifying that, as a principle, no safeguards would be applied against other AC countries (see Echavarría and Gamboa, Vol. II).

Much of the unease stems from the ambiguity of the multilateral agreements, which do not specify commitments for regional or sub-regional groups. Regional integration arrangements may pose a challenge insofar as AD rules included in such arrangements could give rise to questions of interpretation of national treatment (Article I) and formation of free trade zones and customs unions (Article XXIV) (Thorstensen, 1995). Future WTO agreements on the use of trade-remedy measures in an integration scheme notwithstanding, the issue must be tackled among members of each regional agreement, so as to avoid unclear situations which may damage both the letter and the spirit of the integration process. In fact, in many instances, countries have recognized just how antithetical commercial defense measures may be to integration. Some self-restraint is evident, in order not to mar the image of open economy in open regionalism. The likely damage was probably deemed to be greater than the possible benefits of temporary protection to domestic firms. Quite to the contrary, regional initiatives' trade-remedy rules against third parties may provide just the solidarity that intra-use of these measures is wearing away.

The general framework of Mercosur AD, CVD and safeguard rules, as established in the Treaty of Asunción (1991) and the Protocol of Ouro Preto (1994), build upon the precedents of the LAIA, members' domestic laws, and the URAs. In addition to the basic provisions included in Mercosur by-laws, regulations on safeguards and AD measures regarding third countries' imports were drafted in 1996 and 1997, but have not yet been adopted into domestic legislation. Following the surge of Asian imports in 1998, Argentina and Brazil announced a review of those regulations aimed at preparing a truly 'common code', but the subject has faced a rocky road. It is interesting to note that in the 1996 Chile–Mercosur Agreement, whereby Chile became a Mercosur associate member, there are no specific provisions on unfair practices; Article 151 of this agreement provides that WTO rules will be applied. However, there are provisions for notification: when a party adopts trade-remedy measures against a third country, it will inform the other party in order to monitor the imports in its own market. Consultations can be held if 'unfair' imports from a third country are introduced into the market.

For third party trade the AC adopted a framework in 1991 that represented a 'minimum common ground' among domestic trade-remedy laws regarding third countries. The framework was included in Decision 283 (dumping and subsidies), Decision 284 (import restrictions) and Decision 285 (restrictions on free competition). Given their supranational nature, all decisions are automatically incorporated into domestic laws, without legislative approval. The Secretariat is the only authority to determine trade-remedy measures and to decide the imposition of duties.

Decision 283 on dumping and subsidies builds on national laws, but two important differences stem from customs union requirements and the supranational nature of decisions. First, when practices by a third country threaten or cause material injury to products protected by the Common External Tariff (CET), corrective measures in only one member country will not suffice. The second difference relates to the competence given to the Secretariat in the steps leading to the imposition of duties. The Secretariat receives dumping or subsidy complaints and informs the liaison institutions of the country in which the petitioner is doing business. The Secretariat is asked by governments or firms to authorize measures and determines the margin of dumping, the subsidy amount and the existence or threat of injury. The Secretariat drafts a Resolution indicating what duties shall be imposed on which imports for what amount of time.

Common safeguards against third countries were adopted by Decision 452 in 1999, in reaction to the Asian financial crises and the Brazilian devaluation. The basic provisions of Decision 452 on safeguards are the following:

- The common safeguard measures are aimed at protecting industries injured by imports from non-member countries.
- Firms may request safeguard measures in two or three member countries when the significant import increase from third countries threatens to injure or severely injures the common production of a similar good or a directly competitive good. The injury will be considered as circumscribed to a common production when the exports of one or more producers of similar or directly competitive goods requesting the safeguard represent, on an individual or a collective basis, at least 40 per cent of the internal market of said good, in each country for which the enforcement of safeguards is requested.
- Specific provisions are included on the determination of injury to the 'common production'.

- In case of 'critical circumstances', the Secretariat may adopt a provisional safeguard measure in less than 15 days after a petition is introduced by a member country, based on the presumption of a severe injury.
- The Secretariat has the authority to determine the final measures to be applied only in the 'relevant market' and in accordance with the injury.
- The safeguard measures can not exceed three years but may be extended for up to six years.
- Treatment of imports from non-WTO members differs in regard to non-discriminatory treatment, consultations, notifications, developing countries, gradual liberalization of the measures, renewal and trade compensation.

All told, these safeguard mechanisms have breathed some life into the common market. From a political perspective, rules that can be activated in defense of the group's rather than the individual countries' interests contribute to the consolidation of integration.

9.3   Room to maneuver and issues at stake

Clearly, there is a decisive political element involved in the application of these ad hoc instruments, in direct response to pressure from domestic interests. However, an assessment of costs and benefits should refrain from focusing solely on costs borne by exports from developing countries to northern markets. Latin American countries have resorted to these instruments as second or even third best measures to cope with competitive devaluation, losses in domestic GDP growth and unstable macroeconomic conditions. Hence starker and more complex issues are at stake today than in the comparatively simpler world of the pre-1990s as viewed through the North–South lens. Research shows that when trade leads to persistent wage, income and welfare disparities, the less developed country's use of distortionary industrial policy may in fact be welfare enhancing (Skott and Sethi, 1997). Other researchers revisit the need for infant-industry protection during 'learning periods' (Benchekroun, Long and Tian, 1998, and Miravete, 1997) and for some temporary relief from imports to allow the domestic competing industry the opportunity to take the necessary adjustment measures. What newly demand attention are the possible dynamic effects; AD use may attract FDI from 'tariff-jumping' industries seeking to enter the market and reap benefits from the artificially high prices, and thus substantially lessen the benefits afforded the domestic industry (Blonigen and Prusa, 2001). The welfare-enhancing and investment-attracting possibilities that AD offers to developing countries should not be overlooked in an assessment of commercial defense measures.

Together with this assessment of trade relief measures, new light must be shed on trade promotion in the context of development. The importance of subsidies as a domestic policy tool was demonstrated by the significant time spent in philosophical debates between the EU and the US during the UR.

Evidently, the debate transcends the commercial dimension to deal with the role of the state and the protection of vulnerable sectors, be they sunset or sunrise sectors. Latin America regards maintenance of subsidies with economic and social objectives as at least as important as the EU does. It is important to remember that at the end of the 1980s the role of the state was severely reduced in Latin American countries, not only because of the new mindset but also for fiscal reasons. Some authors have argued that Latin American governments may have gone too far in wiping out subsidies as an export promotion tool (Ventura Dias, 2001). Together with the institution-building undertaken as part of the 'second generation' of reforms, many types of subsidies may well be reconsidered (Tussie and Lengyel, 1998). Special and Differential Treatment (S&D) benefits could also be gained from the actionable subsidy that requires export subsidies be eliminated if the country's exports amount to at least 3.25 per cent of world trade for two consecutive years for industrialized countries, and for eight years for developing countries with a per capita GNP of less than US$1000.

> Developing countries should urge for the inclusion of a new provision which stipulates that if the export falls below the criterion of export competitiveness the phasing out of a subsidy should be halted immediately and the country be allowed to re-apply an export subsidy. (Thorstensen, 1995: 267)

The inclusion of export subsidies in the list of prohibited subsidies not only affects a country's capacity to support 'strategic' industries and to compete in international markets. It also affects its capacity to formulate a trade policy complementing its industrial policy. Nevertheless, how this provision has been implemented in practice, particularly in Latin America, should be examined together with the validity of the original idea contained in the agreement.

To sustain a position in favor of deepening multilateral standards, as well as of prudence and reluctance *vis-à-vis* new commitments, Latin American countries need solid technical arguments and political preparation. Their negotiating objectives in the WTO (and other bilateral or regional fora) need to be clarified once some 'sticking points' such as the following are resolved:

- *The problem of 'politicization'*. Although trade-remedies represent an obvious loophole in world trade rules, particularly in AD measures, it is a loophole all have an interest in preserving. In Latin America, defense measures are the political margin left after trade liberalization, and the sine qua non condition to making trade openness feasibly sustainable.
- *The link between antidumping and competition policies*. From a theoretical point of view, the contradiction between the concepts should be easily solved with the adoption of a multilateral regime on trade and competition

policy. However, that depends on the preparedness of developing countries' legal and institutional frameworks to forge multilateral 'common ground' on competition rules (see Tavares de Araujo, Chapter 8).

- *Reopening discussion on the Antidumping Agreement.* First, the impact on trade must be addressed, as there are a considerable number of loopholes left which have made antidumping action the preferred means of imposing restrictions on imports. Second, there are significant asymmetries in the impact that dumping may cause. Dumped imports, even in small quantities, can have damaging effects in developing countries in just a few days. Therefore, timeframes may be too long to protect domestic markets. Third, AD actions – with or without the effective imposition of duties – may more directly affect small or 'infant' export industries of developing countries: first, because new entrants are obliged to keep prices low and thus expose themselves to dumping accusations; and second, because such enterprises are less able to (i) fight off such cases in the political and bureaucratic arenas, or (ii) absorb the measures' economic impact. Finally, it is crucial to keep in mind that in disputes concerning antidumping the role of the panels is limited to determining whether the facts have been properly and objectively established by the domestic authorities (see Weston and Delich, Chapter 10).

- *Review the 'standing of complainants'.* The criteria to determine if complainants are representative of national interests may need to be revisited, since producers related to the exporters and importers are excluded from the calculation. The Antidumping Agreement does not require that domestic producers manufacture original products in order to file a complaint, and the footnote to Article 1 of the Agreement on Rules of Origin seems to reaffirm that origin determination does not apply to domestic industries. A double standard is thus applied: on one hand, origin is examined on allegedly dumped exports but not on the local industry that files the complaint; on the other hand, domestic industries complaining about dumping are allowed to manufacture the same product with parts imported from the allegedly dumping country. This question arose in AD proceedings carried out by the European Commission during the 1980s, and calls into question the extent to which complainants that import a large portion of their inputs or import advanced technological goods are representative of national interests.

- *Improvement of rules in customs unions.* Latin American countries have devoted too little attention to coordinating their regional and multilateral commitments. Though there is not yet enough evidence to reliably assess these rules, recent discussions in Mercosur, the AC and the FTAA on the contradictions between the concepts of trade-remedies and free trade areas or customs unions may bring some elucidation. For the time being, adapting multilateral rules to the reality and the needs of Latin American trade should be the priority, rather than moving towards WTO-plus disciplines.

- *Establish commercial defense rules in services.* The issue is more than purely a technical one, since all Latin American countries are net service importers. Some services deserve more technical research, such as trade in tourism, health services, maritime services, telecommunications, environmental services, accountancy and other professional services. More importantly, the impact of systemic financial crises raised many concerns about the vulnerability of Latin American banking systems and the pace of the financial opening. The main response has been to insist on macroeconomic stability, sound monetary policies and stronger banking supervision as a recipe to minimize both external and domestic risks. The WTO 1997 Agreement on Financial Services, some argue, should have allowed for 'emergency safeguard' provisions or restrictions to 'national treatment' when there is a crisis in the financial system in order to guarantee stable and balanced liberalization (see Fanelli, Vol. II).

- *The link between investment and competition policies.* WTO members need to consider whether the Trade Related Investment Measures (TRIMs) agreement should be complemented with additional provisions on investment regimes and competition policies. Latin American competition policies were significantly improved over the last decade, as the attraction of foreign direct investment became a priority. However, a concrete link between these issues must be resolved, such as the extent to which performance requirements restrict competition, the possibility of a multilateral competition code replacing the usage of trade-remedies (see Chudnovsky and López, Chapter 7).

- *Institutional challenges.* Implementation reveals that the effectiveness of trade-remedy laws depends more on the institutional capacity to enforce them than on the accuracy of their provisions. One of the main imbalances between developed and developing countries relates to the experience, credibility, and technical and financial resources of domestic institutions. Therefore, the costs of implementing legal and institutional frameworks, together with the training of public officials and private users, may hamper the use of trade defense laws, especially for small developing countries. Technical cooperation is still needed if multilateral agreements are to be implemented in a balanced manner, such as the establishment of shared legal services financed by many developing countries (see Weston and Delich, Chapter 10).

- *Reliance on the Dispute Settlement Mechanism.* The abusive use of trade-remedy laws may necessitate a clearer mandate for WTO DS mechanism to monitor possible 'harassment' or abusive use of trade-remedies. The DS mechanism has increased its capacity to identify unfair national discretionary decisions, particularly in AD disputes where the WTO panel is limited to determining whether domestic authorities properly and objectively established the facts and whether their evaluation was objective (see Weston and Delich, Chapter 10). The possible restriction of the panel's capacity in areas besides AD is cause for concern. Since discretion clearly exists in AD and safeguard laws, and to a lesser extent in CVD laws, any trend or intent to weaken the DS mechanism will prove detrimental to the international trade system. A more active participation by the DS mechanism in the monitoring of domestic implementation of commercial defense rules would be beneficial, given the current abuse of these measures.

The long-term trend is clearly towards more control, more uniform standards, and less discretionary margins in all trade-remedy rules, both multilateral and regional. Nevertheless, in the medium term, commercial defense measures as second or third best instruments will likely be left unchanged. At least in the short term, it is unrealistic to think that governments will abandon their use, particularly in the presence of a private sector able to combine economic arguments with political pressures. Governments may prefer to run the risk of facing the 'politicization' of trade policy, that is, of an abusive use by their trading partners or by their domestic firms, than to give them up. At the same time, their increasing use as second or third best instruments to cope with financial pressures augur continued inclinations to hold onto them. Thus multilateral rules will be unable to establish a regime where governments rely solely on multilateral mechanisms, no matter how sound the theoretical argument for elimination is. In the medium term, bilateral and regional free trade initiatives will probably pave the way before the WTO agrees to stricter disciplines. Though Latin American countries seem to have many reasons to support such a trend, they may legitimately hope for an improvement in the transparency and equity of industrialized countries' laws before introducing changes in their own. Both a round in the WTO and the FTAA will converge on clarifying issues of interpretation, but legitimate or illegitimate protectionist sentiment for hard-pressed sectors will not subside.

Notes

* The views expressed are those of the author and do not necessarily reflect the views of the UNCTAD Secretariat, where Manuela Tortora works.

1. This section draws largely from Van Grasstek (1999b).
2. The Compendium fails to include the sub-regional rules of the AC, Mercosur, the Central American Common Market (CACM), and the Caribbean Community (Caricom). For a comparison, see ALADI (1998).

10
Settling Disputes

Ann Weston and Valentina Delich

10.1 Introduction

Effective and efficient dispute settlement (DS) is fundamental to the international trading system. While trade negotiators may seek to achieve clear and fair rules with a broad degree of consensus and commitment, a DS system is needed to ensure that commitments are honored. In the early days of the General Agreement on Tariffs and Trade (GATT), differences were addressed through bilateral consultations. However, this approach proved inadequate over the years, and in the 1970s and 1980s an increasing number of cases were brought before GATT panels. But many countries did not even bother to contest cases given the delays, different procedures for different issues, and particularly the ability of the defending country to block panel findings. The new rules needed to be more clearly enforceable so that the time invested in developing new rules in the Uruguay Round (UR) would not be wasted by a weak DS system. Most observers hailed the World Trade Organization's (WTO) new DS rules as a major achievement of the UR. For smaller economies, which had made little use of the GATT DS system, the changes seemed particularly significant. One question to be addressed in this chapter is to what extent the new WTO DS system has lived up to such expectations, and especially in the eyes of the Americas. Parallel to the multilateral process, several regional trading arrangements have been signed since the late 1980s, each with its own system for dealing with disputes. With the proliferation of regional mechanisms, the other question for this chapter is what are their relative strengths and weaknesses and what does experience with their use imply. If there is to be free trade within the hemisphere, what would be the most appropriate approach to DS?

Section 10.2 provides a background of the WTO system as it evolved under the GATT, changes under the Uruguay Round, and subsequent experience with its usage. Section 10.3 turns to the regional DS mechanisms within the Western Hemisphere, focusing on the North American Free Trade Agreement (NAFTA), Mercosur and the Andean Community. Section 10.4

considers the strengths and weaknesses that have become apparent with experience, and a number of proposals for change. Section 10.5 concludes with possible directions for a hemispheric trade agreement.

10.2   Dispute settlement in the GATT/WTO

The GATT DS system revolved around Articles XXII and XXIII, dealing with consultations and, if this failed, referral to the full membership (technically the contracting parties) for an investigation and recommendation. The system had two hallmark characteristics: full consensus (including the defendant) was needed to move the process forward and adopt the recommendations, and the last resort for a country to pressure implementation of a recommendation was suspension of concessions. Although initially disputes were referred to a working party, beginning in the early 1950s they were referred to a panel of experts (Stewart, 1993). A number of other modifications in practice and amendments to the rules were adopted in subsequent years, several at the request of developing countries. However, contracting parties never accepted reforms of the system that would allow financial compensation or collective retaliatory actions. Until the Dispute Settlement Understanding (DSU) was negotiated in the UR, countries could easily block adoption of panel recommendations. Few cases were brought before panels in the first 25 years: in the 1950s there were some 40 complaints and only ten in the 1960s, leading to even fewer panels. Uruguay brought a number of complaints in the 1960s, in 'a broad-scale attack' according to Dam (1970: 361), identifying over 500 developed country policies that had injured Uruguayan exports, even if they did not violate specific GATT rules. Following Uruguay's lead, there was a proliferation of GATT DS use in the 1970s. Nonetheless there were frustrations as larger importing countries forced many smaller exporting countries to accept 'voluntary' restraint agreements or other grey-area measures that proved difficult to contest in the GATT. Many non-tariff measures were not covered by GATT rules or were explicitly allowed, like Multifibre Arrangement (MFA) restraints.

During the Tokyo Round (1973–79), Brazil played an active role in the Framework Group, which discussed new rules for dealing with disputes. It sought rules to redress the imbalance between developed and developing countries, notably greater involvement of the Director-General in such cases, mandatory prior notification of measures affecting developing countries, and improved surveillance. The US supported an annual trade review of member policies, tighter timelines for cases, and a roster of government experts for consideration as panelists, although it opposed mandatory notification. There were greater differences with the EU and Japan which resisted negotiating DS outside the other negotiating groups, and the EU opposed differential DS rules for developing countries (Stewart, 1993). The Tokyo Round produced a new understanding on general DS cases and a variety of special rules under the plurilateral codes. The understanding clarified the work, procedures and composition of the panels. Differences in the code rules included requiring a minimum amount of consultations before proceeding to a committee review (subsidies), using a technical panel (customs valuation), and quicker procedures for perishable products (standards). These special provisions were not available to non-signatories of the codes, mostly developing countries.

The number of disputes taken to the GATT rose sharply following the Tokyo Round changes, reflecting the growth in protectionism, especially in the US and its unilateral action in areas over which the GATT had no jurisdiction (such as services). Countries like Canada, which had previously sought to deal with issues bilaterally, now found litigation in the GATT necessary to resolve disputes. Several cases were successfully resolved, with 19 of 29 panels from 1979 to 1986 producing reports that were adopted (Stewart, 1993), suggesting that the GATT could work to discipline trade even in cases involving the US and EU. Nonetheless there was general agreement about the need for improvements in the DS process. Proposals were submitted at various meetings and in the Leutwiler Report of 1985 on ways to strengthen the DS system, such as creating a short-list of panelists, encouraging conciliation, tighter timelines for submitting documents to panels, surveillance or enforcement of compliance with panel rulings, and penalties for non-compliance.

When the Uruguay Round was launched in 1986, DS formed one of the 13 (later 15) topics for negotiation, with the aim of strengthening the rules and procedures and improving surveillance to ensure compliance. Widespread support placed procedural changes and increased surveillance of member policies amongst the 'early harvest' results of the UR implemented in May 1989. Within the Americas, Argentina, Brazil, Canada, Jamaica, Mexico and Nicaragua were active in the DS negotiations. Nicaragua and Brazil pressed for measures to strengthen the special and differential (S&D) treatment of developing countries. Jamaica advocated that third parties be able to participate in cases involving grey areas. Argentina proposed removing disputants from panel report approval. Mexico drafted a comprehensive proposal to be the basis of a consensus. Meanwhile, a unanimous proposal was submitted by the De la Paix group, a 13-country coalition, which included Canada, Colombia and Uruguay from the Americas. To bridge the differences between developing country hardliners and the major powers, the group suggested a tighter timetable for different stages of the DS process, using the Director-General to resolve differences in panel selection, removing the right of disputing countries to block any findings and introducing binding arbitration (Finlayson and Weston, 1990). The US favored changes to make panels virtually automatic and more legalistic (using more non-governmental experts) and to ensure that their findings set precedents. In contrast, the EU and Japan sought to increase consultation, conciliation and mediation.

Several changes were accepted and implemented in 1989 on a trial basis, including specific timelines for various stages of the dispute process with a total time limit of 15 months from the initiation of consultations; longer time limits for cases involving developing countries; and legal advice for developing countries involved in a dispute. The following two years focused on the procedure for adopting a panel report, the timeline for its implementation, compensation and retaliation, unilateral measures, rules for 'non-violation' cases, and S&D. A key suggestion in 1990 was the adoption of panel reports unless there was a consensus not to do so or if one of the disputants appealed the findings. Compliance with panel rulings was left undefined; it was to be 'prompt' although 'if it is impracticable to comply immediately ... the contracting party shall have a reasonable period of time in which to do so' (GATT, 1989: 158). In subsequent discussions Mexico proposed a two-year time limit (Stewart, 1993). Others argued that if an appeal found the defendant guilty then retaliation should be allowed automatically. Another key idea, for a single or integrated DS system to govern disputes in all areas, was raised by Canada in 1990. This was linked to countries accepting all the GATT trade rules in a single undertaking and allowing cross-retaliation. Few of the suggestions for S&D treatment were supported. Proposals ranged from mediators considering developing country developmental needs and a review of bilateral solutions to ensure that they met the principle of S&D, to compensation rather than retaliation if the non-complying country is developing, and compensation in excess of injury where it is the affected country. Special treatment for least-developed countries was also raised, including the creation of a separate conciliation body for disputes involving them (GATT, 1990).

The WTO DSU

The final agreement on Dispute Settlement produced the following key results:

- Establishment of the Dispute Settlement Body (DSB).
- Automatic right to a panel unless rejected by consensus (Article 6.1).
- An opportunity for the disputants to review the panel's interim report – if there are no comments this becomes the final report (Article 15).
- All panel reports to be adopted unless opposed by consensus or appealed by the disputants (Article 16).
- The creation of a standing appellate review body with seven members having expertise in law, international trade and GATT, broadly representative of the membership but not attached to any government, of whom three would sit on any single case. The appellate report would be issued in 60 days (or 90 days if necessary) and adopted in 30 days unless opposed by consensus (Article 17).
- Panel reports to be passed by the DSB within nine months of the panel formation, and appellate reports within 12 months (Article 20).
- Implementation of panel/appellate findings may be decided by binding arbitration and usually within 15 months from adoption. Disagreement over the measures implemented is to be assessed by the original panel within 90 days (Article 21).

- If policy changes are not implemented and compensation not agreed upon, the complainant may suspend equivalent concessions. These should usually be in the disputed sector, but if not feasible or effective, they may be in other sectors under the same agreement. If 'the circumstances are serious enough' the suspended concessions may relate to another agreement. The suspensions will be approved by the DSB unless there is a consensus against them. If the defendant objects, the matter will be sent for arbitration by the original panel or by an arbitrator within 60 days, during which time concessions may not be suspended (Article 22).
- Countries agree to take any disputes relating to the agreements first to the WTO for resolution (Article 23).

Other elements of note were:

- Automatic right of a third party to make submissions and to see the disputants' submissions to the panel at its first meeting (Article 10).
- Panels can seek factual advice on scientific or technical issues from experts, excluding employees of governments involved in the dispute and even non-governmental experts unless agreed upon by both parties (Article 13 and Appendix 4).
- Both panel deliberations and appellate proceedings are to be confidential and the opinions anonymous (Articles 14, 17.10–11).

The few specific references to developing countries can be listed as follows:

- During consultations the problems and interests of developing countries shall be given special attention (Article 4.10).
- In a case involving a developing and a developed country, the former may request that at least one panel member be from a developing country (Article 8.10).
- The panel shall make explicit reference to how its report takes into account whatever S&D treatment for developing countries is included in the relevant GATT/WTO provisions (Article 12.11).
- In implementation of any measures following a panel ruling, particular attention should be given to developing country interests (Article 21.2).
- For disputes over the follow-up to panel findings where the complainant is a developing country, there shall be consideration of economic as well as trade impacts of the measures in question (Articles 21.7–8).
- In cases involving least-developed countries, others are to 'exercise due restraint', whether raising matters or asking for compensation/suspension of concessions. They will be given assistance, for example, from the Director-General in resolving disagreements persisting after consultations, by conciliation or mediation rather than through a panel (Article 24).

Initial reactions were generally favorable, though various complaints were registered. For example, penalties remained weak; even if retaliation was more likely to be sanctioned, few countries would pose a credible threat (Weston, 1995). DSB powers were also considerably weakened by limiting its reviews to the procedures, rather than the substance, of national antidumping (AD) and countervailing duties (CVDs) investigations. Moreover, there are concerns that the DSB might lack the capacity to handle the large volume of complaints expected to result from ambiguities and loopholes in the substantive rules. Another critical concern involves the US's ability to use Section 301 of the 1974 Trade Act to initiate WTO cases, to implement WTO-approved retaliation, and to pursue complaints in areas not covered by WTO law.

Experience with the WTO

The number of cases before the WTO has increased sharply; there were 204 complaints involving 161 distinct matters between 1995 and September 2000. As many as 38 cases were solved through panel and Appellate Body (AB) procedures, and there were another 19 active panels (WTO, 2000e). Many developing countries have used the system to bring cases against developed countries as well as other developing countries, suggesting that the new system provides greater equality of access than under the GATT (Brazil, 1998). Many smaller countries have brought and won cases against larger trading partners like Costa Rica's underwear case against the US. In terms of regional distribution, no cases were brought by African WTO members, though a few were involved as third parties in cases like bananas against the European Union (EU) and shrimp against the US, while South Africa was a defendant in a case brought by India. Of the total number of complaints, 26 per cent were brought by developing countries compared to 16 per cent under the GATT. The bulk of developing country cases were against developed countries (see Table 10.1).

Overall, developed countries brought the most cases, and more than their share of world exports. The largest number of cases were still between developed countries (43 per cent of the total); but the share of total cases brought by developed against developing countries has increased the most – from 10 per cent in the GATT to 31 per cent in the WTO. Over 40 per cent of developed country cases were against developing countries, which is more than the developing countries' 27 per cent share of developed countries' exports in 1998. Likewise for developing countries, their cases against developed countries were higher than might have been expected (66 per cent of all developing country complaints compared to 57 per cent of developing country exports). Developed countries have frequently brought the same or similar complaints against a single developing country; for instance, six countries brought separate cases against India's quantitative restrictions, four against Indonesia's measures concerning autos, and three countries against Brazil's auto investment regime. Developing countries have not coordinated their complaints in the same way (Michalopoulos, 1999), though a few examples include the banana and shrimp cases.

Table 10.1 Developed and developing complainants and defendants in WTO DS (1995–2000)

| | Complainant | | Total | % | (% of world imports, 1998) |
	Developed countries	Developing countries			
Defendant					
Developed countries	89	35	124	60	(68)
Developing countries	65	18	83	40	(32)
Total	154	53	207	100	
%	74	26	100		
For comparison: share of GATT DS cases	84%	16%	100%		
(% of world exports, 1998)	(67)	(33)			

Note: Based on cases brought between January 1995 and September 2000. The EU and member countries are counted jointly.

Source: WTO (2000), Kuruvila (1997), and IMF (1999).

The largest single user has been the US, bringing 61 cases. It has also been a leading defendant, with 42 cases, and has been involved in many others as a third party. Second most active has been the EU (with 51 and 41 cases respectively), followed by Canada (10 and 16) which was a third party in 32 cases. Latin America was involved in 33 cases (counting each complainant country separately) as complainants and 43 as defendants. Brazil was the most implicated, with seven cases as complainant and 11 as defendant, followed by Argentina (2 and 12 respectively) and Mexico (6 and 5). Twelve other countries were involved in cases either as complainants or defendants. Although most countries were involved individually, examples of joint complaints include Brazil and Venezuela against US gas standards and similarly US, Canada, Honduras and El Salvador acted jointly as third parties in the Mexican cement case against Guatemala.

10.3   Dispute settlement in regional trade agreements

CUSFTA/NAFTA

A critical impetus in Canada's signature of the Canada–US Free Trade Agreement (CUSFTA) was to reduce the possibility of disputes disrupting bilateral trade, and to ensure that those disputes that did arise were resolved effectively and more expeditiously than possible under the GATT. Similarly, the prospect of speedier DS was one attraction of NAFTA for Mexico.

In NAFTA, there are four different types of dispute resolution processes: those relating to complaints by private investors (under Chapter 11), financial services (Chapter 14), AD and CVDs (Chapter 19) and all other matters (Chapter 20). If a private investor from a NAFTA country claims that another NAFTA government has failed to meet its obligations, Chapter 11 allows the investor to use the host country's domestic courts and arbitration awards are enforceable in domestic courts. In the case of financial services disputes, Chapter 14 establishes that panelists will be selected from a special roster of financial services experts. For AD and CVD cases, instead of appealing a final determination to a domestic court such as the Tribunal Fiscal de la Federación in Mexico, under Chapter 19 a company may request that its government take the case to a binational panel review consisting of two representatives from each country and a fifth selected jointly from a roster of 75 active or retired judges. Once a panel has been requested, its final decision should be reached within 315 days, following a strict timeline for the different stages. The panel reviews the case against national standards, so that in the US the panel considers whether the dumping/subsidizing, injury or the duty was determined according to US law and whether substantial evidence supports the facts. If national standards have not been applied, the panel sends the case back to the national authorities to be reconsidered but it cannot order the duty to be changed (Howse, 1998). An extraordinary challenge is allowed in cases of impropriety or gross error, whereby three judges or former judges selected from a 15-person roster may re-examine virtually the entire case, including the factual and legal analysis, for up to 90 days. Finally, for all other cases, consultations are handled through the various committees created under the agreements. If these fail, the matter may be reviewed by an arbitration panel as established by Chapter 20. The panel involves five members with experience in law, trade or other relevant matters usually selected from a pre-agreed roster of 30 people nominated for renewable three-year terms; the five are selected inversely whereby each country picks panelists from the other country and the chair is a national of the third country. The panel may ask a scientific review board to provide a factual report. The third country may join the consultations if it has substantial interests, or it may attend hearings and receive others' submissions. The final report is due within 160 days of the request for a panel.

If members disagree over whether to resolve differences under the WTO or NAFTA, the dispute shall be settled under NAFTA (Article 2005). In cases involving environmental agreements, sanitary/phytosanitary measures, or standards, the defending country may choose to use NAFTA. Once cases have been directed to NAFTA, they cannot be resubmitted to the WTO or vice versa. The NAFTA side-agreements, although not strictly part of NAFTA, have provided a regional framework for dealing with disputes concerning the environment and labor. This has not satisfied all groups, but it has reduced the use of unilateral mechanisms, and provided useful experience for both hemispheric and multilateral contexts.

Table 10.2 Complainant and defendant countries in NAFTA DS (1994–May 2000)*

	Complainant			Total	100%	(% share of intra-regional imports, 1998)
	Canada	*Mexico*	*US*			
Defendant						
Canada	–	2	14	16	27	(31)
Mexico	3	–	8	11	18	(15)
US	14	19	–	33	55	(54)
Total	17	21	22	60	100	
100%	28	35	37	100		
(% share of intra-regional exports, 1998)	(35)	(20)	(45)			

* Active and completed.

Source: Canada DFAIT (1997) and NAFTA (2000).

The large number of NAFTA DS cases speaks to its success. Some 60 cases have been brought under Chapters 19 and 20, as shown in 10.2. The US has been both the most frequent complainant and defendant, while Canada came second as defendant and Mexico second as complainant. The share of cases defended by all three countries is roughly proportionate to their share of imports from within the region. Mexico brought nearly twice as many complaints relative to its share of exports to the region (see Ortíz Mena, Vol. II for a discussion on Mexico's use of DS under NAFTA), while both Canadian and US complaints were less than might have been expected.

As Table 10.3 shows, four of the 60 cases were under Chapter 20, and none involved the extraordinary challenge committee. According to the Canadian government, the Chapter 19 process has worked well: in nine of 14 cases, the duties were reduced following a binational panel review (Mercury in Howse, 1998). Nonetheless the government still advocates significant reform if not elimination of the trade-remedy system within NAFTA. 'Despite the clear success of Chapter Nineteen ... Canada continues to believe that the application of trade remedies has no place in a free-trade area' (Canada DFAIT, 1997: 3).

Procedures for investor–state disputes are not in the public domain, making it difficult to obtain information about the number of complaints that have been brought and resolved. Most of those shown in Table 10.3 have been subject to a NAFTA tribunal, though without public hearings. By September 2000, of ten complaints known to have been raised, one was resolved privately, and the rest were the subject of a NAFTA tribunal, with three decisions rendered.

Mercosur

The Mercosur DS system set-up by the Brasilia Protocol in 1991 was to be temporary until the negotiation of a new Mercosur institutional structure to

Table 10.3 DS cases in NAFTA (1994–99)

	Chapter 19 cases		Chapter 20 cases		Chapter 11 cases*
	Initiated	Concluded	Initiated	Concluded	
1994	9	0	0	0	–
1995	10	7	1 (agriculture)	0	–
1996	5 (14 panel reviews in 9 months from 1996–97)	8 panel decisions	11 consultations on 10 issues; 1 went to arbitration	1 panel report (agriculture)	–
1997	11	3	1 (corn brooms)	0	Fuel additive: US v Canada
1998	9	4	2 (cross-border trucking services and cross-border scheduled bus services)	1 panel report (corn brooms)	Funeral homes: Canada v US Metal waste: US v Mexico PCB waste: US v Canada Water: US v Canada
1999	10	6	0	0	Lumber: US v Canada Gas additive: Canada v US

* Cases are brought by investors against a government; two additional cases have involved Mexico.

Note: In May 2000, there were 13 active cases under Chapters 19 and 20. The table excludes 17 cases terminated without any decision.

Source: Canada DFAIT (1997), NAFTA (2000) and various newspaper reports.

deal with the customs union (to become effective in January 1995). However, the Ouro Preto Protocol, which set out Mercosur's institutional structure and came into force in December 1995, ratified the system created under the Brasilia Protocol, adding new DS possibilities. Together, the two protocols provide four ways to deal with disputes: bilateral negotiations, consultations with the Trade Commission (a creation of the Ouro Preto Protocol), claims before the Trade Commission and the Common Market Group (CMG), and arbitration. As Mercosur bodies are intergovernmental and make decisions by consensus of all members, legal conflicts between a state and a Mercosur resolution are avoided since a country's consent is required to pass each binding decision. Also, states must always be involved in the conflict; conflict among individuals is left to national laws while conflicts between states and individuals or companies require 'sponsorship' of the state.

Under the Brasilia Protocol, state to state disputes must first undergo direct negotiations for 15 days. If disagreement continues, the dispute may be submitted to the CMG for a recommendation within 30 days. The CMG hears all affected parties and may ask for technical advice. Failing agreement, the parties may resort to binding arbitration. The Arbitration Tribunal is constituted ad hoc each time with three arbiters, one from each country involved and one from a third country chosen by the Administrative Secretariat from a list of candidates who acts as President of the Tribunal. If more than one state holds the same position in a dispute, they must unify their representation before the Tribunal. Should evidence suggest that one party risks irreversible damages, the tribunal may make an interim ruling to end the existing situation. Otherwise, it has 60 days to rule and settle the conflict, with an extra 30 days if needed. The judgement must be adopted by a majority and the decision is binding, with no scope for appeal or resubmission for a second arbitration. The votes are secret, as are the details of any opposing views. The judgement must be honored within 15 days, unless otherwise decided by the tribunal; also, the defendant may ask for clarification of the judgement. If it does not comply in time, the complainant may withdraw trade concessions or adopt temporary retaliatory measures.

In cases involving individuals and companies, Chapter V of the Brasilia Protocol requires a claim be submitted to their respective National Bureau of the CMG with evidence that a member has acted contrary to the treaty. If the National Bureau takes up the case, it may consult with the National Bureau of the other country or submit the matter to the CMG. The CMG, after an evaluation, may reject the claim or call for a panel of experts to consider the case in 30 days and request that the member modify the rules or measures. If the country does not comply within 15 days, the case may go to arbitration directly, avoiding direct negotiations and the CMG hearings.

The Ouro Preto Protocol created the Trade Commission, an intergovernmental body to advise the CMG and make binding decisions by consensus requiring the consent of the defending member. It includes four members from each country and four alternates. The Trade Commission handles consultations and claims, whether by a state, company or individual, involving situations foreseen by the Brasilia Protocol (Articles 1 to 25), and related to the Commission's area of expertise. Claims made to the Commission can also be pursued through the CMG. After discussion at the first Commission meeting, it is submitted to one of nine Technical Committees if no decision is reached. Within 30 days, the Technical Committee must issue its opinions (whether joint or individual in the absence of consensus). If the Trade Commission cannot reach a consensus, it must submit an outline of the different positions to the CMG, which has 30 days to decide on the matter. If the CMG, by consensus, agrees with the complainant, it will set a time by which the defending state must comply with its recommendations. If there is still no consensus, the matter can be taken to the Arbitration Tribunal (Chapter IV of the Brasilia Protocol).

Table 10.4 DS consultations, claims and tribunals in Mercosur (1995–2000)

	1995	1996	1997	1998	1999	2000	Total
New consultations in the Trade Commission	128	84	71	32	39	54	408
Satisfactorily concluded	121	74	52	17	2	–	266
(%)	(94)	(88)	(73)	(53)	(5)		
Unsatisfactorily concluded before Dec. 2000	7	5	8	6	1	–	27
(%)	(5)	(6)	(11)	(19)	(2.5)		
Pending up to Dec. 2000	0	5	11	9	36	–	61
(%)	(0)	(6)	(15)	(28)	(92)		
Claims before the Trade Commission	–	1	2	3	1*	–	7
Claims directed to the CMG	–	–	2	3	1	–	7
Arbitration tribunals	–	–	–	–	2	1	3

Source: Actas de la Comisión de Comercio to 31 December 2000.

By far the most active procedure has been the consultation and claim process before the Trade Commission. Sensitive cases such as autos and sugar are being resolved through bilateral negotiations. Only four cases have been brought for arbitration (2 in 1999, 1 in 2000 and 1 in 2001). The largest initiator of consultations has been Argentina, initiating more than half of all cases, two-thirds of them against Brazil. In some cases there have been references to the GATT/WTO to justify the policies under investigation. This was the case in 1995 with Uruguay's complaint about Argentina's treatment of paper imports and with Brazil's complaint about Argentina's payments on textile exports, while in 2000 the arbitration case on textiles resulted from Argentine safeguards applied under the WTO Agreement on Textiles and Clothing (ATC) (for a more complete discussion on each country's use of Mercosur's DS mechanism, see case studies in Vol. II).

The number of consultations has declined sharply (Table 10.4), from 128 during 1995 to 36 in 1999. One reason might be a greater familiarity and understanding of the rules and workings of the customs union; 80 per cent of the cases in 1995 were settled after members provided the required information. However, the share of cases satisfactorily concluded has fallen, with a growing number pending resolution. This reflects a lack of political will to deal with disagreements through the claims process.

Andean Community

Andean Pact members created a permanent Court of Justice in 1979 to declare community law, solve differences and interpret the Cartagena Agreement, which founded the Pact. However, the Court only began work in 1984. In May 1987, through the Quito Protocol, members agreed to reform the institutional framework and there were further institutional changes in 1996 through the Trujillo Protocol. The Andean Pact was renamed Andean Community (AC) and three new organisms were established in addition to the pre-existing Commission, an intergovernmental executive body: the General Secretariat, the Andean Presidential Council and the Andean Foreign Relations Ministers Council. Finally, in 1999 the Cochabamba Protocol gave the Court new functions, like arbitration.

Two principles governing the AC legal system make its DS procedures quite different from those of NAFTA and Mercosur. First, AC norms directly affect a member's domestic legal system as they have full effect domestically without any government or legislative action. Community law has supremacy over national norms; if there is a contradiction between a domestic and community norm, the latter prevails. Second, the Court's applications and interpretations of community norms bind states without consent. Besides Court rulings, the sources of community law include treaties among AC members, decisions by the Foreign Relations Ministers Council and the Commission, and General Secretariat resolutions.

The Court consists of one judge from each AC country (Bolivia, Colombia, Ecuador, Peru and Venezuela) elected for six years with one possible re-election. It has jurisdiction over cases involving non-compliance, nullification, and pre-trial interpretation. In cases of non-compliance with AC norms, a mandatory administrative procedure must be followed before a case goes to the Court. The General Secretariat may initiate a case prompted by its own research or in response to a request by member states or individuals. An 'observation note' detailing possible non-compliance is sent to the member under investigation, to which a response is required. It may then issue a 'non-compliance report' requiring prompt corrective action. The report may be appealed to both the General Secretariat and the Court, but meanwhile compliance is required. Failing this, the Secretariat may take the matter to the Court, which may order suspension or restriction of AC benefits for the non-complying member. The Court may also consider cases of nullification, where Commission decisions or General Secretariat resolutions violate norms of the AC legal system. Such cases may be brought by the Commission, the General Secretariat, individual members (if they had not voted for the Commission decision being challenged), and corporations or individual people directly affected by the AC norms. Finally, prejudgement interpretation by the Court may be sought by domestic courts in cases involving AC norms, as it is the only tribunal authorized to do this interpretation.

Once a case is admitted the Court notifies the defendant, which has 30 days to respond. After a period for evidence and hearings with the parties, the Court has 15 days to rule. It may nullify a norm, decision or resolution, or, in cases of non-compliance, establish corrective measures to be taken the day after the public reading of the ruling, though appeals are allowed. The Cochabamba Protocol extended the functions of the Court to include resolution of cases involving an AC body's negligence of obligations, arbitration of disagreements upon disputants' request, and the hearing of labor disputes within AC institutions. Also, individuals can submit a case directly before the Court in cases of country non-compliance and the Court's ruling allows them to sue for damages.

Thus member states have transferred conflict resolution to the Court under the AC DS system. The Court's jurisdiction is compulsory and the process adjudicatory. An interesting characteristic is the General Secretariat's capacity to act without a member's request to ensure compliance with community rules. This contrasts sharply with Mercosur where states retain control with negotiation at the core of the system, and arbitration only as a last resort.

Between 1969 and 1979 the Andean Commission was in charge of negotiation, mediation and conciliation. Once the Court was in operation, only the administrative step of the system was used for several years: the General Secretariat considered some non-compliance cases and issued a number of 'observation notes'. It was not until 1996 that the first case of non-compliance was submitted to the Court (Lloreda Ricaurte, 1998). As Table 10.5 shows, the prejudicial interpretation is the resolution method most commonly used.

Table 10.5   Nullity, non-compliance and prejudicial interpretation in Andean DS (1985–2000)

	Nullity cases	Non-compliance cases	Prejudicial interpretation
1985	1	–	–
1986	2	–	–
1987	–	1[a]	1
1988	–	–	4
1989	–	–	6
1990	–	–	6
1991	–	–	3
1992	4[b]	–	3[c]
1993	–	–	7[d]
1994	–	–	10
1995	–	–	34
1996	1	3	33
1997	5	3	32
1998	3	10	45
1999	3	14	41
2000	6	17	51
Total	25	48	236

Note: To August 2000; (a) the Court rejected the case; (b) three cases were rejected; (c) the three cases were rejected; and (d) one petition was rejected.

Source: Derived from www.comunidadandina.org, and the Andean Community Court of Justice.

The largest number of rulings against a single country in non-compliance cases was six against Ecuador, largely due to breaches of the common external tariff. The three most frequent causes for disputes are restrictive measures (including additional duties on imports), the common external tariff, and payment of AC duties (Fairlie, 2001). See country case studies in Vol. II for a more in-depth discussion on each country's use of the AC DS mechanism.

10.5   Evaluation and proposals

NAFTA

Initially, NAFTA appeared to offer advantages over both domestic and GATT review processes in terms of scope, timelines and effectiveness (binding DS of trade-remedy cases). For instance, without remands, the average review process in the US was 734 days, while in Canada the average was 462 days. Some of these relative advantages were diminished with the new WTO rules and with the shortening of domestic review timelines (Penner, 1996). Nevertheless, NAFTA mechanisms have been effective in resolving many disputes with a third of the cases terminated before a decision was issued. In several AD cases, the panels have led to duty reductions. To date, none of the panel decisions have been appealed to the extraordinary challenge process, whereas three such challenges accrued under CUSFTA. But the remanding of decisions to national authorities has caused delays, as have the withdrawal of panelists and late depositions, motions and brief filings. On average, though, the NAFTA mechanisms have produced findings more quickly than the national judicial review mechanisms.

There have been various criticisms of the NAFTA dispute system.

- Financial capacity to bring a case can be a constraint, as the firm requesting the government to bring the case often has counsel present throughout (costing US$200,000 to US$600,000, according to estimates in Howse, 1998).
- Panelists may not have the capacity necessary to fully analyze a case's facts following the shift from experts in trade law or economics in CUSFTA to judges or retired judges in NAFTA.
- The Chapter 19 process has not been able to overturn inappropriately applied AD or CVD duties. Some products have been the subject of several cases as new complaints may be submitted leading to new investigations.
- The limited authority of binational panels, which can only review AD and CVD within national laws where the standards of review are different, has led to suggestions of asymmetry. Canadian law requires much greater errors for an agency's decision to be overturned, and therefore Canadian complaints are more likely to be supported by a panel than US complaints.
- The ad-hoc nature of panels may make their findings inconsistent. Options to increase coherence include creating a standing body with

technical support resources available and broadening panel membership to avoid national bias.

- Transparency and accountability questions have been raised in Canada, partly in response to cases involving investor–state disputes under Chapter 11. In a fuel additive case, the Canadian government paid C\$20 million in compensation to a US company in return for it dropping its NAFTA challenge. The settlement of the dispute behind closed doors, as allowed under NAFTA, was criticized by the financial press as well as traditional NAFTA opponents. Other transparency and accountability concerns have been raised in the US and Canada, even when cases were taken to NAFTA tribunals.

Finally, a number of disagreements, in particular between Canada and the US, have not been addressed within NAFTA or the WTO. Instead, the governments and industries involved have chosen to address politically sensitive issues such as lumber, wheat and autos through bilateral agreements outside NAFTA or through a blue ribbon panel.[1] Some cases, like wheat, were discussed bilaterally following Canadian requests for WTO and NAFTA consultations (Canada DFAIT, 1999b).

Mercosur

Initially, Mercosur's system received praise because of its flexibility and limited bureaucracy. The process was designed to use the agreement's pre-established institutions and form ad-hoc tribunals for each case instead of constructing a permanent arbitration tribunal. Also, the initial negotiation phase allowed countries to accommodate interests without resorting to legal proceedings. Two factors contributed to the initial approval of a flexible system: the poor performance of a strict rule-oriented approach to DS in the Andean Pact and the belief that liberalization towards a customs union in Mercosur could be better managed if a political window were kept open. However, when the transition period formally concluded in December 1994, few changes were made besides the creation of the Trade Commission in January 1995. Over time it became clear that the DS process was not evolving towards a more institutionalized and procedurally rigorous approach. On the contrary, the political and diplomatic traits of the system were accentuated, making overall policies, including the management of disputes, heavily dependent upon each member's domestic political context.

A review of the working of the Mercosur DS system shows that various problems have emerged:

- The number of consultations not satisfactorily concluded has been increasing every year except in 1999, when the share of pending cases rose to 92 per cent of cases brought for consultation. Similarly, the share of cases pending resolution has also grown from year to year.

- Very few cases were taken beyond the consultation stage to become claims (seven of 354).
- The Trade Commission no longer considers consultations in plenary, but rather automatically passes them on to a Technical Committee. Moreover, the Technical Committees (formed by government officials) are almost never able to reach a joint opinion.
- The role of the private sector is limited to presenting the claim and subsequently lobbying government officials.
- While there have only been four arbitration tribunals, two problems have already emerged. First, because tribunals are ad hoc, there are divergent interpretations of Mercosur norms. Second, the system does not allow for appellate action against tribunal findings except for minor clarifications.

Given these systemic problems, it is understandable that governments, since 1995, have preferred to resort to diplomatic and presidential intervention and even leave consultations pending. Two amendments could strengthen and streamline the Mercosur DS system. First, a permanent arbitration tribunal without supranational powers would solve problems of divergent interpretations and rulings that can't be repealed without creating a large bureaucratic entity. Of five permanent members, three arbitrators could hear each case and their interpretation of the norms could be appealed to the full tribunal. Second, private sector participation through the observation of Trade Commission sessions by the firms whose case is presented would pressure its government to make a strong presentation. Another option to augment private sector participation would be to allow the firm to present its own case during the initial consultation.

Andean Community

The 1980s was a lost decade for economic integration in Latin America and the Andean Pact countries were not an exception; deadlines to achieve a free trade area and customs union were not met, many exceptions were negotiated, and business lost faith in the process. Court proceedings were rare prior to 1995, though evidence suggests that an informal agreement to not use the system prevailed rather than widespread compliance with regional commitments (Aninat del Solar, 1992). High rates of non-compliance, 92 cases before 1983, were largely caused by economic crises (Hurtado Larrea, 1985). A three-month moratorium was then declared and members agreed not to bring charges against each other (Cárdenas, 1994). Non-compliance cases were not presented again until 1996. Despite the inherent virtues of retaliation as provided by the Andean Pact, Jaramillo Rojas (2000) attributes its disuse to three factors: a generalized non-compliance among members, difficulties in compliance posed by the economic crises, and fears of deteriorating political and diplomatic relationships among members. With the new energy injected into the integration process, as well as the recent reforms in the DS system, an increase in its use is likely.

The relatively frequent use of prejudicial interpretation as the most often used DS action steps up AC harmonization. More than other resolution methods, it guarantees a homogenous interpretation of community norms at the domestic level, resolving a problem that is still pending in Mercosur and that the WTO solved through the creation of the Appellate Body. Consistent interpretation of the norms will become ever more important as FTAA negotiations proceed, since the coexistence of multiple norms at different levels on the same subject could pose new legal problems. Community norms are being formulated for intra-bloc relations, while third-party relations are left to national legislation. FTAA agreements, in antidumping for instance, would supersede AC norms, making them applicable to neither intra-AC relations or relations between an AC member and a non-AC FTAA member. However, the AC norm could still be valid for relations with countries outside of the FTAA. On the contrary, if the FTAA were only to enunciate principles or minimum standards instead of full-fledged agreements, then AC countries could apply community norms to intra-bloc trade and national legislation to trade with other countries. In response to these two drastically different roles for AC norms, González Vigil (2001) highlights the relevance and importance of harmonization of domestic and AC norms.

The WTO

In many respects the high hopes of the WTO mechanism have been borne out. As a Brazilian diplomat noted, countless aspects of the DSU could be improved, but on the whole it is a well-conceived mechanism that has promoted the fulfillment of WTO objectives (Brazil, 1998). The Canadian government has stated that, 'as a frequent user of the system, Canada believes the Dispute Settlement Understanding has clearly demonstrated its fundamental effectiveness and viability' (Canada DFAIT, 1999a: 1) and consequently refrained from proposing major changes during the 1999 review. Nevertheless, experience has subsequently tempered the initial enthusiasm and led to several suggestions for change, revolving around issues of capacity, implementation and authority. To these issues we turn.

Capacity

The DS mechanism may become overloaded without additional resources at many levels. The number of disputes is projected to continue rising, particularly as exemptions covering developing countries' commitments expire. Also, submissions and reports are becoming more technical and lengthier than the 20 to 30-page GATT average. There is also major concern about the capacity of developing countries, especially smaller WTO members, to protect their interests given the level of technical expertise required and the tighter deadlines.[2] In turn, the WTO Secretariat's technical assistance is seriously limited relative to the number of active cases.[3] Moreover, the Secretariat is meant to advise on issues rather than specific cases. Hence many developing countries have sought external legal counsel from international law firms at considerable cost (ACWL, 1998). Initially governments had to have their own lawyers represent them; this requirement changed with the AB decision to allow the St Lucia government to be represented by a private lawyer in one of the banana cases. This position was supported by Canada, but opposed by the US. For these reasons, the new Advisory Center on WTO Law will play a useful role, providing governments with an assessment of how to proceed with a case and thus reducing legal costs. It could advise countries, particularly smaller ones, about joint presentation of complaints or joint participation as third parties. Several donor countries provide trade-related technical assistance, some of which addresses DS, but the amounts and effectiveness of the training have been criticized, particularly where it is managed bilaterally rather than through the WTO (Rajapathirana *et al.*, 2000). Bilateral assistance tends to be tied to the use of a donor's experts, and it involves a certain amount of duplication rather than complement of effort.

Capacity issues must also be considered if the process is opened to non-state actors such as NGOs or the private sector. To promote transparency, some have argued for the right to make submissions and even appear independently before panels. This may entrench the 'laissez-litigez' nature of the DS (Ostry, 1999) and would increase WTO costs, panelists' workloads, and panel timetables (Canada DFAIT, 1999a). Without additional resources to cover training and other costs, southern NGOs would not be able to participate in a more open WTO, which would merely exacerbate the existing 'structural asymmetry' (Ostry, 1999).

Finally, the roster of panelists must be expanded. With more countries involved in cases as third parties, it will be increasingly difficult to find panelists since nationals of countries involved cannot be used. Lengthy cases can place overwhelming demands on official representatives of smaller, developing countries who often have other non-WTO business in Geneva. A solution may be to create a permanent roster of panelists and AB members.

Implementation of DSB recommendations and retaliatory measures

While many panel and AB reports have been adopted on schedule, their findings have not been implemented as expeditiously as intended, and some delays have irreversibly damaged trade. Various parts of the WTO, notably trade remedies, limit the scope for reversing trade restrictions. For example, the AD agreement leaves ample margin for investigators with virtually no possible reinstatement under the DSU (see Tortora and Tussie, Chapter 6, for a discussion on loopholes left in the AD agreement).[4] Another problem is that neither the panel nor the AB is required to rule on remedial action nor a reasonable time for compliance.[5] Panels may limit themselves to recommending that the defendant bring an offending measure into conformity with its WTO obligations, which gives the defendant room to determine what approach to adopt in its compliance. The offending policy has not been withdrawn in some instances, leaving complainants with no other option than retaliation. This has raised questions about the appropriateness of proposed retaliatory measures, and whether they provide a solution for smaller, undiversified economies. Should a defendant introduce a new measure, there are no clear procedures as to whether a complainant can request retaliation before the consistency of the new measure is assessed (Herman in Canada House of Commons, 1999).[6] In the banana case, in which there was more than one claimant, the strongest country asked for retaliatory action while the others asked the panel to review the defendant's implementation of the recommendation.

Three alternatives have been proposed for dealing with retaliation among asymmetrical countries: financial compensation, multilateralization of sanctions, and the withdrawal of retaliation for alternative compensation. Financial compensation is a traditional response, and would benefit smaller, developing countries. While such compensation may offset damages, the multilateralization of sanctions may be needed to ensure the offending policy is changed (Rodrik, 1995, and Das in Raghavan, 2000). Multilateralization is perhaps a more feasible option, especially given its precedence in the United Nations collective security provisions. Multilateralization would level the field in developing countries' favor, making an eventual retaliatory action credible. The US has proposed another alternative, and the House of Representatives passed it in the Trade Promotion Authority Act, to offer a more palatable method of compensation: trade-expanding compensation. By allowing non-compliance in one area in exchange for concessions in another area, this alternative pursued in the US may offer a win-win solution.

Authority

Panel and AB authority has been questioned. Many panels have resulted in substantive interpretations of WTO agreements, involving an expansion of member rights and/or obligations. This judicial interpretation departs from rule-making through multilateral negotiation as intended in the WTO. Even if the countries involved can be satisfied, there is a question about how to address the interests of other countries. One suggestion is that other countries be allowed to make limited submissions to the AB even if they had not previously registered a 'third-party' interest (Canada DFAIT, 1999a). Another is that the results from a panel or AB should only apply in that case; more radically, where changes in rights and obligations are at stake, the matter should be brought to the General Council for approval by all member countries (Das in Raghavan, 2000). Others have argued that panel and AB decisions might be more acceptable if their deliberations were open to the public, and if members of the public were able to participate through submissions. However, also at issue is the capacity of panels and ABs to cope with additional inputs, and developing country NGOs' capacity to participate.

10.5 Final remarks

The WTO DS system provides developing countries with the opportunity to defend their rights and to pressure other countries to meet their obligations in a more balanced way than in the GATT. However, the review of the rules and experience with them, has called attention to four kinds of problems: developing countries' limited technical capacity and scarce financial resources to make effective use of the system; loopholes and ambiguities in substantive rules (for AD, for instance, see Chapter 6); discrepancy among procedural rules such as sequencing problems with Articles 21 and 22; and controversial AB interpretations of WTO agreements.

Technical capacity problems can be solved in the medium term through assistance with technical training and capacity building. Advisory centers on international trade law within the hemisphere, whether at the national, sub-regional or even regional level, could be created to advise both private sector (and NGO) interests and governments about trade disputes. Valuable advice could be offered on the best way of seeking redress, that is on what basis and at what level: nationally, regionally, hemispherically or through the WTO. Such centers could provide poorer, smaller countries in the hemisphere with the legal expertise to bring or defend cases and could also train judges, panelists and others involved in the adjudication of disputes.

However, the problems of loopholes, discrepancies and controversial interpretations are more difficult to solve because they rely on the consensus of all members to change both substantive and procedural rules. The AB interpretations that allegedly augment or diminish rights are particularly serious, as all WTO rule-making supposedly requires negotiations among all members. If the AB augments the rights of some members outside the WTO-negotiating framework without counter-concessions, it unfairly changes the balance of rights and obligations under the agreements. Rather than requiring a consensus of all members for adoption of the AB reports or a vote on the new rules, the problem could be prevented by a search for common interpretations of ambiguous provisions in the WTO Councils that could then be submitted for approval by all members.

The final shape of the hemispheric system will depend upon the substantive results achieved in the FTAA negotiations. First, the deeper the commitments the more rule-oriented the system should be. Second, it is still unclear whether it will be a unified DS system or whether each chapter will have its own institutional arrangement according to the subject matter. The five years of experience with the WTO system and the FTAA text's similarity to the DSU text could allow for improvement on questioned aspects of the WTO system including transparency and clarity in the compliance process in the scope of a similar hemispheric system.

The FTAA should also build upon sub-regional experiences. First, it should be acknowledged that success is not guaranteed from mere replication of a successful model. DS must take into account the idiosyncrasies of each integration initiative, so that it may be truly effective. Second, experience underlines that a system's effectiveness and the political will to comply with commitments are closely related; no system can right the wrongs of countries fully failing to comply with commitments because of a massive economic crisis. The AC system was dysfunctional in the 1980s precisely because of such non-compliant behavior, and Mercosur also experienced DS disuse in 1999 and 2000 when the economic crisis reduced the political will to cement the trade bloc. A more constructive lesson to be learned from the AC system is the practicality of pre-judicial interpretation, as harmonized interpretation of community norms greatly benefits the integration initiative. Similarly, Mercosur offers an example of the utility of an appellant body, in that it offers both reaffirmation of the decisions for unconvinced governments and it may cushion the losing country from further domestic pressure.

Notes

1. See Weston (1996). In the case of lumber, however, Canada has decided to take its long-standing dispute with the US forest industry to the WTO.
2. Brazil suggested changing the timelines from calendar days to business days to provide some breathing room (Brazil, 1998).
3. The WTO's regular budget for technical assistance is CHF0.74 million and the Director-General has called for an increase to CHF10 million by 2003. Meanwhile, the WTO has a trust fund for extra-budgetary contributions for technical assistance.
4. The AD Agreement allows investigators to 'construct' the prices of the exporter, leaving antidumping at the discretion of the investigating authorities, with virtually no possibility for reinstatement under the DSU (Brazil, 1998).
5. Arbitration has determined that a reasonable timeframe can range from eight to 15 months (Zuijdwijk, 1999).
6. EU remedial action in the banana case addressed the immediate concerns of the panel but also introduced new measures that were opposed by the complaining countries. Article 21.5 is unclear about whether such new measures should be reviewed by a new panel and then a new appeal.

Bibliography

Abare (1995) *US Farm Bill 1995*, Canberra, Abare Policy Monograph No. 5.

ACWL (1998) 'An Advisory Centre on WTO Law. A Working Proposal developed by Bangladesh, Colombia, Hong Kong, China, The Netherlands, Norway, The Philippines, South Africa, Tanzania, Tunisia, Turkey, United Kingdom and Venezuela', October.

Ahnlid, A. (1997) 'Performance Requirements and Investment Incentives' at the OECD Symposium on the MAI, Seoul, April.

ALADI (1998) *Cuadro comparativo de las Legislaciones Nacionales sobre Salvaguardias de los Paises Miembros de la ALADI*, ALADI/SEC/dt 390.2/Rev.1 (Montevideo: ALADI), 4 September.

Amsden, A. (1989) *Asia's New Giant* (New York, NY: Cambridge University Press).

Anderson, K., Erwidodo and M. Ingco (1999) 'Integrating Agriculture into the WTO: the Next Phase' presented at The WTO-World Bank Conference on Developing Countries in a Millennium Round, Geneva, 20–21 September.

Aninat del Solar, A. (1992) 'La institucionalidad en el Grupo Andino', LC/R.1151 (Santiago, Chile: ECLAC) 10 June.

Annan, K. (1997) 'Secretary General Stresses International Community's Objective of Harnessing Informatics Revolution for Benefit of Mankind' in UNCSTD Inter-Agency Project on Universal Access to Basic Communication and Information Services, 3rd Session, Geneva, 12 May.

Aranda, V. and K. Sauvant (1996) 'Incentives and Foreign Direct Investment' *UNCTAD Current Studies Series A*, No. 30 (Geneva: UNCTAD).

Armentano, D. (1996) *Antitrust and Monopoly* (Oakland, CA: The Independent Institute).

Bachtler, J. (1996) 'Policy Competition and Foreign Direct Investment in Western Europe' presented at the OECD Workshop on Policy Competition and Foreign Direct Investment, Paris.

Baumol, W. (1990) 'Entrepreneurship: Productive, Unproductive and Destructive', *Journal of Political Economy*, Vol. 98, No. 5.

——, J. Panzar and R. Willig (1982) *Contestable Markets and The Theory of Industry Structure* (New York, NY: Harcourt Brace).

Becker, G. (1983) 'A Theory of Competition among Pressure Groups for Political Influence', *Quarterly Journal of Economics*, Vol. 98, No. 3, pp. 371–400.

Benchekroun, H., N.V. Long and H. Tian (1998) *Learning by Doing and Strategic Trade Policy* (Montreal: Centre Universitaire de Recherche et Analyse des Organisations).

Bergsten, C.F. (1998) 'Fifty Years of the GATT/WTO: Lessons from the Past for Strategies for the Future' presented at the WTO Symposium 'Fifty Years: Looking Back, Looking Forward', Geneva, April. Available at http://www.iie.com/papers/bergesten0498.htm.

Bhagwati, J. and T.N. Srinivasan (1996) 'Trade and Environment: Does Environmental Diversity Detract from the Case for Free Trade?' in J. Bhagwati and R. Hudec (eds), *Fair Trade and Harmonization. Prerequisites for Free Trade?* Vol. 1. *Economic Analysis* (Cambridge, MA: The MIT Press).

Blonigen, B. and T. Prusa (2001) 'Antidumping', *National Bureau of Economic Research (NBER) Working Paper* No. 8398 (Cambridge, MA: NBER) July.

Bonisteel, S. (2001) 'Digital Divide Growing for Latin America', *Newsbytes* available at http://www.newsbytes.com/news/01/164536.html consulted 16 April 2001.

Brazil (1998) 'The Brazilian Government's Perspectives on the DSU' presented at the First Annual US Conference on Dispute Resolution in the WTO, Washington, 24 June.

Brown, D., A. Deardorff and R. Stern (1996) 'International Labor Standards and Trade: a Theoretical Analysis' in J. Bhagwati and R. Hudec (eds) *Fair Trade and Harmonization. Prerequisites for Free Trade?* Vol. 1. *Economic Analysis* (Cambridge, MA: The MIT Press).

Butkeviciene, J. (2000) 'Movement of Natural Persons under the GATS: Perspectives for New Negotiations' presented at the Sub-regional Seminar for Member Countries of East African Cooperation, Kenya, 2–3 March.

——— and D. Diaz (1998) 'Trade in Services: a Positive Agenda for Developing Countries' presented at Taller Comercio de Servicios, Panama, 25–26 October.

Canada DFAIT – Department of Foreign Affairs and International Trade – (1997) 'NAFTA: A Partnership at Work' available at http://www.infoexport.gc.ca/nafta/partners-e.asp consulted 24 August 1998.

——— (1999a) 'Dispute Settlement Understanding' *DFAIT Discussion Paper* available at http://www.infoexport.gc.ca/discussion/dsu-e.asp.

——— (1999b) *Opening Doors to the World: Canada's International Market Access Priorities 1999* (Ottawa: DFAIT).

Canada House of Commons (1999) 'Canada and the Future of the World Trade Organization: Advancing a Millennium Agenda in the Public Interest. Report of the Standing Committee on Foreign Affairs and International Trade' (Ottawa: Canada House of Commons) June.

Cárdenas, M. (1994) 'Implicaciones del regionalismo abierto en el ordenamiento jurídico del Acuerdo de Cartagena' in *Integración Latinoamericana* (Buenos Aires: BID-INTAL) November.

Castells, M. (1996) 'The New Business World: Networks and Firms' presented at The ILO Enterprise Forum, Geneva, 8–9 November.

Caves, R. (1998) 'Industrial Organization and New Findings on the Turnover and Mobility of Firms', *Journal of Economic Literature*, December.

CEI – Centro de Economía Internacional – (2000) *New Trade and Investment Opportunities* (Buenos Aires: Ministry of Foreign Affairs).

CEPAL – Economic Commission for Latin America – (1996) 'Nota Bibliogràfica sobre el Comercio de Servicios: Conceptos y Principios de Liberalizaciòn', DOC. CEPAL/ALCA/GTS/001, 3 December.

Chadha, R., B. Hoekman, W. Martin, A. Oyejide, M. Pangestu, D. Tussie and J. Zarrouk (2000) 'Developing Countries and the Next Round of WTO Negotiations', *The World Economy*, Vol. 23, No. 4, April.

Chudnovsky, D. and A. López (1997) 'Las estrategias de las empresas transnacionales en Argentina y Brasil: ¿qué hay de nuevo en los años noventa?' *Centro de Investigaciones para la Transformación (CENIT) Documento de Trabajo*, No. 23 (Buenos Aires: CENIT).

——— (1998) 'La inversión extranjera directa en la Argentina en los años 1990: tendencias, determinantes y modalidades' in *Argentina de cara al mundo 3. Aportes para un debate necesario* (Buenos Aires: Centro de Economía Internacional).

——— (2001) *La transnacionalización de la economía argentina* (Buenos Aires: EUDEBA).

CNCE – Comisión Nacional de Comercio Exterior – (1997, 1999) *Annual Report* (Buenos Aires: CNCE).

Cohen, W. and R. Levin (1989) 'Empirical Studies of Innovation and Market Structure' in R. Schmalensee and R. Willig (eds), *Handbook of Industrial Organization*, Vol. II, North-Holland.

Cowhey, P. and M. Klimenko (1999) 'The WTO Agreement and Telecommunication Policy Reforms', *World Bank Trade Policy Support Paper* available at http://www1.worldbank.org/wbiep/trade/papers_2000/bptelecom.pdf.

Dam, K. (1970) *The GATT: Law and the International Economic Organization* (Chicago, IL: University of Chicago Press).

David, M. and M. Nonnemberg (1997) 'Mercosur: Integração Regional e o Comércio de Produtos Agrícolas' (Instituto de Pesquisa Economica Aplicada (IPEA): Rio de Janeiro), May.

De la Guardia, E. (1997) 'El Acuerdo Multilateral de Inversiones y la Argentina: de la OCDE a la OMC' (Buenos Aires: Permanent Argentine Mission to International Organizations in Geneva).

Dedrick, J. and K. Kraemer (1998) *Asia's Computer Challenge: Threat or Opportunity for the United States and the World* (New York, NY: Oxford University Press).

Dedrick, J., K. Kraemer and J. Palacios (1999) 'Impacts of Liberalization and Economic Integration on Mexico's Computer Sector' (Irvine, CA: Center for Research on Information Technology and Organizations (CRITO), University of California, Irvine). Mimeo.

Demsetz, H. (1973) 'Industry Structure, Market Rivalry, and Public Policy', *Journal of Law and Economics*, Vol. 16, April.

Djankov, S. and B. Hoekman (1998) 'Conditions of Competition and Multilateral Surveillance', *The World Economy*, Vol. 21, November.

Easterbrook, F. (1992) 'Ignorance and Antitrust' in T. Jorde and D. Teece (eds), *Antitrust, Innovation, and Competitiveness* (New York, NY: Oxford University Press).

EC – European Commission – (1997) *Competition Law in the European Communities*. Volume IIB: Explanation of the Rules Applicable to State Aid (Brussels: EC).

EU – European Union – (2000) 'Negotiating Guidelines: Drafting Elements', Informal Paper, 12 July.

Evans, P. (1995) *Embedded Autonomy: States and Industrial Transformation* (Princeton, NJ: Princeton University Press).

Fairlie, A. (2001) 'Informe Andino'. Mimeo.

Falvey, R. and P. Lloyd (1999) 'An Economic Analysis of Extraterritoriality'. Mimeo.

FAO – Food and Agricultural Organization of the United Nations – (various years) Statistics.

Fiani, R. (1998) 'Uma abordagem abrangente da regulação de monopólios: exercício preliminar aplicado a telecomunicações', *Universidade Federal do Rio de Janeiro, Instituto de Economía Discussion Paper*, No. 408, April.

Finlayson, J. and A. Weston (1990) *The GATT, Middle Powers and the Uruguay Round. No. 5. Middle Powers in the International System* (Ottawa: North–South Institute).

Fox, E. and Ordover (1997) 'The Harmonization of Competition and Trade Law' in L. Waverman, W. Comanor and A. Goto (eds), *Competition Policy in the Global Economy: Modalities for Cooperation* (New York, NY: Routledge).

FTAA – Free Trade Area of the Americas – (2000) *Official Hemispheric Database*.

Ganesan, A.V. (1998) 'Strategic Options Available to Developing Countries with regard to a Multilateral Agreement on Investment', *UNCTAD Discussion Paper* No. 134, Geneva.

Gardner, R. (1969) *Sterling-Dollar Diplomacy: the Origins and Prospects of Our International Economic Order* (New York, NY: McGraw Hill).

GATT – General Agreement on Trade and Tariffs (1989) *Activities 1988* (Geneva: GATT).

—— (1990) *Activities 1989* (Geneva: GATT).

Geroski, P. and J. Schwalbach (1991) *Entry and Market Contestability* (Cambridge, MA: Basil Blackwell).

Gibbs, M. (1985) 'Continuing the International Debate on Services', *Journal of World Trade Law*, Vol. 19, No. 3, pp. 199–218.

—— and M. Mashayekhi (1989) 'Elements of a Multilateral Framework of Principles and Rules for Trade in Services' in *Uruguay Round: Papers on Selected Issues* (New York, NY: United Nations).

Gilpin, R. (2000) *The Challenge of Global Capitalism* (Princeton, NJ: Princeton University Press).

Goldstein, J. (1998) 'International Institutions and Domestic Politics: GATT, WTO and the Liberalization of International Trade' in A. Krueger (ed.), *The WTO as an International Organization* (Chicago, IL: University of Chicago Press).

González Vigil, F. (2001) 'La comunidad Andina de Naciones (CAN) ante el ALCA' presented at the IDB – INTAL II Coloquio Academico de las Amèricas, 3–5 April.

Granados, J. (1999) 'El ALCA y la OMC: especulaciones en torno a su interacción' *INTAL–ITD Documento de Trabajo*, No. 4, August.

Grieve, W. and S. Levin (1996) 'Common Carriers, Public Utilities and Competition' in *Industrial and Corporate Change*, Vol. 5, No. 4, pp. 993–1011.

Grilli, E. (2000) 'The Asian Crisis: Trade and Trade Policy Consequences', *Latin American Trade Network (LATN) Working Paper* No. 2 (Buenos Aires: LATN), January.

Hertel, T. and W. Martin (1999) 'Would Developing Countries Gain from Inclusion of Manufactures in the WTO Negotiations?' presented at The WTO–World Bank Conference on Developing Countries in a Millennium Round, Geneva, 20–21 September.

Higgins, R., M. Glueck, D. Kaplan and M. McDonald (1996) 'The Causes and Consequences of the Aluminum MOU' in F. McChesney (ed.), *Economic Inputs, Legal Outputs: the Role of Economists in Modern Antitrust* (New York, NY: John Wiley & Sons).

Hoekman, B. (1988) 'The Uruguay Round Negotiations: Investigating the Scope for Agreement on Safeguards, Services and Agriculture', Unpublished PhD thesis (Ann Arbor, MI: University of Michigan).

—— (1996) 'Assessing the General Agreement on Trade in Services' in Martin and Winters (eds), *The Uruguay Round and the Developing Countries* (Cambridge: Cambridge University Press).

Howse, R. (1998) 'Settling Trade Remedy Disputes: When the WTO Forum is Better than the NAFTA', *Commentary* No. 111 (Toronto: C.D. Howe Institute), June.

Hurtado Larrea, E. (1985) 'Los incumplimientos y la acción asignada a la competencia del tribunal' in *El Tribunal de Justicia del Acuerdo de Cartagena* (Buenos Aires: BID-INTAL).

IMF – International Monetary Fund – (1998) *Direction of Trade Statistics Yearbook 1998* (Washington, DC: IMF).

—— (1999) *Direction of Trade Statistics Yearbook 1999* (Washington, DC: IMF).

—— (2000) *Direction of Trade Statistics Yearbook 2000* (Washington, DC: IMF).

Jackson, J. (1998) *The World Trading System. Law and Policy of International Economic Relations*, second edition (Cambridge, MA: The MIT Press).

Jacquemin, A., P. Lloyd, P. Tharakan and J. Waelbroeck (1998) 'Competition Policy in an International Setting: the Way Ahead' *The World Economy*, Vol. 21, November.

Jaramillo Rojas, G. (2000) 'Solución de controversias, el caso andino' presented at the Interamerican Development Bank, 26 October. Available at www.Iadb.org/mif/conferences/speeches/jaramillo.

Jatar, A.J. and L. Tineo (1998) 'Competition Policy in the Andean Region: Ups and Downs of a Policy in Search of its Place' in M. Mendoza, P. Correa and B. Kotschwar (eds), *The Andean Community and the United States: Trade and Investment Relations in the 1990s* (Washington, DC: Organization of American States).

Jun, K.W. and H. Singh (1996) 'The Determinants of Foreign Direct Investment in Developing Countries: New Empirical Evidence', *Transnational Corporations*, Vol. 5, No. 2, Geneva.

Ken, P. (1996) *Guia Gerencial para a Tecnologia da Informação* (Rio de Janeiro: Editora Campus).

Kumar, R. (1995) 'Developing-Country Coalitions in International Trade Negotiations' in D. Tussie and D. Glover (eds), *The Developing Countries in World Trade* (Boulder, CO: Lynne Rienner).

Kuruvila, P. (1997) 'The GATT/WTO DS Mechanism', *Journal of World Trade*, Vol. 31, No. 6, December.

Lall, S. (1984) 'Exports of Technology by Newly Industrializing Countries: an Overview', *World Development*, Vol. 12, No. 5/6, pp. 471–80.

—— (1986) 'Comparative Advantage in Trade in Services', in S. Lall and F. Stewart (eds), *Theory and Reality in Development: Essays in Honour of Paul Streeten* (London: Macmillan – now Palgrave Macmillan).

Laplane, M. and F. Sarti (1997) 'Investimento Direto Estrangeiro e a Retomada do Crescimento Sustentado nos anos 90', *Economia e Sociedade*, No. 8, Sao Paulo.

——, F. Sarti, C. Hiratuka and R. Sabbatini (2001) 'El caso brasileño' in D. Chudnovsky (ed.), *El boom de la inversión extranjera directa en el Mercosur* (Buenos Aires: Siglo Veintiuno).

Lee, K. (1996) *Global Telecommunications Regulations: a Political Economy Perspective* (London: Pinter).

Lengyel, M. and D. Tussie (2000) 'Promoción de Exportaciones y Disciplinas Multilaterales: Posibilidades e Interrogantes' in M. Olarreaga and R. Rocha (eds), *La Nueva Agenda de Comercio en la OMC* (Santa Fé de Bogotá: World Bank Institute/ Universidad del Rosario).

Lloreda Ricaurte, N. (1998) 'Las instituciones comunitarias andinas' in *Comunidad Andina y Mercosur, Desafíos Pendientes de la Integracion en America Latina* (Bogota: Ministerio de Relaciones Exteriores de la Republica de Colombia).

Lloyd, P. (1998) 'Multilateral Rules for International Competition Law?', *The World Economy*, Vol. 21, No. 8, pp. 1129–49.

—— and K. Vautier (1999) 'Regional Approaches to Cross-Border Competition Policies'. Mimeo.

Low, P. and A. Subramanian (1995) 'TRIMs in the Uruguay Round: an Unfinished Business?' in *The Uruguay Round and the Developing Economies World Bank Discussion Papers* No. 307, Washington, DC.

Mannheim, K. (1952) *Ideology and Utopia*, Second Edition (New York, NY: Harcourt).

Mansell, R. (1993) *The New Telecommunications: a Political Economy of Network Evolution* (London: Sage Publications).

—— and U. Wehn (eds) (1998) *Knowledge Societies: Information Technology for Sustainable Development* (New York, NY: Oxford University Press).

Mark, J. and G. Helleiner (1988) *Trade in Services: the Negotiating Concerns of the Developing Countries* (Ottawa: North–South Institute).

Mattoo, A. (1999) 'Developing Countries in the New Round of GATS Negotiations: from a Defensive to a Pro-Active Role', presented at the WTO-World Bank Conference on Developing Countries in a Millennium Round, Geneva, 20–21 September.

—— and M. Olarreaga (n.y.) 'Reciprocity across Modes of Supply in the WTO: a Negotiating Formula', World Bank. Mimeo.

Medhora, R. (1998) 'Emerging Issues in International Trade Relations: Some Research Directions', *International Development Research Centre (IDRC) Trade Employment and*

Competitiveness (TEC) Research Program Working Paper available at http://www.idrc.ca/tec/emerging.html.

Michalopoulos, C. (1999) 'The Developing Countries in the WTO', *The World Economy*, Vol. 22, No. 1, January, pp. 117–43.

Miravete, E.J. (1997) 'Time-Consistent Protection with Learning by Doing', *Universidad Autonoma de Barcelona Department of Economics Working Paper* available at http://ideas.uqam.ca/ideas/data/Papers/aubautbar395.97.html.

Moran, T. (1998) *Foreign Direct Investment and Development. The New Policy Agenda for Developing Countries and Economies in Transition* (Washington, DC: Institute for International Economics).

Motta Veiga, P. (1999) 'Brasil: el reciente ciclo de inversiones y las políticas de atracción', *Latin American Trade Network (LATN) Brief* No. 3 (Buenos Aires: LATN) January.

—— and R. Iglesias (1997) 'Policy Competition and Foreign Direct Investment in Brazil' (Paris: OECD). Draft.

NAFTA – North American Free Trade Agreement – (2000) *Status Report. NAFTA and FTA Dispute Settlement Proceedings* available at http://www.nafta-sec-alena.org/english/index.htm consulted 8 September 2000.

Narlikar, A. (2000) 'Bargaining Together in Trade: Developing Countries in Coalitions', DPhil Thesis (Oxford: University of Oxford).

Nelson, R. and S. Winter (1982) *An Evolutionary Theory of Economic Change* (Cambridge, MA: Harvard University Press).

Network Wizards (2001) 'Distribution of Top-Level Domain Names by Host Count, January 2001' at http://www.isc.org/ds/WWW-200101/dist-bynum.html consulted 27 July 2001.

OAS – Organization of American States – (1996) 'Provision on Trade in Services in Trade and Integration Agreements of the Western Hemisphere', SG/TU/WG: SER/DOC.1/96, updated May 1997.

OECD – Organization of Economic Cooperation and Development – (1998a) *Harmful Tax Competition: an Emerging Global Issue* (Paris: OECD).

—— (1998b) *Foreign Direct Investment and Economic Development – Lessons from Six Emerging Economies* (Paris: OECD).

—— (1999) 'Review of Tariffs' TD/TC/(99)7/FINAL (Paris: OECD).

—— (2000a) *Agricultural Outlook 2000–2005* (Paris: OECD).

—— (2000b) 'Assessing Barriers to Trade in Services: Using 'Cluster' Approaches to Specific Commitments for Interdependent Services', TD/TC/WP(2000)9 (Paris: OECD), 9 March.

Oman, C. (1999) 'Policy Competition and Foreign Direct Investment' (Paris: OECD Development Centre).

Ostry, S. (1999) 'Future of the WTO' prepared at the Brookings Institution Governing in a Global Economy Trade Policy Forum, 15–16 April.

Oyejide, T.A. (2000) 'Interests and Options of Developing and Least-Developed Countries in a New Round of Multilateral Trade Negotiations', *G-24 Discussion Paper Series on International Monetary Affairs*, No. 2, United Nations, May.

Penner, A. (1996) 'Why We Were Right and They Were Wrong: an Evaluation of Chapter 19 of the FTA and NAFTA', *DFAIT Trade and Economic Policy Paper* SP78A (Ottawa: DFAIT), September.

Polanyi, K. (1944) *The Great Transformation: the Political and Economic Origins of Our Time* (Boston, MA: Beacon Press).

Prieto, F. (1999) 'Chile, el ALCA y el GATS 2000', Chilean Ministry of Foreign Relations, International Economic Relations Bureau, 21 June.

—— (2000) 'The GATS, Sub-Regional Agreements and the FTAA: How Much is Left to be Done' in S. Stephenson (ed.), *Services Trade in the Western Hemisphere: Liberalization, Integration and Reform* (Washington, DC: Brookings Institution Press).

—— and S. Stephenson (1999) 'Regional Liberalisation of Trade in Services by Countries of the Western Hemisphere' in M. Rodriguez, P. Low and B. Kotschwar (eds), *Multilateral Trade Rules in the Making* (Washington, DC: Brookings Institution Press).

Qian, Y. (2000) 'Analysis of the Commitments under the GATS and the World Trade Organization', 8 February. Ying.a.qian@aexp.com.

Raghavan, C. (2000) 'The World Trade Organization and its Dispute Settlement System: Tilting the Balance against the South', *Trade and Development Series*, No. 9 (Penang: Third World Network).

Rajapathirana, S. *et al.* (2000) 'Review of the Framework for Technical Assistance for Trade Development of Least Developed Countries'. Mimeo.

Rashid, S. (1988) 'Quality in Contestable Markets: a Historical Problem?', *Quarterly Journal of Economics*, February.

Ricupero, R. (2000) 'La integración y el regionalismo en las américas' in P. Kruger *et al.* (eds), *Las américas: Integración económica en perspectiva* (Bogota: InterAmerican Development Bank).

Rodrik, D. (1995) 'Developing Countries after the Uruguay Round' in *International and Financial Issues for the 1990s*, Vol. VI (New York, NY: UN).

—— (1997) 'Sense and non sense in the globalization debate', *Foreign Policy*, Summer.

—— (2000) 'How Far Will International Integration Go?', *Journal of Economic Perspectives*, Vol. 14, No. 1, pp. 177–86.

Rogowski, R. (1989) *Commerce and Coalitions* (Princeton, NJ: Princeton University Press).

Ruggie, J. (1982) 'International Regimes, Transactions and Change: Embedded Liberalism in the Postwar Economic Order', *International Organization*, Vol. 36, No. 2, Spring.

Salop, S. (1979) 'Strategic Entry and Deterrence', *American Economic Review*, May.

Scherer, F. (1994) *Competition Policies for an Integrated World Economy* (Washington, DC: The Brookings Institute).

Schmalensee, R. and R. Willig (eds) (1989) *Handbook of Industrial Organization*, North-Holland.

Schumpeter, J. (1912) *The Theory of Economic Development* (Cambridge, MA: Harvard University Press, 1934).

—— (1928) 'The Instability of Capitalism', *The Economic Journal*, September.

—— (1939) *Business Cycles* (New York, NY: McGraw-Hill).

—— (1942) *Capitalism, Socialism and Democracy* (London: George Allen & Unwin, 1976).

Scott-Joynt, J. (1998) *EMAP Media*, 19 March. info@total.emap.com URL: http://www.totaltele.com

Singleton, R. (1997) 'Competition Policy for Developing Countries: a Long-Run, Entry-Based Approach' *Contemporary Economic Policy*, Vol. 15, April.

Skott, P. and R. Sethi (1997) 'Uneven Development and the Dynamics of Distortion', *University of Aarhus Department of Economics Working Paper* available at http://ideas.uqam.ca/ideas/data/Papers/aahaarhec1997-23.html.

Spar, D. (1998) 'Attracting High Technology Investment. Intel's Costa Rican Plant', *World Bank Foreign Investment Advisory Service (FIAS) Occasional Paper* No. 11 (Washington, DC: FIAS).

Srinivasan, T.N. (1999) at the Symposium on Trade and Development, Geneva, March.

Stephenson, S. (1998) 'Approaches to Services Liberalization by Developing Countries' (Washington, DC: Organization of American States). Mimeo.

—— (2000) 'Regional Agreements on Services and Multilateral Disciplines: Interpreting and Applying GATS Article V' in P. Sauve and R. Stern (eds), *GATS 2000: Liberalization of Services* (Washington, DC: Brookings Institution Press).

—— (2001) 'Multilateral and Regional Services Liberalization by Latin America and the Caribbean', *OAS Trade Unit Working Paper*, OEA/Ser.D/XXII, SG/TU/TUS-9, March.

Stewart, T. (1993) *The GATT Uruguay Round. A Negotiating History (1986–1992)*, Vol. II (Boston, MA: Kluwer Law and Taxation Publishers).

Strange, S. (1994) *States and Markets*, Second edition (London: Pinter).

Sutton, J. (1991) *Sunk Costs and Market Structure* (Cambridge, MA: The MIT Press).

Tan, A. (1998) 'Managing Liberalization, Regionalism and Globalization in the Next 50 Years', presented at the WTO Symposium on the World Trade System, Geneva, April.

Tavares de Araujo, J. (1998) 'Trade, Transparency and Competition: FTAA and CER', *Journal of Latin American Competition Policy*, Vol. 1, Special Issue, December.

—— and L. Tineo (1998) 'Harmonization of Competition Policies among Mercosur Countries', *The Antitrust Bulletin*, Vol. XLIII, No. 1.

——, C. Macario and K. Steinfatt (2001) in 'Antidumping in the Americas', OEA/SER.D/XXII, SE/TU/TUS-10, March.

Thomas, K. (1998) 'International Control and Discipline of Subsidies: the EU and WTO Surveillance Exercises', *STI Review*, No. 21, Paris.

Thorstensen, V. (1995) *Commercial Defense Policy and Its Instruments* (Washington, DC: Interamerican Development Bank).

Tigre, P. (1992) 'Current Dilemmas and Future Options for Informatics Policy' in P. Evans, C. Frischtak and P. Tigre (eds), *High Technology and Third World Industrialization: Brazilian Computer Policy in Comparative Perspective* (Berkeley, CA: International and Area Studies, University of California at Berkeley).

Tussie, D. (1987) *Less Developed Countries and the World Trading System* (London: Pinter).

—— (1998) 'Globalization and World Trade: from Multilateralism to Regionalism', *Oxford Development Studies*, Vol. 26, No. 1, pp. 33–45.

—— and D. Glover (eds) (1993) *Developing Countries and World Trade: Policies and Bargaining Strategies* (Boulder, CO: Lynne Rienner).

—— and M. Lengyel (1998) 'WTO Commitments on Export Promotion', *Latin American Trade Network (LATN) Working Paper* No. 1 (Buenos Aires: LATN) November.

—— and M. Lengyel (2001) 'Developing Country Participation versus Influence' in B. Hoekman, P. English and A. Mattoo (eds), *Trade Policy, Economic Development and Multilateral Negotiations: a Handbook* (Washington, DC: World Bank).

UNCTAD – United Nations Conference on Trade and Development – (1985) 'Services and the Development Process', TD/B/1008, Rev. 1 (New York, NY: UN).

—— (1988) *Trade and Development Report* (New York, NY: UN).

—— (1992) *The Determinants of Foreign Direct Investment. A Survey of the Evidence* (New York, NY: UN).

—— (1993) 'The Impact of Subsidies on Trade in Services: Background Note by the UNCTAD Secretariat', UNCTAD/SDD/SER/3, 4 October.

—— (1994) 'Trade-Related Investment Measures' in *The Outcome of the Uruguay Round: an Initial Assessment*. Supporting papers to the Trade and Development Report 1994 (Geneva: UNCTAD).

—— (1995a) 'Impact of Progressive Liberalization and on Services Imports on the Development of Competitive Services Sectors, and the Difficulties Faced by

Developing Countries Which Prevent Them from Increasing Their Participation in World Trade in Services', TD/B/CN.4/43 (Geneva: UNCTAD Secretariat), 31 July.

—— (1995b) *World Investment Report 1995. Transnational Corporations and Competitiveness* (Geneva: UNCTAD).

—— (1998) *World Investment Report 1998. Trends and Determinants* (Geneva: UNCTAD).

—— (1999a) 'Analysis of Experiences in Selected Services Sectors', TD/B/COM.1/28, 17 August.

—— (1999b) 'Report of the Ad Hoc Expert Group Meeting on Efficiency and Cost Benefit Assessment of Host Country Tax Incentives and Technical Assistance Needs', Geneva, 8–9 July.

USDA – US Department of Agriculture – (1997) *Paraguay: Annual Situation and Outlook* (Washington, DC: USDA).

—— (2000) *Brazilian Sugar Sector Annual Report 2000 Gain Report* (Washington, DC: USDA).

USDC – US Department of Commerce – (2001) 'Antidumping and Countervailing Duty Statistics' available at http://www.ita.doc.gov/import_admin/records/stats/iastats1.html, consulted 17 August 2001.

US Government (1998) 'Impact of Anti-Competitive Practices of Enterprises and Associations on International Trade', presented at The WTO Working Group on the Interaction between Trade and Competition, Geneva, 11–13 March.

USTR – United States Trade Representative – (2000) Press Release 00–57, 28 July.

Van Grasstek, C. (1999a) 'In US Plans for the New Round: Negotiating More Agreements with Less Authority', Report to UNCTAD, 30 July.

—— (1999b) 'The Resolution of Economic Disputes'. Mimeo.

Ventura Dias, V. (2001) 'Las reglas multilaterales sobre subsidios a la luz de algunos fallos de la organización mundial del comercio' (Santiago, Chile: ECLAC). Mimeo.

Vogel, S. (1996) 'International Games with National Rules: Competition for Comparative Regulatory Advantage in Telecommunications and Financial Services', *Berkeley Roundtable on International Economy (BRIE) Working Paper* No. 88 (Berkeley, CA: BRIE, University of California at Berkeley) June.

Weston, A. (1995) 'The Uruguay Round. Unraveling the Implications for Least-Developed and Low-Income Countries' in *International and Financial Issues for the 1990s*, Vol. VI (New York, NY: UN).

—— (1996) 'CUSFTA and NAFTA Viewed from a Spoke', *Integration & Trade*, Buenos Aires, January.

Wilson, W. (1918) World War I Speech delivered in Joint Session to the US Congress on 8 January 1918.

Wohlers, M. and C. Plaza (2000) *Informe Anual Telecomunicações e Tecnologias da Informação, 2000* (São Paulo: CELAET/NIEP).

World Bank (1994) *World Development Report 1994: Infrastructure for Development* (New York, NY: Oxford University Press).

—— (2000) *World Development Report 2000–2001* (Washington, DC: World Bank).

WTO – World Trade Organization – (1996) 'Trade and Foreign Direct Investment', PRESS/57 (Geneva: WTO) 9 October.

—— (1997) *Trade Policy Review: Brazil, 1996* (Geneva: WTO).

—— (1999a) 'Domestic Support: Brazilian Response to US's question concerning the effects of Proalcool program on sugar sector', G/AG/N/BRA/13 (Geneva: WTO) 5 March.

—— (1999b) 'Preparations for the 1999 Ministerial Conference: Services: Communication from Brazil', WT/GC/W/333 (Geneva: WTO), 23 September.

—— (1999c) 'Preparations for the 1999 Ministerial Conference: WTO Services Trade Negotiations: Communication from Australia', WT/GC/W/353 (Geneva: WTO), 11 October.

—— (1999d) 'Preparations for the 1999 Ministerial Conference: Focus and Priorities of the New Round of Services Negotiations: Communication from Hong Kong, China', WT/GC/W/215 (Geneva: WTO), 22 June.

—— (2000a) *Trade Policy Review: Brazil, 2000* (Geneva: WTO).

—— (2000b) 'Cairns Group Negotiating Proposal', G/AG/NG/W/35 (Geneva: WTO), 22 September.

—— (2000c) 'Communication from Hong Kong, China: Scope and Coverage of the Services Negotiations and their Guidelines', S/CSS/W/6 (Geneva: WTO), 29 September.

—— (2000d) 'Communication of Mauritius on Behalf of the African Group: Negotiating Guidelines and Procedures', S/CSS/W/7 (Geneva: WTO), 4 October.

—— (2000e) 'Overview of the State-of-play of WTO Disputes' available at http://www.wto.org/wto/dispute/bulletin.htm consulted 8 September 2000.

Yeats, A. (1998) 'Does Mercosur's Trade Performance Justify Concerns about the Effects of Regional Trade Arrangements? Yes!', *The World Bank Economic Review*, Vol. 12, No. 1, pp. 1–28.

Young, A. (1999) 'Labour Mobility and the GATS: Where Next?' Services 2000: New Direction in Services Trade Liberalization.

Zuijdwijk, T. (1999) 'Note on WTO Panel and Appellate Body Reports: Implementation', presented at the Centre for Trade Policy and Law (CTPL) Conference, Ottawa, March.

Index